Oxford Socio-Legal Stu…

Realistic Socio-Legal Theory

OXFORD SOCIO-LEGAL STUDIES

General Editor: Keith Hawkins, Reader in Law and Society, and Fellow and Tutor in Law of Oriel College, Oxford

Editorial Board: John Baldwin, Director of the Institute of Judicial Administration, University of Birmingham; William L. F. Felstiner, Professor of Sociology, University of California-Santa Barbara; Denis Galligan, Professor of Socio-Legal Studies and Director of the Centre for Socio-Legal Studies, Oxford; Sally Lloyd-Bostock, Senior Research Fellow, Centre for Socio-Legal Studies, Oxford; Doreen McBarnet, Senior Research Fellow, Centre for Socio-Legal Studies, Oxford; Simon Roberts, Professor of Law, London School of Economics.

International Advisory Board: John Braithwaite (Australian National University); Robert Cooter (University of California-Berkeley); Bryant Garth (American Bar Foundation); Volkmar Gessner (University of Bremen); Vittorio Olgiati (University of Milan); Martin Partington (University of Bristol).

Oxford Socio-Legal Studies is a series of books exploring the role of law in society for both an academic and a wider readership. The series publishes theoretical and empirically-informed work, from the United Kingdom and elsewhere, by social scientists and lawyers which advances understanding of the social reality of law and legal processes.

REALISTIC SOCIO-LEGAL THEORY

Pragmatism and a Social Theory of Law

BRIAN Z. TAMANAHA

UNIVERSITY PRESS

OXFORD
UNIVERSITY PRESS

Great Clarendon Street, Oxford OX2 6DP

Oxford University Press is a department of the University of Oxford.
It furthers the University's objective of excellence in research, scholarship,
and education by publishing worldwide in

Oxford New York

Athens Auckland Bangkok Bogotá Buenos Aires Calcutta
Cape Town Chennai Dar es Salaam Delhi Florence Hong Kong Istanbul
Karachi Kuala Lumpur Madrid Melbourne Mexico City Mumbai
Nairobi Paris São Paulo Singapore Taipei Tokyo Toronto Warsaw

with associated companies in Berlin Ibadan

Oxford is a registered trade mark of Oxford University Press
in the UK and in certain other countries

Published in the United States
by Oxford University Press Inc., New York

© Brian Z. Tamanaha 1997

The moral rights of the author have been asserted

Database right Oxford University Press (maker)

First published 1997
First published new as paperback 1999

All rights reserved. No part of this publication may be reproduced,
stored in a retrieval system, or transmitted, in any form or by any means,
without the prior permission in writing of Oxford University Press,
or as expressly permitted by law, or under terms agreed with the appropriate
reprographics rights organisation. Enquiries concerning reproduction
outside the scope of the above should be sent to the Rights Department,
Oxford University Press, at the address above

You must not circulate this book in any other binding or cover
and you must impose this same condition on any acquirer

British Library Cataloguing in Publication Data

Data available

Library of Congress Cataloging in Publication Data

Data available

ISBN 0-19-826560-3
ISBN 0-19-829825-0 (Pbk.)

Printed in Great Britain
on acid-free paper by
Bookcraft Ltd., Midsomer Norton, Somerset

For Elizabeth

General Editor's Introduction

In earlier days, many of those who worked in the field of socio-legal studies were perhaps less given to scholarly introspection than their colleagues located more centrally in some of the fields of social science or philosophy. One reason for this may have been the heavy imprint left upon the field in its formative years by those who held a very instrumental view of law, and who were interested in conducting empirical research for the purpose of law reform or to contribute to the development of social policy. One consequence of this approach was that there were until quite recently relatively few programmatic analyses of the socio-legal field, its paradigms, its key questions and assumptions, its direction, and so on. But as the field of socio-legal studies has moved from its place in the 1970s as a rather offbeat pursuit on the fringes of conventional legal scholarship to its current position of orthodoxy, so it has begun to enter a more reflective and questioning phase. Some commentators, indeed, have already written of a crisis in socio-legal scholarship.

Brian Tamanaha's provocative book explores the present position of socio-legal studies, and presents a large-scale and fundamental reappraisal of socio-legal theory. The work argues for the development of a pragmatic realist approach to theory, drawing from behavioural and interpretive positions in social science, and it in turn recruits the insights of social science to revisit some of the major problems in legal theory. Professor Tamanaha's analysis also serves as a critique of critical legal theory, which the author regards as having been more of a force for harm, rather than good. The programmatic analysis of this book serves to complement the work of Roger Cotterrell, whose *Law's Community* also appears in *Oxford Socio-Legal Studies*.

Professor Tamanaha makes a plea in this book for an approach to the analysis of legal phenomena characterised by a commitment to pragmatism. He argues also for more community of interest and communication in socio-legal scholarship so that legal theory may be informed more fully by socio-legal studies, so that socio-legal studies in turn may be more fully informed by philosophy and legal theory, and, finally, so that both legal theory and socio-legal studies may be better informed by the practice of law.

Keith Hawkins

Contents

Foreword		xi
1.	Introduction: the Problematic State of Socio-legal Studies	1
2.	Pragmatism and Realistic Socio-legal Studies	26
3.	Behaviourism and Interpretivism in Complement	58
4.	An Analytical Map of the Concept of Law	91
5.	A Social Theory of Law by Comparison to Legal Positivism	129
6.	The Internal/External Distinction and the Notion of a 'Practice'	153
7.	Studies of Judicial Decision-Making	196
8.	Legal Theory and the Practice of Judging	228
Three Last Words		245
Bibliography		257
Index		275

Foreword

To put it in the most ambitious terms, this book attempts to identify and develop foundations for the social scientific study of law in the age of anti-foundationalism. When reading legal theory, social theory, or the philosophy of social science, it is easy to begin to feel as if everything concrete is being destabilized, crumbling away before the corrosive onslaught of postmodernism. Nothing it seems is certain any more, not truth, fact, objectivity, right and wrong, not even science, and certainly not law. However, once you put the theory book down and walk on the hard ground, a sense of realism creeps back to suggest that there must be something amiss with all this talk of no foundations since nothing much seems to have changed in the real world. Everything is as solid as it ever was. That, anyway, is what I hope to demonstrate in a philosophically and empirically sound way.

Throughout this book I pursue three distinct, interwoven aims. My first aim is explicity programmatic: to present in comprehensive form a realistic approach to socio-legal studies. I build upon philosophical pragmatism to lay an epistemological foundation which specifies the nature of social science and its knowledge claims, and to establish a methodological foundation which partakes of both behaviourism and interpretivism. Owing to this objective, I engage in more detailed discussions of the philosophy of social science than is normal for a socio-legal work, and certainly far more than usually appears in discussions of legal theory.

My second aim is to bring an infusion into legal theory of insights based upon social science. I attempt to carry out the social scientific approach to law promoted by the Legal Realists, though I also add insights about science which were not fully appreciated at the time they wrote (and the answers provided are not always consistent with the views espoused by the Realists). This aim shaped the structure and content of this book. Except for the Introduction and Chapter Three, each Chapter is built around questions which occupy legal theory. This is an attempt to reach legal theory from social science in a way that understands and strives to respond to the issues which concern legal theory. Socio-legal scholars insist upon the independence to explore their own concerns without being dictated to by the interests of law or legal theory. I try to bring the two fields closer together.

These first two aims are joined in my presentation of the social theory of law, a symbolic interactionist-based view of law which serves as a common analytical baseline for socio-legal studies and legal theory. I apply the social theory of law to offer answers to many of the core issues in jurisprudence, including: what is law? what is law's relation to society? what is the nature of legal positivism? is law indeterminate? is law just politics? While I cannot claim to have conclusively resolved any one of these questions, what I have done is show how they can be approached and understood from a realistic, informed social science perspective.

My third aim is to mount a response to the increasing influence of the self-avowed critical school of socio-legal theory. I argue that this critical approach is epistemologically unsound, potentially harmful to the socio-legal enterprise, and does little to advance the political causes critical scholars tout. Because my political views substantially overlap with those of critical scholars, in this work I find myself in the uncomfortable position of being most critical of scholars for whom I have a great deal of sympathy. But my conviction that the critical approach does more harm than good for the political causes we share compels me to present this response.

Chapter One is the Introduction, in which I briefly describe the intellectual currents that surround the field of socio-legal studies, and I elaborate on the most prominent problems the field currently suffers from. This Chapter will set the scene for the foundation laying to come. The realistic approach I elaborate will respond to the problems that dog the field.

Chapter Two establishes the theoretical foundation for realistic socio-legal studies by laying out and then drawing upon philosophical pragmatism. I discuss the current popularity of pragmatism in legal theory, and I use pragmatism and its connections to Legal Realism to locate the position of socio-legal studies in relation to the current schools of legal theory, especially Critical Legal Studies and Law and Economics. An important aspect of this discussion will be to ground the fact-value distinction in the only way it can be understood consistent with postmodernism.

Chapter Three discusses behaviourism and interpretivism, with their respective emphases on behaviour and meaning, as they have been invoked in legal theory and socio-legal studies. A realistic approach draws equally from both, though that is easier said than done since so much of their past interaction has been antagonistic. I articulate the strengths and weaknesses of each, demonstrating how they each presuppose and need the other. Complex issues surrounding the notion of meaning and its relationship to behaviour will be taken up in detail.

Chapter Four deals with the age old issue at the centre of legal theory, the question of the concept of law, which I approach from the social science perspective rather than legal theory. I provide an explanation for why the attempt to locate a universally acceptable concept of law has proven so elusive. Using studies of law from legal anthropology and legal sociology, especially those informed by behaviourism, I set out two fundamental categories of the concept of law, then I map the relations between these categories. The end product is an overview not just of the concept of law but of law's relationship to society.

Chapter Five develops what I call a social theory of law, set out by comparison to legal positivism. Socio-legal scholars have traditionally been opposed to legal positivism. But I will build upon the fact that these approaches share a common reference to social practices to join the two in their view of law. To accomplish this, I demonstrate the ways in which H. L. A. Hart's legal positivism is normative despite his claims that it is descriptive, and I argue that a strict legal positivism would be grounded in the social theory of law I set out. The social theory of law serves as the backdrop for the remainder of the book which develops different aspects of this theory in greater detail in relation to issues of particular concern for legal theory.

Chapter Six discusses the internal-external distinction and the notion of a practice. Although its significance has yet to be widely recognized, the internal-external distinction is becoming increasingly pivotal in legal theory. This poorly understood distinction—which is a function of the interpretivism-behaviourism divide—can be fully apprehended only by returning to its source of origin in the philosophy of social science. In the course of this discussion I indicate how the issue of indeterminacy arises in the social science context. I develop the notion of a practice, which serves as an activity-based linch pin for the internal-external distinction. Then I analyse various issues in which the distinction is implicated, both in legal theory and in socio-legal studies.

Chapter Seven examines behaviourist and interpretivist social scientific studies of judicial decision-making, comparing them with accounts by judges and observations by legal theorists. I set up the discussion in terms of the central obsession of US legal theory: the issue of the indeterminacy of rules as it relates to the practice of judging. A wealth of studies have been conducted on judicial decision-making, but they have never been systematically examined for what they say to the legal theory debate. That is what I do in this and the following Chapter. These Chapters are intended to demonstrate, through application, the value of the general approach I prescribe.

Chapter Eight draws upon the findings of the social scientific studies of judging, as well as upon accounts by judges and legal theorists, to formulate a portrait of judicial decision-making. The findings extend beyond the issue of indeterminacy to suggest that judicial decision-making (in the United States) has changed in the last hundred years, and that the implications of this change, which involve a shift in the balance between rule application and instrumental rationality, must be taken notice of and more carefully attended to.

In the final Chapter I begin by pointing out the strengths and weaknesses of the pragmatic approach as revealed in this sustained application of pragmatism to law and to the social scientific study of law. Then I conclude with a final word on each of the three themes woven through this work.

The genesis of many of the ideas elaborated in this work can be traced back to my experience as a practising lawyer, first as a law clerk to a federal judge in Virginia, then as a public defender in Hawaii, and finally as a assistant attorney-general in Micronesia. My experience in Micronesia, in particular, led me to question everything I had learned about law from legal theory. Almost none of it seemed to fit. The quest to understand the situation led me on an intellectual journey through 'law and the social sciences', where I found a wealth of information (especially in the older works), of which legal theorists seemed generally unaware. Legal theory needs to be more fully informed by socio-legal studies, and that is what I have set out to do.

However, in the course of this intellectual journey, which extended beyond law and the social sciences to delve deeply into the philosophy of social science, and into philosophy and social theory, I also became increasingly aware of the limitations of socio-legal studies. In particular, notions of truth and meaning are implicitly or explicitly relied upon, yet they remain poorly developed; under pressure from postmodernism, the field seems to be moving away from its strength in social science, toward an embrace of politics; and, broadly speaking, the field reflects a limited understanding of, and failure to engage, legal theory. The field of socio-legal studies needs to be more fully informed by philosophy and legal theory, and that is also what I have set out to do.

Finally, in this search for answers I was struck by the fact that, despite their differences, both legal theory and socio-legal studies share one trait: neither strongly resonated with my experience of law. Both fields often seemed unrealistic, out of touch. Although 'realism' has several technical usages which I later identify, plain everyday realism is the dominant sense in which I apply this term. In this work I approach legal theory and socio-legal studies from a realistic perspective, close to and informed by the practice of law. Both fields, I argue and attempt to demonstrate, would benefit from a correction in this direction.

Although this book was conceived and written as a single continuous text, modified versions of several Chapters were extracted and published separately. A version of Chapter Two will appear in "Pragmatism in United States Legal Theory: Its Application to Normative Jurisprudence, Sociolegal Studies, and the Fact-Value Distinction," 41 *American Journal of Jurisprudence* (forthcoming 1996); a version of Chapter Four appeared in "An Analytical Map of Social Scientific Approaches to the Concept of Law," 15 *Oxford Journal of Legal Studies* 501 (1995); and a version of Chapter Six appeared in "The Internal/External Distinction and the Notion of a 'Practice' in Legal Theory and Sociolegal Studies," 30 *Law and Society Review* 163 (1996). I thank the publishers for allowing me to use material from those articles.

For their critical comments on earlier drafts of various Chapters of this book, I would like to thank John Eekelaar, Lawrence Friedman, Donald Black, Gordon Woodman, Andre Hoekema, Roger Cotterrell, Keith Hawkins, Mark Cooney, David Gregory, Elizabeth van Schilfgaarde, and the anonymous reviewers of Oxford University Press. I would also like to thank Keith Hawkins for his help during the editorial process, and Laura Aglietti for her meticulous research assistance. Finally, I would like to give a special thanks to Lawrence Friedman, Roberto Unger, Morton Horwitz, and John Leubsdorf. Without their support, I would not have had the opportunity to embark upon an academic career, and this book would not have been written.

1 Introduction: the Problematic State of Socio-legal Studies

An odd duality characterizes the field of socio-legal studies. By all external appearances it is booming, with increasing numbers of scholars, journals, conferences, associations, books and series dedicated to the subject. There are 'more people attracted to the field than ever,' with 'new law and society programs springing up at colleges and universities' (Merry 1995: 11–12).[1] A leading socio-legal scholar has even declared that '[l]aw is entering an age of sociology' (Black 1989: 4). The field is doing so well, or at least is perceived as such, that it prompted a highly publicized backlash in legal academia in the United States. A respected federal judge recently lamented the increase in non-doctrinal courses taught in law schools, including those focusing on law and the social sciences, which he argued have little to contribute to the practice of law and are leading to the demise of legal education (Edwards 1992, 1993). Socio-legal studies—so long shunted to the margins of the legal academy as well as social science departments—are becoming a real presence in a way that was not so just a decade ago.

Despite this healthy glow and the energetic flurry of activity which generates it, however, closer scrutiny reveals that all is not well with the field. An implicit sign of the unease is the proliferation of review articles addressing 'Where We Have Been Going and Where We Might Be Going' (Simon and Lynch 1989).[2] Robert Tremper put it vividly: 'Wracked by anguish, self-doubt, role confusion, and occasional impotence, the field has been undergoing a decade-long analysis session in the literature' (Simon and Lynch 1989: 826, quoting Tremper). There is widespread recognition that few concrete reforms have come from the reams of social scientific studies that have been completed on law

---

[1] The labels law and society studies or law and the social sciences have also been applied to this field, but current usage appears to favour socio-legal studies. I should note that certain participants in the individual disciplines listed would object to being placed under the label socio-legal studies. In Britain, Marxist legal sociologists have sharply criticized socio-legal scholars as liberals whose work is deficient and conservative. See Travers (1993). The weight of conventional usage will likely prevail over such objections.

[2] For other recent review articles on various areas of socio-legal studies, see Friedman (1986); Travers (1993); Merry (1992); Just (1992); Starr and Collier (1989); Snyder (1981); Lloyd-Bostock (1981); Munger (1993); Conley and O'Barr (1993).

in the last fifty years. Lawyers, judges, and lawmakers simply are not paying much attention. A few social scientists have begun to express concerns that their interests and the interests of law are so far apart that there are dangers to overly close collaboration (Carson 1988). Others have charged socio-legal studies with a tendency to support the status quo (Trubek and Esser 1989). Articles suggesting 'new directions' or 'new formulations' have begun to appear with regularity. It is a field in transition, pleased with its new-found prominence yet dissatisfied with the present state and not quite certain where the future lies.

The label socio-legal studies has gradually become a general term encompassing a group of disciplines that applies a social scientific perspective to the study of law, including the sociology of law, legal anthropology, legal history, psychology and the law, political science studies of courts, and science-oriented comparativists. These various approaches to law are joined by more than just their scientific orientation. Broadly speaking, the glue which bonds this diverse group is a left-to-far-left critical orientation to law. Most socio-legal scholars are 'progressives'. Building upon the solidarity and commonality of interests derived from this politically-informed critical stance, socio-legal scholars are in the process of forming a genuine community of discourse, developing a shared baseline of knowledge derived from work produced in the different contributing disciplines.

Although the field is gradually becoming a truly international one, with contributors from all over the world, I will approach it primarily from the Anglo-American experience, and decidedly more American than Anglo. This emphasis is justified because the Anglo-American contribution has had a major role in shaping the field; but more so because approaching the subject from this angle is the best way to introduce the many connections between socio-legal studies and American-born philosophical pragmatism and Legal Realism. Equally important, it will provide a link with current themes in US legal theory, many of which share the same inspiration and source of origin. The limitations of this parochial orientation should be offset by the depth of understanding gained by a narrowed focus, and by the fact that philosophical pragmatism is becoming increasingly influential outside the United States. What I analyse relates most directly to the US experience, but has implications beyond.

The Postmodern Transitional Moment in Socio-legal Studies and Legal Theory

Socio-legal studies 'is undoubtedly in a transitional phase in which there is much radical rethinking to do' (Cotterrell 1995: 296). 'It is a time of self-reflection and reevaluation of our methodological and theoretical legacies, a time of self-criticism and skepticism not only about the validity of our traditional approaches but also, it seems, about the validity of the endeavor itself' (Calavita and Seron 1992: 770). A major factor contributing to this transitional moment in socio-legal studies is the fact that the social sciences generally are in a state of reassessment and change. Above all else, they are struggling to absorb the interpretive challenge to the long dominant positivist view of science. Interpretivism (or hermeneutics) urges recognition that social action largely consists of the meaning-oriented behaviour of social actors, that the sources of this meaning are the different social groups within which we are socialized, and that when we see and interpret the world it is inevitably from within this group-informed perspective.[3] The core methodological prescription of interpretivism is that social scientists should strive to understand the meaning-infused contexts in which social action takes place, rather than attempt to formulate 'laws' of social action. The shift to interpretive analysis raises complex questions about the relationship between interpretivism and positivism, objectivity and subjectivity, action and structure, and micro and macro, that have yet to be resolved. Moreover, it places at the centre of social science that mysterious and obtuse thing called 'meaning'.

Another factor contributing to this transitional moment is the pervasive influence of anti-foundationalism[4]—the notion that there are no ultimate foundations for knowledge, no absolute truths. In technical terms, 'Anti-foundationalism is a view about epistemic justification that denies that knowledge can have foundations in the following sense: chains of justification can never end in a proposition that, unlike every other step in the chain, enjoys a non-inferential epistemic warrant' (Leiter 1992: 97). Or more simply, in the final analysis beliefs are grounded in nothing more firm than other beliefs, or webs of beliefs. This notion is the culmination of many different streams of thought in

---

[3] Excellent articles on the impact interpretivism has had in various fields can be found in Hiley, Bohman, and Shusterman, eds. (1991); Rabinow and Sullivan, eds. (1979).

[4] A classic text of modern anti-foundationalism is Rorty (1979). See also Baynes, Bohman, and McCarthy, eds. (1987).

twentieth-century philosophy, including hermeneutics, philosophical pragmatism, Wittgenstein's language analysis, and Kuhnian philosophy of science.

Postmodernism is the label attached to the convergence of these various streams of thought, the label attached to this transitional moment. The name implies that we have reached the end of the project of modernity and the cluster of beliefs it represents, beliefs about progress, rationality, objectivity, and universal humanistic notions of right and wrong. Despite its slippery resistance to being characterized, Richard Tarnas (1991: 95-9) has captured the themes underlying postmodernism and its extraordinarily far-reaching implications:

> There is an appreciation of the plasticity and constant change of reality and knowledge, a stress on the priority of concrete experience over fixed abstract principles, and a conviction that no single a priori thought system should govern belief or investigation. . . .
>
> The human subject is an embodied agent, acting and judging in a context that can never be wholly objectified, with orientations and motivations that can never be fully grasped or controlled. The knowing subject is never disengaged from the body or from the world, which form the background and condition of every cognitive act. . . .
>
> The mind is not the passive reflector of an external world and its intrinsic order, but is active and creative in the process of perception and cognition. Reality is in some sense constructed by the mind, not simply perceived by it, and many such constructions are possible, none necessarily sovereign. . . . There is no empirical 'fact' that is not already theory-laden, and there is no logical argument or formal principle that is a priori certain. All human understanding is interpretation, and no interpretation is final. . . .
>
> The subject of knowledge is already embedded in the object of knowledge: the human mind never stands outside the world, judging it from an external vantage point. Every object of knowledge is already part of a preinterpreted context, and beyond that context are only other preinterpreted contexts. . . . Hence the nature of truth and reality, in science no less than in philosophy, religion, or art, is radically ambiguous. The subject can never presume to transcend the manifold predispositions of his or her subjectivity. . . .
>
> Basic to this perspective is the thesis that all human thought is ultimately generated and bound by idiosyncratic cultural-linguistic forms of life. Human knowledge is the historically contingent product of linguistic and social practices of particular local communities of interpreters, with no assured 'ever-closer' relation to an independent ahistorical reality. Because human experience is linguistically prestructured, yet the various structures of language possess no demonstrable connection with an independent reality, the human mind can never claim access to any reality other than that determined by its local form

of life. . . . Moreover, linguistic meaning itself can be shown to be fundamentally unstable, because the contexts that determine meaning are never fixed, and beneath the surface of every apparently coherent text can be found a plurality of incompatible meanings. No interpretation of a text can claim decisive authority because that which is being interpreted inevitably contains hidden contradictions that undermine its coherence. Hence all meaning is ultimately undecidable, and there is no 'true' meaning. . . .

Postmodern philosophers can compare and contrast, analyze and discuss the many sets of perspectives human beings have expressed, the diverse symbol systems, the various ways of making things hang together, but they cannot pretend to possess an extrahistorical Archimedan point from which to judge whether a given perspective validly represents the 'Truth'.

Postmodernism apparently destabilizes all the core certainties of our existence—truth, reality, meaning, the world out there. It unceremoniously dumps the notion of objectivity and the fact-value distinction and reason itself into the rubbish bin of no longer believable Enlightenment illusions. The pessimistic postmodern vision harkens back to the Tower of Babel: an anarchic clash of incommensurable perspectives, each bearing its own standards of reason and right, impervious to criticism from others. The only evident 'solution' to this postmodern condition is the unreassuring proposal that we should continue to engage in conversation in the hope that somehow one perspective—preferably the 'right' one (that is, *our* perspective)—can prevail over the others in a way that leads to a consensus. This convergence of views, however, cannot occur through reasoned persuasion (because reason itself, and the premises upon which it operates, are likewise perspective bound), but only through a process of conversion grounded in rhetoric.

The effect of postmodernism is to challenge all claims to authority, especially those of science and philosophy. If there are no ultimate truths, both disciplines lose their longstanding (and sometimes competing) claims to be the diviners of true knowledge. In response, academic philosophy is presently undergoing an uncertain transformation which may lead to the end of philosophy or, more likely, to a shift to a more sociologically informed theory which focuses its attention on social rather than epistemological problems (see Baynes, Bohman, and McCarthy 1987). The natural sciences will undoubtedly survive unscathed by the collapse of their epistemological props because they *work*. Computers, robotics, genetics, space travel, advanced weaponry, and all the other products of scientific-technological development will not disappear with the postmodern message that absolute truths don't exist.

6 Realistic Socio-legal Theory

But the always weaker social sciences are directly threatened. Under the postmodern view, social science becomes just one more perspective or jumble of perspectives,[5] without any special method or reasoning capacity, and thoroughly tainted by the influence of values. Since they lack the instrumental power of the natural sciences, if the social sciences are to survive postmodernism, the above suggests that they will do so on the basis of their rhetorical skills, not on the strengths of the purported 'truths' they reveal. And deviously, the rhetorical strategy applied by the social sciences to boost their persuasive power is precisely their claim to be able to identify true knowledge through objective examination and the rigourous application of reason, claims which postmodernism says are necessarily false. Postmodernism, in effect, condemns social scientists to the posture of being either self-deluded or hypocritical.

Science and philosophy are not alone in being threatened by postmodernism. This complex of ideas also challenges claims essential to law's self-identity: that the rules, texts, concepts and principles, which form the corpus of law in modern society, have determinate meaning; that the interpretation and application of law can be a neutral or objective process; that law is good or right.

For reasons related to the above developments—related by virtue of the early influence of pragmatic philosophy and the present influence of postmodern ideas—legal theory in the United States is also in a state of transition, with two different aspects, a long term one and a short term one. The long term change has been ongoing for almost a century, and was notably instigated by Oliver Wendell Holmes. Drawing upon philosophical pragmatism (see Grey 1989), Holmes irreverently pierced the prevailing mode of analysing common law concepts as if they were essentialist notions of timeless provenance with a necessary internal structure and set of external relations. His favourite debunking mechanism was to employ historical analysis to demonstrate that these abstract concepts have a terrestrial origin in a specific context, derived from particular and contingent needs, and not infrequently based upon mistake (Holmes 1955). Holmes argued that legal rules should serve human purposes and must therefore be shaped to meet these purposes.

The change wrought by Holmes, which was carried through by Roscoe Pound and the Legal Realists, was to render law and legal theory increasingly instrumental oriented (see Summers 1982). With the

[5] Bauman (1992) contains an informative collection of articles exploring the relationship between postmodernism and social science.

exception of a handful of remaining classical natural law theorists, few legal theorists today discuss law exclusively in terms of abstract concepts. The focus is on whether law works the way we desire and if not how it can be made to do so. Many judicial decisions raise the same kinds of questions, and are routinely filled with discussions of social policy. One consequence of this shift toward instrumentalism is that the current state of US legal theory consists of what some have called 'postmodern jurisprudence' (Minda 1995), a plethora of competing approaches, each representing a particular normative or interest group perspective, each arguing that law should serve the interests they tout. Legal theory has become thoroughly and openly politicized.

The short term transition in US legal theory is the seemingly overnight convergence upon pragmatic philosophy of many of these competing jurisprudential schools, again with the exception of natural law theorists (Moore 1985).[6] Prominent representatives of the left, centre, and right in US legal theory—of critical legal studies (Singer 1988; Horwitz 1992; Minow and Spelman 1990), critical feminism (Radin 1990), critical race theory (Matsuda 1990), law and economics (Posner 1990a), and of the mainstream[7]—scholars who otherwise hold sharply divergent opinions about law, have begun to assert that pragmatism points the way. The most revealing aspect about this rush to pragmatism is precisely the fact that it can accommodate such divergent positions. Anything which appeals to the entire spectrum of political views *must* be empty of substance. For that reason, as I will later demonstrate, pragmatic philosophy has little to offer to normative legal theory.

The final element in this threshold description is socio-legal theory itself. Socio-legal theory, broadly defined, involves theoretically informed social science applied to law theoretically informed. It is the speculative side of socio-legal studies, in contrast to the empirical research side. So broad is this definition that a good deal of what now falls under the label socio-legal studies qualifies, as do many sociologically oriented works in legal theory.

In this Chapter, and throughout the course of this book, I will be presenting and arguing for one particular brand—not the only one

---

[6] Ronald Dworkin has also taken a stance against pragmatism, but Smith (1990) has persuasively argued that Dworkin's position is pragmatic in many respects.

[7] As with all centrists, mainstream scholars see a bit of truth in everything, including pragmatism. Articles touting pragmatism that arguably represent different spectrums of the centre include West (1985); Kronman (1990); Grey (1989).

possible—of socio-legal studies—for realistic socio-legal studies. The term 'realism' is meant to allude to an allegience with both Legal Realism and scientific realism, with reservations noted. The Legal Realist connection is an actual historical fact: in the sense I have defined it, many of the Legal Realists were socio-legal scholars who applied scientific concepts like functionalism and behaviourism to law. 'For most legal realists social science was realism' (Duxbury 1995: 97). Socio-legal studies are thus, in important respects, 'the most direct descendant of Legal Realism' (Singer 1988: 504 n. 129). The particular brand of socio-legal studies I argue for builds upon the approach championed by the Realists. The allusion to scientific realism refers to the specific sense in which scientific realists accept that there is 'a world out there', and the way to understand this world is through close observation, though I depart from strict scientific realism by also recognizing that in a certain sense we contribute to making this world what it is (to us) through our perception of it and our activities within it. Finally, I mostly mean 'realism' in the common sense usage. Being realistic is trying to keep your feet on the ground, which we know to be solid regardless of the sense of destabilization brought on by postmodernism; by 'ground' I mean recognizing the conditions of our existence, and going from there.

My thesis is that the role of realistic socio-legal theory in the context of postmodern jurisprudence is to be a non-political source of knowledge about the nature, function, and effects of legal phenomena. As such, it will be the only predominantly descriptive, non-normative alternative available among the current schools in legal theory, with a critical capacity which plays no favourites among the competing schools of normative legal theory, be they on the left, centre, or right. Realistic socio-legal theory, I venture to assert, best captures, explains, and grounds the intuitions of and attitudes towards their work held by many socio-legal scholars, at least those who feel uncomfortable with the overly politicized atmosphere that currently pervades the field.

To make such claims today sounds at best old-fashioned and at worst reactionary, but they will be buttressed by a philosophical tradition which meets postmodernism on its own terms. The theoretical underpinnings for this realistic socio-legal theory will be the philosophical pragmatism of John Dewey and William James, and its most realistic modern proponent, Hilary Putnam (as distinct from the pragmatism of Richard Rorty), supported by the pragmatism of Williard Quine and Donald Davidson. There are many deep connections between pragmatism and the above described flow of ideas, both with regard to science and law. Important aspects of pragmatism were integrated into Legal Realist thinking, especially the instrumentalist emphasis, and pragmatism is consistent with the (conditional) scientific realism just described (James 1975: 270–3).

Pragmatism is essential for two further reasons. First, it is a direct predecessor to current anti-foundationalist thought in philosophy, and it was long ago incorporated into interpretive social science through the work of George Herbert Mead and Alfred Schutz, so there are well-developed existing sources to draw upon at the level of theory and methodology. Secondly, pragmatism contains the same underlying elements as postmodernism—all of the pragmatic theorists identified above have actually been cited as postmodern theorists (see Patterson 1992; Schanck 1992)—but does not suffer from the pessimism and sense of paralysis which permeates postmodernism. The difference is so great that the common identification of pragmatism with postmodernism is misleading—the classical pragmatists, at least, were consummate modernists who believed in progress. This modernism was the backbone of their constructive orientation, their melioristic approach, and provides a needed antidote to postmodernism.

It may seem unusual that I earlier asserted that pragmatism is empty of substance and has little to offer to normative legal theory, but now propose to contruct realistic socio-legal theory on the same edifice. Pragmatic philosophy *is* exceedingly thin, as I will later show. Nonetheless, what makes pragmatism perfectly suited for supporting a realistic socio-legal theory is that the method of inquiry touted by the pragmatists is none other than the *scientific* method. Unlike legal theory, which is thoroughly normative and hence substantively rich, the scientific method is empty of content. Rather than a sign of weakness, however, this is the source of its particular strength, the essence of its identity. Pragmatic philosophy contains the resources for a scientific approach to law regardless of postmodernism.

I will draw upon pragmatism to demonstrate that while many of the insights underlying postmodernism are correct, their import is limited mostly to philosophical discourse. They do not rule out everyday or scientific usage of notions like truth, fact, reality, neutrality, and right and wrong. To the contrary, a central point made by pragmatism is that the grounding for these terms is not to be found in the abstract realm of philosophy but in these very everyday usages and practices.

From a pragmatic perspective, many references to postmodernism, especially the most skeptical ones,[8] represent yet another attempt by those engaged in philosophical discourse to legislate for everyone else what can or cannot be done based upon a claimed special insight into the nature of things (including the pronouncement that things have no nature). Talk of postmodernism, in other words, often smacks of the continuance of metaphysics under the guise of the rejection of metaphysics.

This suggests that talk of postmodernism within the socio-legal community and the social sciences generally should itself be studied as a sociological phenomenon. Socio-legal scholar Rosemary Coombe (1995: 600) hinted at this when she observed that the postmodern 'subjectivity itself occupies a space of unacknowledged socioeconomic and cultural privilege'. As Zygmunt Bauman (1992: 101) remarked in relation to the feeling of anxiety and loss of direction generated by postmodernism, 'intellectuals tend to articulate their own societal situation and the problems it creates as a situation of the society at large.'

Talk of postmodernisim, which is limited mostly to the academic community,[9] and even then to distinct subsections thereof, is in no small part an expression of the disaffected state of progressive intellectuals who see their work ignored and hopes dashed in an age when 'it no longer seems relevant to repeat the old battlecries of the variant forms of the socialist movement' (Hunt 1990: 511). From a marginalized position where one's own theoretical base and claims to authority has been eviscerated, attacking all forms of authority—as skeptical postmodernism indiscriminantly does—seems empowering, or at least equalizing. Through this (purported) undermining of authority, the comfortable radical can claim to 'enhance the possibilities for the powerless to engage in the essential dialogue of world re-making,' to act as 'front-line combatants in the daily struggle to resist, reproduce or change the world' (Hunt 1990: 534, skeptically quoting Allan Hutchinson).

---

[8] An excellent study of the different forms of skepticism supported, and not supported, by Wittgenstein, can be found in Smith (1992).

[9] Recognizing this objection, Austin Sarat (1994: 620) pre-emptively but without argument declares that 'Postmodernism is an emergent fact; it is not a fad of academic discourse.' My response to this assertion is to point out that even for postmodern theorists themselves, at least for those functioning in society, postmodernism is a feature only of their theoretical deliberations, not of their everyday thought and discourse.

The Problems with Socio-legal Studies

Several observers have recently declared the field to be in a state of 'crisis'. 'Just as this movement seems to be reaching maturity, it has been seized with doubts about its purpose, accomplishments and future' (Trubek and Esser 1989:5). In this Section I will explore the sources of this crisis. This over-emphasis on the negative should not obscure the many substantive accomplishments of the field, which have been exhaustively reported elsewhere,[10] and a good deal of which I draw upon later in this book. Moreover, it should be noted that opinions differ over whether the field is ailing, and how so, and the situation differs by country and subject. Necessarily, this attempt to encapsulate the situation will suffer from the flaws of superficiality and overstatement, though not to the extent of inaccuracy.

A threshold problem with discussing the field of socio-legal studies as such is that there have been important differences in the development of its individual sub-disciplines. Thirty or forty years ago they were much more separate than they are now. Legal anthropology, for example, followed a path quite different from that of legal sociology. The former had its origin in the study of indigenous systems of normative order in non-western societies, whereas the latter has primarily been occupied with the study of various aspects of state law in the West. Despite these and other contrasts, however, there have been shared experiences, especially in the fact that both have had to deal with the collapse of structural-functional analysis, the rise of interpretivism, and the implications of postmodernism. And now that anthropologists are increasingly turning their attention to home, the differences between the two disciplines are fading, a process that is helped along by close interaction through joint conferences and membership in common organizations. Legal history also has its own tradition (one much more strongly entrenched in law schools), though it has also been influenced by some of the same theoretical changes which affected legal anthropology and sociology. Political scientists who study the court have drawn upon the same basic theoretical sources, except that behaviouristic studies have dominated the field. More so than any of the others, psychology and the law has developed along its own distinct path, which focused on specific areas like the insanity defence, judge and jury decision-making, and serving as expert witnesses at trial, and it has its own distinct

---

[10] See n. 2 and sources cited therein.

theoretical foundations, though it too has begun to join the socio-legal fold. In the following discussion I have gleaned from the literature problems that apply to all of the social scientific approaches to law except law and economics (which, for reasons of divergent political orientation, remains largely outside the group of socio-legal studies),[11] though to differing degrees depending on the discipline.

Diagnoses of the situation highlight three basic themes: the questionable value of the work produced by socio-legal scholars, underdeveloped theory in the field, and the influence of the political predispositions of socio-legal scholars upon their work. The first two themes were summarized by Lawrence Friedman (1986: 779) in his review of law and society studies:

People who study the legal system seem to be marginal, wherever they are. Sociology of law, students of judicial systems in political science, anthropology of law, psychology of law—all of these, alas, are not in the 'mainstream' of their disciplines; they are not 'where the action is.' . . . To many observers, the work done so far amounts to very little: an incoherent or inconclusive jumble of case studies. There is (it seems) no foundation; some work merely proves the obvious, some is poorly designed; there are no axioms, no 'laws' of legal behavior, nothing cumulates. The studies are at times interesting and are sporadically useful. But there is no 'science'; nothing adds up. . . . Grand theories do appear from time to time, but they have no survival power; they are nibbled to death by case studies. There is no central core.

It is a rather damning compilation of observations, to which Friedman added his assessment that 'to be sure, there is some truth to these complaints' (ibid.). Closer examination will shed a bit more understanding light.

Before directly addressing the above three themes, however, I must identify the overarching dynamic which has profoundly influenced the field. This dynamic involves the fact that participants in the effort to apply social science to law come from very different backgrounds—social science and law—with contrasting interests, paradigms, knowledge, language, ways of thinking and modes of action. This dynamic operates on two levels, external and internal. The internal level involves cross-disciplinary interaction within the community of socio-legal scholars, which consists of participants from social science faculties and from law faculties; the external level involves the interaction between the

---

[11] Law and economics has been more integrated into the British socio-legal community than in the US Cotterrell (1995: 83–90).

socio-legal community and legal professionals, academics as well as practising lawyers.

A generalization which applies to both levels is that, because few of the social scientists who study law are actually trained in law, and few of those in law faculties have extensive backgrounds in science (though the number is increasing), participants from both sides—even as collaborators—have too often been partially blind to the views of the other, deaf to their manner of discourse, and ignorant of their interests and concerns. Commenting on the less than successful partnership between law and the social sciences, Simon and Lynch (1989: 832) observed that '[e]ach came to the enterprise with their own objectives that never quite melded. Lawyers regarded social scientists as technicians, and social scientists viewed the law as an opportunity to explore issues of general theoretical interest.'

This attempt to intermix such radically different pursuits has sometimes led to second class status within and abuse from both sides. From social science departments come charges that socio-legal scholars lack scientific sophistication (see e.g. Berends 1992; Travers 1993); and from law departments come complaints that their work is largely irrelevant to the concerns of law (see e.g. Edwards 1992; Johnson 1991). Inevitably, this divergence of interests also generates conflict and frustration within the community of socio-legal scholars; as when law professor Richard Abel (1980: 135) excoriated legal anthropologists for the tendency to 'allocate disproportionate effort to gathering and presenting data' without enough attention to theory—for being too anthropological—and suggested that unless this is remedied 'anthropologists of law will be condemned to rediscovering what we already know and merely illustrating it with further examples.' This dismissive attitude was returned in kind when a sociologist reviewing Abel's three volume comparative study of the sociology of the legal profession suggested that work in the field 'hardly deserves the name "sociology" ' (Berends 1992: 167).

The difference between the two sides to this partnership also extends to contrasting temperaments. To put it in slightly caricatured terms, social scientists are wont to find knowledge in all its minutia interesting for its own sake ('Hmm, isn't it fascinating?'); whereas those trained in law tend to view knowledge in instrumental terms ('What's the point and how can I use it?'). It is as if their respective temperaments are locked in a negative relation: talk of habitus or autopoeisis or the kula exchange raises the interest level of the social scientist in direct proportion to the degree to which it induces sleep or impatience in the legal mind; the more the lawyer or legal scholar insists upon specific and definite answers to particular problems, the more the social scientist stammers, hems and haws, and introduces cautionary asides or conditions, before finally offering up an answer phrased in probabilities.[12] While many socio-legal scholars from the law side have a more speculative turn of mind than the average person trained in law, there are limits to their appetite for social science fare. Likewise, many socio-legal scholars from the social science side assiduously avoid dealing with positive law rules and read very little legal theory.

A. Questionable Value of the Work Produced

In a variety of different ways, this gulf between those trained in social science and those trained in law has been a significant contributing factor to the first theme mentioned above—the questionable value of the work produced, at least in relation to the concerns of legal professionals. Every reflective socio-legal scholar must wonder whether anyone outside the group is reading or cares about his or her work. 'Most academic lawyers are at best uninterested, and at worst hostile to socio-legal research. The same applies to practising lawyers.' (Lloyd-Bostock 1988: 11). In their review of more than a half century of work in the sociology of law, the most that Rita Simon and James Lynch (1989: 843) could (ever so cautiously) assert is 'there is some evidence, at least on the criminal side, that social science research on legal institutions is being used in policy debates and in the implementation of policy;' though 'courts place little weight on empirically based research findings.'[13]

One reason for this indifference is that, consistent with the tradition of the social sciences, a good deal of socio-legal work gathers information with no direct instrumental value. Most work in legal anthropology, for example, takes the form of case studies, which have a limited capacity for generalization or application to other contexts; and legal anthropologists have tended to ignore the study of state law itself, focusing instead on non-state systems of order and how they interact with state law, which goes outside the self-enclosed legal world of legal pro-

---

[12] As Simon and Lynch (1989: 827) put it, social scientists were 'discouraged at the treatment they received' when called upon by legal collaborators 'to answer specific questions with a definite yes or no'.

[13] Sally Lloyd-Bostock (1988: 1) described the reception of law and psychology studies in a way that is apt for socio-legal studies generally: 'Lawyers, if they are aware of developments in the field at all, often remain sceptical of their value.'

fessionals. Furthermore, critical socio-legal works which emphasize exposing (or constructing) unheard or dominated 'subjectivities' lie, by design, outside the domain of legal professionals.

Psychology and psychologists have actually been called upon extensively in law, especially to testify in court on various issues like insanity or repressed memories, or to consult on matters like jury selection, though questions about use value are rampant. The science of psychology is relatively weak, with little theoretical agreement and a high rate of theory turnover; psychologists testify on subjects which lay people are competent to judge for themselves; their conclusions are too often based upon shaky studies of questionable real world application; and it is often possible to find experts who will testify on either side of an issue (see Lloyd-Bostock 1981). Psychology in law suffers from a mercenary image.

The general legal indifference to the sociology of law can be partially explained in terms of the kinds of issues sociologists have focused on: various aspects relating to crime, the jury, the legal profession, access to law, and studies of lay knowledge and opinions about law (Simon and Lynch 1989: 832–42). Although these are worthy subjects, and they fit well within sociological specializations (like small group dynamics or the effects of professionalization), not one of them falls within the core concerns of the legal profession or legal theory. Crime studies have more to do with (and tend to be produced by) criminology departments; the jury, as far as the legal profession is concerned, is a black box that exists for traditional reasons more so than logical; the composition and nature of the legal profession has little or nothing to do with the positive law issues that occupy the legal profession; access to law problems are interesting mostly to legal reformers, not to the average legal practitioner or legal theorist; and knowledge and opinion studies tell lawyers what they already know from interacting with clients—that the general public has a vague and limited understanding of the law. Thus, from the perspective of most in the legal profession, academics as well as practitioners, what sociologists have produced to date may be interesting, but much of it is already known or mostly beside the point. Trying to convince the lawyers that they *should* be more concerned with these subjects appears futile.

Asking legal professionals to set jointly the research agenda with the social scientists might help insure greater attention to the results. It is no accident that the socio-legal works that have received the most attention in the legal community—notably Stuart Macaulay's (1963) study of non-contractual relations in the business community—have been produced by scholars located more on the law side. And legal history, substantially conducted by persons trained in the law, has been relatively successful in reaching a legal audience, at least among legal theorists. Lawyers know what lawyers find interesting. But even explicitly setting out to investigate issues of direct interest to lawyers is no assurance that anything will come of the study. Political scientists have conducted many studies on judicial decision making, an issue of central signficance to legal theorists as well as to judges. But these studies have had no noticeable impact within the confines of legal theory or with regard to judicial reform.

The truth might well be that legal professionals wouldn't care about social scientific studies no matter what they produced, except in those instances when a study happens to lend support to their position in a particular case. Legal professionals live predominantly in the world of positive law rules, within the practice of law. As Richard Posner (1990a: 431) observed about the general failure of Legal Realist proposals for legal reform through social science: 'In particular, the lawyer's weak sense of fact—that lack of scientific spirit in law—was bound, sooner or later, to tell against the efficacy of legal reform.'

It is possible for socio-legal scholars to rationalize the indifference of judges and lawyers to their scholarship as necessary or even good, as the price of remaining free from the stultifying influence of the legal community's narrow concerns. There is a strong, though not unanimous (see Whitford 1989), view within the socio-legal community, especially reflected in the recent spate of studies focused on ideology critique, that socio-legal scholars should not produce legal reform oriented studies. The objective should instead be consciousness raising, and changing the world by changing the vocabulary. Whether for this purpose or for concrete reform, however, there is little indication of substantial interest by any audience outside the socio-legal community, by legislators, administrators, social activists, or members of the public.

This across-the-board rebuff suggests that there might be another over-arching factor in the failure of socio-legal studies to generate outside interest: people have become less receptive to the message. For at least the last twenty years—marked in law by the end of the Warren Court, in politics by Reagan-Thatcher, and in economics by the worldwide capitulation of Marxism (and increasingly of welfare socialism) to capitalism—political sentiment in the West, and beyond, has steadily shifted towards the right, away from the interests and concerns of socio-legal scholars. As socio-legal theorist Alan Hunt (1990: 510–11) put it, 'The closing years of the twentieth century are proving to be an epoch fraught with difficulties for progressive intellectuals. Contemporary Western societies seem further than ever away from the major structural transformations necessary for dismantling of the hierarchies of class, gender and race and the achievement of social justice.'

Interestingly, as another sign of the differences in temperament between the two sides, social scientists who study law appear less troubled by the apparently negligible impact of their work than socio-legal scholars from the law side. Those on the law side have a more directly instrumental, reformist bent, and are therefore more inclined to adjudge the socio-legal effort to date to be a disappointment. The social scientists are doing what they do in every field: conduct research projects, accumulate information, publish books and articles; if reform follows therefrom, fine, but regardless they will carry on collecting knowledge, which provides its own contentment. From the standpoint of the social scientists, such failure is not primarily the fault of the scientific effort—which has, after all, taught us much about law—but of the lack of political will to carry through suggested reforms, and of the peculiarly insular and thickheaded tunnelvision of the legal mind, which fails to take notice of the wealth of available information.

B. *Underdeveloped Theory*

The second theme—underdeveloped theory—is perhaps the most prominent. 'Today, some fear the movement is becoming an intellectual backwater, drawing on outmoded ideas about law and social inquiry and cut off from strong currents of thought in legal and social theory' (Trubek and Esser 1989: 6–7). This concern is not new. Max Travers (1993: 448) pointed out that a number of writers have 'noted the theoretically and methodologically underdeveloped nature of the field over the last thirty years'. Simon and Lynch (1989: 843) took a more positive view: 'in the recent past, attempts have been made to develop a theory of law, and while it is not complete, it is a useful step in the right direction.'

In one respect complaints about underdeveloped theory are strange. Socio-legal studies pieces are filled with references to fancy theories and theorists. On the first page of her article, 'A New Social Constructionism for Sociolegal Studies', Elizabeth Mertz (1994: 1243) cites, among other influences on the new constructionist approach to the study of law, Schutz, Berger and Luckman, Husserl, Weber,

Bourdieu, Foucault, Gramsci, Habermas, and Durkheim, all noted members of the pantheon of social theory. Too often, however, references to theory pay insufficient attention to the compatibility of the different theoretical sources identified, or are tacked on to the beginning and end of a study without being well integrated into the study itself.

Charges of underdeveloped theory fall into two categories, one relating to social science concerns and the other to legal concerns. Complaints in the former vein are that socio-legal scholars fail to appreciate the implications of longstanding debates in the philosophy of social science, like the problematic relationship between action and structure. The specific objection is not so much that there is an absence of theory, but that theories are applied by socio-legal scholars in an '*ad hoc* and instrumental way, rather than as part of a commitment to a principled and systematic investigation of social life' (Travers 1993: 443). Critics stressed 'the need to locate studies of law clearly within frameworks of inquiry indicated by sociological theory' (Cotterrell 1995: 84). In addition, socio-legal scholars have been specifically criticized for lagging behind in recognizing and implementing the new insights generated by the interpretive revolution in social science.

These charges are not entirely undeserved. In fairness, however, it should be recognized that interpretive analysis is now *the* hot mode in the field. 'Stories, not statutes or statistics, have become the subject matter of much sociolegal scholarship' (Ewick and Silbey 1995: 198). Moreover, condemnations emanating from social science departments about the deficient theorizing of socio-legal scholars carry overtones of over-zealous doctrinal policing, of self-appointed theoretical sophisticates looking down upon their supposedly less aware half-brethren. Nothing whatsoever prohibits a pragmatic '*ad hoc* and instrumental' use of theory, as long as it proves informative and does not give rise to internal contradictions. The longstanding academic tradition of defending the purity of schools and paradigms has directly contributed to the current state of disagreement in the social sciences. Finally, considering the recent influx into law faculties of persons with law degrees as well as doctorates in social science (the development which incited the backlash in US legal academia mentioned at the outset), combined with the greater interest in law as a subject of study within social science departments, it seems reasonable to project that the level of social science theory within socio-legal studies will quickly advance.

Complaints in the law vein are that socio-legal studies 'fall very short with their theories on law' (Ziegert 1979: 235; see also Snyder 1981:

163). That is, socio-legal studies have produced little theoretical work on law as such or on the relationship between law and society. Again, a case can be made that this often repeated charge is not entirely fair. The neo-Weberian vision of Roberto M. Unger (1976), who sees the development of society through the lens of legal development, the darker views of Donald Black (1976), who views law in terms of inequitable governmental social control, the cautiously optimistic views of Philippe Nonet and Philip Selznick (1978), who project the evolution of law towards lesser repression and greater responsiveness, and the systems analysis of Niklas Luhmann's autopoiesis (1982; see also Teubner 1988), are all filled with theories about law and its relation to society.

Despite these efforts,[14] the impression that theory in the field is inadequate is widespread. In part the problem is these theories are *too* theoretical: the evolutionary frameworks of Unger and Nonet and Selznick, and the systems analysis of Luhmann, are set at too high a level of abstraction to produce testable (verifiable or subject to falsification) hypotheses. This raises the question of whether they even qualify as scientific (not that these theorists would care if this honorific label were withheld); 'ideal type' evolutionary theories have the quality of projected history based upon future-looking prophecy; and Luhmann's systems analysis and his analogy to a biological organism cannot be adjudged in terms of correct or incorrect, but whether or not it is interesting and informative. Of the above theorists, only Black explicitly set out to produce testable hypotheses in a self-consciously scientific vein. However, his concept of law (as governmental social control) is basically limited in scope to criminal law (cf. Sciulli 1995: 809,819); hence his work is seldom mentioned in legal theory, though it has generated interest among criminologists. Moreover, Black formulated 'laws' of legal behaviour at an inopportune time, when behaviouristic analysis and positivism fell into disfavour. Thus he was writing to an unreceptive audience.

Comments about theoretical underdevelopment with regard to law can be interpreted as grumbling that the kind of theory which exists in socio-legal studies is not the kind we can do much with—that these theories are informative but not plausible in their totalizing (cover the universe) vein, nor very useful, either in serving as guidelines for research or in presenting a programme for positive change. We complain about the absence of grand theory, while at the same time our appetite for it,

[14] For an excellent, though slightly dated, overview of these (except Luhmann) and other theories in the field, see Moore (1986).

and belief in it, has waned. 'The authority of "grand theory" styles seems suspended for the moment in favour of a close consideration of such issues as contextuality, the meaning of social life to those who enact it, and the explanation of exceptions and indeterminants rather than regularities in the phenomena observed . . .' (Marcus and Fischer 1986: 8).

The suspicion of and distaste for grand theory is another symptom of the postmodern moment, a consequence of the postmodern privileging of local and micro- over the general. Several socio-legal theorists have forcefully voiced opposition to the disavowal of macro-level theory (Handler 1992; Hunt 1990), but few such theories are being ventured.

C. *The Influence of Politics*

The third and final theme—regarding political influences on socio-legal scholarship—is the most longstanding of the problems with socio-legal studies and may be the most damaging because it threatens the integrity and credibility of the field. Discussion over the tainting influence of the values of social scientists began with the very first issue of the *Law and Society Review*, and has erupted at regular intervals ever since.[15]

Social science generally has long struggled with this problem, but it is much more acute here because, as the recent President of the Law and Society Association, Sally Engle Merry (1995: 13), proclaimed, socio-legal scholars have evinced an 'historical concern for social justice and progressive politics'. And she showed no qualms about characterizing socio-legal work as 'left-liberal scholarship' (ibid.). Moreover, Merry's predecessor in the post, Joel Handler (1992), openly identified socio-legal studies with leftist transformative politics. Yet many of these socio-legal scholars receive grants from the National Science Foundation—which surely does not believe it is subsidizing leftist politics—and routinely preface their findings with observations about their careful methodology to bolster the scientific credibility of their findings.

If socio-legal studies is just leftist or far-left politics, however, it deserves as much attention as the noxious doctrinal tracts produced by the far right. As the latter would assert, the fact that the former bears the stamp of science is not a testament to its greater veracity, only a reflection of the fact that the left populates university social science departments and law faculties (see Duxbury 1995: 428–35). Michael King criticized the use of psychology in law in a manner which applies

[15] See e.g. Auerbach (1966); Skolnick (1966); Nonet (1976); Nelson (1988); Silbey and Sarat (1987).

to socio-legal studies generally: 'what passes for knowledge is often no more than an ideology or value system which some social group seeks to impose in order to maintain the existing social order or to change society in the direction which the group considers appropriate' (quoted in Lloyd-Bostock 1981: 20).

Contrary to the 'status quo v. critical' alternatives expressed by King, however, there is little balance in socio-legal studies, where the dominance of the left is acute. For example, the Introduction to a recent collection of works by many of the most prominent legal anthropologists working today contains unabashed declarations of their leftist faith:

> Because all the contributors hold the view that legal orders create asymmetrical power relations, they also share the assumption that the law is not neutral. The legal system does not provide an impartial arena in which contestants from all strata of society may meet to resolve differences. For example, conflicts between factions of a ruling class may shape the possibilities open to subordinated groups (Starr and Collier 1989: 7).

The very taken-for-granted flavour of these statements reflects the extent to which they are widespread wisdom in the field, at least among the older generation of scholars. Similarly, the radical left notion of 'hegemony' is often repeated, but seldom demonstrated, in socio-legal scholarship.[16]

There is a strong 'critical' wing within socio-legal studies which is explicitly political in orientation (Silbey and Sarat 1987), and a good deal of the work produced in the field consists of leftist criticisms of law or the legal order. So predominant is this trend that socio-legal studies in the United States have been identified as one branch of critical theory (Singer 1988: 536). And at the initial formation of Critical Legal Studies, a movement of the radical left which is avowedly political, socio-legal scholars were an important wing of the group (Duxbury 1995: 435–50; Schlegel 1984).[17] Thus it is not surprising when the editors of the above collection acknowledge that several contributors 'recognize the convergence between their interests and the interests of the Critical Legal Studies Movement' (Starr and Collier 1989: 6).

Peter Just points out the dangers involved when he criticized Laura

---

[16] Perhaps as a sign of growing dissatisfaction, use of the term hegemony, along with other favourite 'buzzwords', has become a source of ridicule among socio-legal scholars (see Macaulay 1992: 826).

[17] According to Mark Tushnet (1991: 1542 n. 102), 'The law and society movement already includes a significant number of feminists and "political economists" who are associated with CLS.'

Nader's claim that the consensual orientation of the Zapotec was a Christian-tradition based, 'anti-hegemonic' strategy to keep the colonial legal system at bay. In the actual ethnographic data presented by Nader, Just (1992: 394) 'found little to connect the operation of Zapotecan legal harmony either with Christian tradition or with "encroaching superordinate powerholders".' Just (p. 406) recognized that this imposition upon the data by Nader is not uncommon in the field, and warned that:

> . . . the anthropologist of law must be even more careful when he or she sees something in the other society that has ideological implications for his or her own, careful not to confuse those ideological implications for either a clear-sighted vision of 'what is going on' in the other society (however elusive and illusory such an objectivist—nay, positivist—sense of ethnographic reality may be) or for indigeneous ideology. We should be careful, in short, not to appropriate *them* simply as a means of talking about *us*.

The social sciences have a long and honourable history of serving as critics of culture and society, and there are convincing arguments that it should have this role (See Marcus and Fisher 1986). But this critical role derives its power from the fact that science has championed the banner of truth. It is fashionable in this postmodern period to dismiss as naïve or too positivist Max Weber's insistence that the values of the scientific investigator should come into play only when selecting the problem to be studied, and that the investigation itself must be conducted as objectively as possible. If not, however, just as CLS charges that 'law is politics,' and for many of the same reasons, socio-legal studies will be nothing but politics.

More to the point, postmodernism would appear to insist upon precisely that. If the objectivity claimed by scientism is necessarily false, and the fact/value distinction cannot be drawn, and scientists inevitably view the world from within their own biases, then it's all politics anyway, so the socio-legal scholar ought to face up to it and embrace politics without reservation, as 'critical empiricists' have argued (Trubek and Esser 1989). A different response, however, and one more consistent with these beliefs, is to give up social science completely, or at least give up the claim that what one is doing can be called science. Otherwise the scientist is operating under a banner that carries a false claim to authority.

Few socio-legal scholars would, or would want to, accept either conclusion. The fact that socio-legal studies regularly assume a critical stance toward the law is not itself the problem. Rather it is the selectiveness of this critical gaze—social scientists should be equally critical (or suspicious, or testing) towards whatever exists in the field of study, and especially towards their own predispositions and activities. No social scientist can sincerely believe that the left alone has a lock on the truth. If postmodernism suggests that there is a degree of irreducible pluralism of interpretations, then socio-legal scholars should recover as many of these as possible. While the currently popular call to articulate the 'oppositional' view is laudable (Ewick and Silbey 1995), an exclusive emphasis on this is not. Social science which shows only the leftist, hyper-critical truth will in fact *be* politics, because all it will be doing is promoting one perspective over the others.[18]

Finally, even theorists who urge that social science should emphasize criticism recognize that 'the critic must be able to *pose alternatives* to the conditions he is criticizing. . . . The traditional rhetorical strategies are increasingly easy to dismiss because they are either so thoroughly pessimistic that no alternative at all can be foreseen, or else so thoroughly idealist or romantic in posing alternatives as to lack credibility' (Marcus and Fischer 1986:115–16, emphasis in original). Socio-legal studies suffer from the failure to heed this advice.

The foregoing portrait of the influence of politics in socio-legal studies, accurate as it may be, is not entirely fair, as it is too onesided. A number of socio-legal scholars have implicitly or explicitly indicated discomfort with the influence of politics in the field (see Tetlock and Mitchell 1993),[19] as reflected in calls for a 'naturalistic' study of law which emphasizes 'dispassionate' description (see Hawkins 1992). And a distance has been maintained between CLS and socio-legal scholars, at least to some degree, because many of the latter take science seriously in a way the former does not. Futhermore, the US socio-legal community goes much further with overt politics than do other socio-legal communities.[20] There is also fragmentation within the US

[18] Farber and Sherry (1993: 844) observes that there is an ideological bias in the narrative literature which discourages the telling of conservative stories.

[19] Tetlock and Mitchell (1993) discuss the strong leftist bias in psychological studies of justice, which results in caricatured portraits of conservatives and threatens the credibility of the field.

[20] For example, articles in a recent special issue of the (British) *Journal of Law and Society* (Special Issue 1995), dedicated to a review of the twenty-one year existence of the Oxford Centre for Socio-Legal Studies, heavily emphasize empiricism with nary a mention of postmodernism. They appear almost quaint by comparison to articles in a contemporaneous issue of the (American) Law and Society Review (Symposium 1995), many of which mention postmodernism and the critical approach.

socio-legal community, as insider Austin Sarat (1994: 617 n. 6) points out: 'The positivists feel unappreciated; the interpretivists feel threatened; critical scholars believe that the work of law and society scholars and the Association is not political enough; traditional social scientists, that it has been too politicized.'

Considering the long history of discussions over the influence of politics in socio-legal studies, it appears likely that this will always be a struggle. There are perhaps three main differences with today's situation. First, the anti-positivist, postmodern challenge to the fact-value distinction has removed an essential source of support for those who take the position that science should be free of politics. Consequently, the critics appear to have the hottest theory on their side. Secondly, they lay claim to being radicals engaged in transforming the world (Ewick and Silbey 1995: 199), by way of contrast to the conformist, old-fashioned and ineffective positivists, thus seizing the high road as champions of the oppressed. Thirdly, an impressive and highly respected clique within the unofficial leadership of socio-legal studies—including prominent scholars, presidents of leading associations, and review editors of journals—are among those most vocal in promoting their political position. Not only does this create an inaccurate image of the field as a whole, it strongly reinforces the notion that socio-legal studies *should* be leftist critical politics, generating pressure on younger scholars to conform, suppressing the expression of alternative views,[21] which portends ill for the future.

Locating a Path Forward

This book will attempt to make a positive contribution in each of the three problem areas discussed above. With regard to the first two problems—underdeveloped theory and the questionable value of the work—interdisciplinary barriers were major contributing factors. The obvious prescription is that each side must learn more about the understanding and concerns of the other, especially with regard to their underlying theoretical presuppositions. This book begins with the lawyers' and legal theorists' perspectives and interests, but strives to work in the social scientists' and social theorists' perspectives and interests in an integrated fashion. While trying to show the many points of

---

[21] This suppression extends to making it more difficult for people who challenge the standard leftist position from having their articles accepted for publication in journals (see Suedfeld and Tetlock (1991)).

connection, the knowledge and terminology of both groups will be drawn upon in almost equal measure. Inevitably, this strategy risks saying more about law than those on the social science side are interested in, and more about social science than those on the law side have patience for; and it risks elaborating aspects of science the scientists take for granted and aspects of law the lawyers take for granted. But the idea is to help create a hybrid vocabulary and set of concepts for socio-legal studies that partakes of both of its contributing influences.

In addition to the general benefit of joining the two realms of discourse in a single piece, through an extended discussion of issues in both the philosophy of social science and legal theory I hope to lessen modestly the theoretical deficit in the field. With regard to social science, I explore issues in epistemology and in the nature of meaning which have not been fully appreciated in socio-legal studies. With regard to law, I selectively have targeted core issues within legal theory, like the concept of law, legal positivism, and the nature of judging. Although socio-legal scholars are correct to insist that the field should not be dominated by the legal perspective, an effort must be made to draw direct connections whenever they exist and are illuminating. In particular, the social theory of law I elaborate in the course of this book provides a bridge between the two disciplines which will allow for communication in relation to a shared baseline.

Finally, the last problem mentioned, the influence of politics in socio-legal studies, is of central relevance to the discussion in the following Chapter, in which I locate the position of socio-legal studies among the current mix of legal theories, identifying its close connections to Legal Realism and philosophical pragmatism. I will draw upon the latter to mount a response to postmodernism and the denial of the fact-value distinction. More generally, the thrust of this book as a whole is to articulate a solid grounding for a realistic approach to socio-legal studies by way of contrast to the critical wing. This realistic approach insists on recognizing the value of old positivist approaches like functionalism and behaviourism, as well as new approaches like interpretivism, with awareness of the faults and limitations of both. And it insists that doing social science is a distinct enterprise with a powerful critical capacity, which should not be collapsed into the narrow political activism represented by the critical empiricism touted by the radical left.

2 Pragmatism and Realistic Socio-legal Studies

Philosophical Pragmatism

Writing at the turn of the last century, William James and John Dewey, building upon the work of Charles Sanders Peirce, set about to construct an alternative to the then dominant schools of philosophical thought: German rationalism and British empiricism. Both theorists believed that philosophy was in a sorry state because these traditions stood at opposite extremes, constructing a false and unresolvable set of philosophical antinomies.

At one extreme were the 'Tender Minded' rationalists, as James labelled them, referring to Kant and Hegel and German philosophy generally, though it also applied to non-German philosophers. These philosophers had an excessive desire for order, first principles, abstraction, the *a priori*, ideas, and certainty, and they were optimistic, religious, monistic and dogmatic (James 1975: 13). They were 'tender minded' because their work evinced the desire to escape the messy, contingent, chaotic reality of everyday life, in favour of the 'more real' realm of the absolute. Striving to locate this absolute realm led to the massive analytical structures constructed by these philosophers.

The problem with rationalist philosophy was not just the excessive degree of abstraction it engendered; the problem was that the philosophers considered the absolute to be *the* ultimate reality, the realm of ordered truth hidden behind the apparent chaos of experience. This belief led philosophers to declare the essential unity and order of things despite the obvious contradiction that everyday reality posed. Occupied with this absolute realm, philosophy had nothing to say, no guidance to offer, to the temporal realm. There is no absolute, James and Dewey argued. The analytical schemes produced by these philosophers are transparently fictional inventions, constructed to provide them with a place of repose from the harsh world outside their third floor study.

At the other extreme were the 'Tough Minded' empiricists, which refered to the British school of empiricism led by David Hume. These philosophers were focused on facts, sensations, the material world, and pluralism, and they were pessimitic, irreligious, fatalistic and sceptical. With a stiff upper lip and shoulders held stout, tough-minded empiricists were prepared to meet the world head on, facing it as it was in all of its contingency. They focused on the immediately real and nothing more, without any comforting illusions.

Philosophical pragmatism is in many respects close to empiricism. Consequently, James and Dewey directed the bulk of their critique at the rationalist tradition. Their major criticism of the empiricists is that they were too atomistic in their focus on discrete sensations as the basis for knowledge. 'Experience carries principles of connection and organization within itself' (Dewey 1948: 91). An atomistic view of experience denies the reality of the pervasive influence of tradition (customs, habits, beliefs) on our experience. Moreover, the empiricists were too austere in their rejection of concepts and generalizations. '[A]bstraction is essential' in the organization of and learning from experience (Dewey 1948: 149–50).[1] As James (1975: 275) put it, the 'pragmatist himself has no objection to abstractions. . . . But he never ascribes to them a higher grade of reality.' Finally, James and Dewey objected that the empiricists were too sceptical—too negative, destructive, and fatalistic, not allowing for the melioristic approach to positive social reform favored by pragmatists.

Dewey (1948: 99–102) summarized the harmful series of contrasts between these two schools of thought:

> By common consent, the effect of English empiricism was sceptical where that of German rationalism was apologetic; it undermined where the latter justified. It detected accidental associations formed into customs under the influence of self- or class-interest where German rational–idealism discovered profound meanings due to the necessary evolution of absolute reason. The modern world has suffered because in so many matters philosophy has offered it only an arbitrary choice between hard and fast opposites: Disintegrating analysis or rigid synthesis; complete radicalism neglecting and attacking the historic past as trivial and harmful, or complete conservatism idealizing institutions as embodiments of eternal reason; a resolution of experience into atomic elements that afford no support to stable organization or a clamping down of all experience by fixed categories and necessary concepts—these are the alternatives that conflicting schools have presented . . . .
>
> A philosophic reconstruction which should relieve men of having to choose between an impoverished and truncated experience on one hand and an artificial and impotent reason on the other would relieve human effort from the heaviest intellectual burden it has to carry. It would destroy the division of men

---

[1] In James' (1975: 300) graphic imagery: 'Without abstract concepts to handle our perceptual particulars by, we are like men hopping on one foot. Using concepts along with the particulars, we become bipedal.'

of good will into two hostile camps. It would permit the co-operation of those who respect the past and the institutionally established with those who are interested in establishing a freer and happier future. For it would determine the conditions under which the funded experience of the past and the contriving intelligence which looks to the future can effectually interact with each other. It would enable men to glorify the claims of reason without at the same time falling into a paralyzing worship of super-empirical authority or into an offensive 'rationalization' of things as they are.

Dewey's words convey the sense in which philosophical pragmatism draws from common sense pragmatism: avoid extremes, and use whatever works. 'Antidualism was one of the leitmotifs of pragmatism' (Joas 1993: 72).

The pragmatic critique of philosophy led to its core tenets, which I earlier characterized as 'thin'. According to James (1975: 37), pragmatism consists of just two basic aspects: a method of inquiry and a theory of truth. Both of these aspects were derived from the pragmatists' observations about knowledge.

Their first, crucial step was to challenge the long dominant philosophical view of knowledge—the view that knowledge of the ultimate, the absolute, the permanent and unchanging true Being, could only be obtained through contemplation, because only in this manner can the 'illusion' of messy existence be escaped. 'There was bequeathed to generations of thinkers as an unquestioned axiom the idea that knowledge is intrinsically a mere beholding or viewing of reality—the spectator conception of knowledge. So deeply engrained was this idea that it prevailed for centuries after the actual progress of science had demonstrated that knowledge is power to transform the world, and centuries after the practice of effective knowledge had adopted the method of experimentation' (Dewey 1948: 112).

Pragmatism replaced the spectator conception of knowledge with an operative one—knowledge is 'the active control of nature and of experience' (Dewey 1948: 122). Action, not contemplation, is the key to knowledge. Knowledge is obtained through experience gained in the course of working in the world to achieve our projects. 'Knowing, for the experimental sciences, means a certain kind of intelligently conducted doing; it ceases to be contemplative and becomes in a true sense practical' (Dewey 1948: 121). Although science provided the most obvious example of operative knowlege, Dewey emphasized that it is no different from the knowledge exemplified by artisans (1948: 110–11, 114–15). Pursuant to this view, knowing is 'conceived of as active and operative, after the analogy of experiment guided by hypothesis, or by invention guided by the imagination of some possibility' (p. 123).

Intelligently conducted doing takes place within a material environment and a context that involves both prexisting ways of doing (knowing) and a community of doers; it takes place within practices. 'For Peirce and Dewey, inquiry is cooperative human interaction with an environment; and both aspects, the active intervention, the active manipulation of the environment, and the cooperation with other human beings, are vital. . . . For the pragmatists, the model is a group of inquirers trying to produce good ideas and trying to test them to see which ones have value' (Putnam 1995: 70–1).

This operative view of knowledge gave rise to the first aspect of pragmatism—a science-based methodology of inquiry. 'The first distingushing characteristic of thinking then is facing the facts—inquiry, minute and extensive scrutinizing, observation' (Dewey 1948: 140).[2] This inquiry is not aimless or random; it is anticipatory, purposeful, 'with some vague sense of the *meaning* of the difficulty' (p. 142, emphasis in original). Dewey (pp. 145–6) warned, however, that 'there is always danger that [such inquiry] will be subordinated to maintaining some preconceived purpose or prejudice. . . . Being precommitted to arriving at some special result, it is not sincere.'

The key is 'disinterested and impartial inquiry', which 'means that there is no particular end set up in advance so as to shut in the activities of observation, forming of ideas, and application' (p. 146). Disinterested and impartial inquiry is crucial to the success of instrumental knowledge; a prejudicial investigation will only tell you what you already believe or want to believe, which may be incorrect; only through open and careful attention to the facts can one discover the best possible way to understand and deal with the problem at hand.

This view of knowledge and the science-based methodology of inquiry led directly to the second aspect of pragmatism—a theory of truth. In Dewey's words (1948: 156, emphasis in original):

If ideas, meanings, conceptions, notions, theories, systems are instrumental to an active reorganization of the given environment, to a removal of some specific trouble and perplexity, then the test of their validity and value lies in accomplishing this work. If they succeed in their office, they are reliable, sound, valid, good, true. If they fail to clear up confusion, to eliminate defects, if they

---

[2] James (1975: 32) described the pragmatic method this way: 'The attitude of looking away from first things, principles, "categories," supposed necesities; and of looking towards last things, fruits, consequences, facts.'

increase confusion, uncertainty and evil when they are acted upon, then are they truly false. Confirmation, corroboration, verification lie in works, consequences. Handsome is that handsome does. By their fruits shall ye *know* them. That which guides us truly is true—demonstrated capacity for such guidance is precisely what is meant by truth.

Truth is what works. Truths can change, and new truths can be created as we work in the world, contributing to and shaping reality through our activities.

This instrumental conception of truth was consistent with a highly sophisticated understanding of science. James (1975: 206–7) described this understanding:

> Up to about 1850 almost everyone believed that sciences expressed truths that were exact copies of a definite code of non-human realities. But the enormously rapid multiplication of theories in these latter days has well-nigh upset the notion of any one of them being a more literally objective kind of thing than another. There are so many geometries, so many logics, so many physical and chemical hypotheses, so many classifications, each one of them good for so much yet not good for everything, that the notion that even the truest formula may be a human device and not a literal transcript has dawned upon us. . . . The suspicion is in the air nowadays that the superiority of one of our formulas to another may not consist so much in its literal 'objectivity', as in subjective qualities like its usefulness, its 'elegance' or its congruity with our residual beliefs.

James wrote these words—which deny the correspondence theory of truth—almost a century ago, and only recently have they become a widely accepted view of the nature of knowledge produced by the natural sciences (though many dissenters remain).

To a large extent our actions are guided by habit or custom. New truths come about when some experience (solving an intractable problem, discovering a contradiction, exposure to an unexplainable fact or phenomenon) puts a strain on old beliefs or existing recipies for action. For each individual, new truths are adopted in a conservative and patchwork fashion, preserving 'the older stock of truths with a minimum of modification, stretching them just enough to make them admit the novelty, but conceiving that in ways as familiar as the case leaves possible' (James 1975: 35). In this process, James asserted (p. 35), the 'first principle' is loyalty to old truths. His view on this matter presages Quine's influential holistic account of knowledge.[3]

---

[3] See Putnam (1995: 11–19) (describing James' holism). Quine's theory will be elaborated in Ch. 6.

Thus, thinking is situated within a particular problem framework,[4] and is governed by the already existing corpus of beliefs, by tradition; though at any given moment the grip on thought of a limited number of this body of old truths can be loosened—through critical reflection or leaps of imagination—when they prove inadequate to the problem at hand.[5]

Finally, the pragmatists limited the scope of truth. Truth, according to Dewey, is restricted to matters-of-fact, to the empirical, which is the realm in which science reigns supreme.

But the realm of meanings is wider than that of true-and-false meanings; it is more urgent and more fertile. When the claim of meanings to truth enters in, then truth is indeed preeminent. But this fact is often confused with the idea that truth has a claim to enter everywhere; that it has monopolistic jurisdiction. Poetic meanings, moral meanings, a large part of the goods of life are matters of richness and freedom of meanings, rather than of truth; a large part of our life is carried on in a realm of meanings to which truth and falsity as such are irrelevant (Dewey 1925: 332).

Accordingly, both truth and science have a circumscribed role in the realm of meaning.

At the time of its promulgation, the pragmatic theory of truth incited ridicule and outrage from the philosophical establishment,[6] and even today it remains controversial. The nuances of the debate cannot be reproduced here. Instead, I will address, in order, three often pressed objections: 1) that pragmatism defines truth in terms of individual utility, making it subjective; 2) that realists embrace a contradiction when they combine holism and realism; and 3) that pragmatism is relativistic and self-refuting.

The pragmatist argument that truth is what works, what satisfies, led many to believe that this definition gave license to each individual to define truth for his or her self, in terms of what satisfied or worked for them. This was a gross misunderstanding, as Hilary Putnam (1995: 24 n. 7) insists:

Some critics even read James—against repeated statements to the contrary, explicit and implicit, in his writings—as holding that if the consequences of

---

[4] Dewey and James argued that in large part we engage in our activities without thinking, through habit; thought was required only when trouble arose (Dewey 1948: 139).

[5] For an excellent discussion of the pragmatist view of thought as situated, practice bound, and largely coloured by existing beliefs, see Grey (1989: 793–805).

[6] An account of the highly dismissive German reaction to pragmatism can be found in Joas (1993: 94–121) ('American Pragmatism and German Thought: A History of Misunderstandings').

believing that *p* are good for *you*, then *p* is 'true for you.' Let me say once and for all that James never used the notion of 'true for me' or 'true for you.' Truth, he insists, is a notion which presupposes a community, and, like Peirce, he held that the widest possible community, the community of all persons (and possibly all sentient beings) in the long run, is the relevant one.

Thus the satisfaction theory of truth does not imply 'a meeting of purely personal need. . . . It includes public and objective conditions. It is not to be manipulated by whim or personal idiosyncrasy' (Dewey 1948: 157). Israel Scheffler (quoted in Flanagan 1991: 37) articulated it in a clarifying way:

> The satisfactory character of a true belief consists in its predictive adequacy. If a given belief is true, then, and only then, if you act on this belief, forming your expectations in accordance with it, experience will *satisfy these expectations or predictions*, it being irrelevant whether or not *you are satisfied also*.

That is why pragmatists emphasized careful scrutiny of the facts. There is a fact of the matter—although we can only perceive this from within a tradition shaped perspective—and beliefs which do not agree with these facts are false.

James (1975: 272) repeatedly pointed out that pragmatists 'carefully posited "reality" *ab initio*;' that is, each individual is up against the world, a world which consists of material objects (including other individuals) that are not 'malleable to thought' (Rorty 1979: 279). The 'notion of reality independent of either of us, taken from ordinary social experience, lies at the base of the pragmatist definition of truth. With some such reality any statement, in order to be counted true, must agree' (James 1975: 283). Where the pragmatists depart from Realists[7] is in their insistence that 'there is no one way the world really is . . . The world is carved up in accordance with human values and interests' (Flanagan 1991: 37).

Critics have seized upon this response to assert that pragmatists cannot subscribe both to holism and to realism, which are contradictory positions. Holism implies giving up sharp dualisms like fact/value, fact/theory, interpretation/fact, which would seem to indicate that pragmatists cannot talk about agreement with the facts or with reality; yet 'James's philosophy contains a strong strain of "direct" realism, that

---

[7] Although the pragmatists posited reality, they were not 'Realists' in the philosophical sense of an absolute reality independent of the human mind. Rather, they believed that reality comes to us through the 'human touch' (James 1975: 119), and that, in a non-idealistic sense, through activity in the world humans participate in creating reality.

is of the doctrine that perception is of objects and events "out there" '
(Putnam 1995: 19). The pragmatic explanation is that while we do
indeed constitute reality through our perception of it, we share and perceive a common world, stabilized through shared experiences, constraining conditions, languages and concepts; within this context we can
talk about facts and about reality. A 'fallibilistic' theory of truth—that
is, being open to the possibility that a truth today may not be a truth
at some later period—as distinct from an absolute theory of truth, or
from its opposite, scepticism (the denial of the possibility of truth), is
what allows pragmatists to straddle this apparent contradiction. As
Putnam (1995: 21) notes, 'this may seem a delicate (some will say
impossible) balancing act, but it represents the situation in which we
live.'

This explanation verifies two important assertions in the previous
Chapter. First, it demonstrates that despite adhering to holism and to
an antifoundationalist view of truth, the pragmatists were not sceptics
in the sense highlighted by postmodernism (Putnam 1995: 68–74).
'Pragmatism has been characterized by *antiscepticism* . . .' (p. 21, emphasis in original). The fact that there are no absolute truths is not a reason to doubt the possibility of truth or to doubt any particular truth;
postmodernism makes these errors. Secondly, it illustrates how pragmatism treats philosophical discourse and everyday discourse separately—holding an anti-realistic position in the former (rejecting
metaphysical Realism, the position that there is a sharp distinction to
be drawn between the properties things have 'in themselves' and the
properties 'projected by us') and holding a realistic one in the latter
(accepting realism about the things we interact with everyday).[8]

[O]nly those who had lost touch with the familiar objects—the citrus fruits . . .
the birds, fish, tables, armchairs, vehicles, machines, and so on—'whose antics
make our sentences and opinions true or false' would think of objecting to being
called realistic. But to say this indicates nothing about what position such a person would (should) take concerning the debate between professional philosophers who claim that an objective world (one that exists independent of our
thought and language) makes our true statements true (the realists) and those
who take issue with that claim (the anti-realists) (Murphy 1990: 114).[9]

To the charge of relativism, the final objection regularly levelled
against pragmatism, pragmatists respond that this critique has no bite

---

[8] See J. Conant, 'Introduction', in Putnam (1990: xliv–xlv).
[9] In this passage Murphy is articulating Donald Davidson's position.

because there is no absolute. The notion of absolute truth can serve as a regulative ideal; what the pragmatists challenge is 'the pretence on anyone's part to have found for certain at any given moment what the shape of that truth is' (James 1975: 309). In practice, given that no absolute truths have ever been demonstrated, there is no difference in consequence between these two views; the absolutist's version of truth works out to the same thing as the pragmatist's. When trying to establish any given truth, both the absolutist and the pragmatist must resort to verification (or attempts at falsification). This response concedes that pragmatism is relativistic, in the sense that relativism is a denial of the absolute, but insists that the absolutists' claims of truth are equally relativistic, regardless of what they assert, because the claim to absoluteness is illusory. Thus, there is really no point in discussing relativism.

At this point, however, critics contend that pragmatists fall into the relativist paradox: the very assertion that truths are relative is prohibited because to assert it is to assert a non-relative truth. James's response is that even this assertion—truths are relative—is meant in the pragmatic sense of truth (1975: 302). That is, it should be tested and discussed to see whether it fits, and it may later be revised or corrected. Adopting a fallibilistic theory of truth means that even that theory is fallible. The paradox is escaped as long as this is recognized.

There are many complicated ramifications to pragmatism; there are differences among the pragmatists which I have suppressed in this account; and pragmatists wrote volumes on a myriad of subjects ranging from the nature of consciousness to education. But the above sets out the core of pragmatic philosophy.

It should now be evident why pragmatism is empty of substance: a methodology of inquiry and a theory of truth do not themselves present any truths about the world (other than the theory of truth itself). Pragmatism does not say what the good is, how to live, what economic or political system to develop, or anything else of that nature. That is why James (1975: 32) asserted that pragmatism 'stands for no particular results. It has no dogmas, and no doctrines save its method'. This is not to deny the power of pragmatism, only to indicate that, as Rorty (1992a: 724) put it, 'much of pragmatism is purely negative and renunciatory,' expended in the critique of existing philosophical traditions and the absolutist view of truth, and limited in import to issues of specifically philosophical concern.

This lack of substantive content is what allows scholars on the left, right, and centre of US legal theory to resort simultaneously to pragmatism. No argument leads from pragmatism to any particular political position. Pragmatism 'is neutral between alternative prophecies, and thus neutral between democrats and fascists' (Rorty 1992b: 75; see also Fish 1990: 1464). What, then, does pragmatism have to offer legal theory and why have so many theorists lined up behind it?

Pragmatism In US Legal Theory

Consistent with the above discussion, I will divide the resort to pragmatism in US legal theory into negative (critical) uses and positive (constructive) uses. Both uses are saturated with irony, as I will show. First I will cover the negative uses, which can be grouped into two basic categories: a critique of essentialist/conceptualist formalism, and an admonition to avoid excessive theorizing or abstractions. Then I will address the constructive uses: more dialogue, traditionalism, attention to context, and the middle way. Finally, I will indicate why legal theorists have converged on pragmatism despite its questionable value for their purposes, and I will identify where socio-legal studies stand in the context of legal pragmatism.

A. Resort to Pragmatism for Negative Purposes

Essentialist/conceptualist formalism, as distinct from rule oriented formalism,[10] is the kind of formalism Legal Realist Felix Cohen long ago dismissed as so much 'transcendental nonsense'. It is the view of law as consisting of a set of abstract concepts and principles with rationally governed internal and external relations which mechanically lead to specific answers in particular cases. This version of formalism consists of two connected components—legal concepts or principles, and mechanistic reasoning. The former component provided legitimation for judge-made common law (which, aside from references to customary social practices, lacked democratic underpinnings) by suggesting that the judges were not making but finding the law as it exists in these abstract concepts and principles. The latter component provided legitimation to the stage of application by removing the active presence of the individual judge, in effect denying that the judge's subjective values infected the 'mechanical' reasoning process.

---

[10] At the most basic level, rule-oriented formalism is the attitude that rules should be considered binding (see Schauer (1988)). There is nothing inherently metaphysical about this notion, although mechanistic understandings of how rules operate can have metaphysical overtones.

Both of these aspects of essentialist/conceptualist formalism have been thoroughly discredited in US legal thought through the influence of the Realists (Singer 1988: 496–503). Consequently, it is difficult to find any formalists of this classical type among US scholars or judges today (Smith 1990: 427). But residual strains of formalism remain. In his 'pragmatist manifesto', Richard Posner (1990a: 455) bemoaned the fact that 'at this writing the formalist style is resurgent in the Supreme Court and in the lower federal courts as well.' Thus, Posner argues (1990b: 1663–4), pragmatism is still needed as a 'powerful antidote to formalism', to combat conceptualism as well as claims of deductive legal reasoning.

Indeed, CLS scholar Joseph Singer (1988: 505–32), in the course of touting pragmatism, persuasively argues that all of the major legal theories formulated since the Realists—from the legal process and reasoned elaboration schools led by Hart and Sacks, to the rights school led by Dworkin and Rawls, to (especially) the law and economics school led by Posner[11]—have reintroduced significant elements of formalism. 'They each attempt to recreate, to some extent, the idea of an objective standpoint that judges can use to adjudicate complex legal issues without taking sides in desperate social struggles' (p. 516).

Law and economics, which bears the brunt of Singer's critique, is a particular villain in this regard, with its mathematical models and objective sounding formulas about efficiency and wealth maximization, and its resort to the free market as a neutral process. Posner (1990b: 1667–8) concedes that law and economics is formalistic,[12] but counters that it represents a good kind of formalism which follows pragmatic injunctions to apply the scientific method, to pay attention to consequences, and to see law in instrumental terms (as a means to maximize wealth). Critical scholars respond that economic analysis of law is hardly if at all scientific in the empirical sense (Singer 1988: 522, 525–6). The only 'facts' in the overwhelming majority of law and economics pieces are stipulated in unrealistic, simplified hypotheticals, and the 'science' involved consists mostly of the manipulation of models, with the 'consequences' predetermined by the economic propositions presupposed at the outset.

Singer is clearly correct that law and economics, as well as other

---

[11] A clear overview of these and other jurisprudential schools, and their relation to the Realists, can be found in Minda 1989; see also Tamanaha 1992.
[12] Posner (1990a: 24) ('Economic analysis of law is a formalist edifice erected upon a realist base . . .').

existing legal theories, contains strains of formalism. However, it does not follow therefrom that CLS is more consistent with pragmatism than the other theories. After a sharply argued critique which persuasively demonstrated that every existing major legal theory—except CLS—is formalistic in one sense or another, Singer arrived at the following supposedly realist/pragmatist-based prescription: we need more *conversation*. This prescription, it should be noted, was not about how judging should be conducted, which was the subject of all the legal theories he criticized, but rather was directed to liberal and critical theorists. The notion that *more conversation among theorists* is a solution to the problems involved with judging is as far as one could get from the practice-oriented approach taken by the pragmatists. But Singer is not entirely to blame for this empty proposal; it reflects the prescriptive emptiness of pragmatic philosophy, as we will see again and again.

Furthermore, it is incorrect to imply that the pragmatists rejected formalism per se, though their instrumentalist/anti-essentialist position does contest aspects of conceptual formalism. A formalism that serves our interests is good. Any system built around rules will require some level of formalism, for at base, rule formalism simply means *following rules*. And a certain degree of rule formalism is desirable in law because, as Dewey (1931: 137) recognized, 'There is of course every reason why rules of law should be as regular and as definite as possible.'

The second negative use of pragmatism in legal theory is the admonition to avoid excessive abstractions. Recall, however, that James and Dewey insisted that abstractions, generalizations and theories are 'essential' to organizing experience and knowledge. Their point was that abstractions should be judged by their instrumental value, and they cautioned against assigning abstractions a higher status than the empirical reality to which they referred.

There are no modern day Kants in legal theory, at least not in the United States. And though certain legal theorists do approach these heights in their love for abstraction, there is no standard for determining when a given level of abstraction is excessive, except perhaps the rough one of checking what percentage of readers are unable to read to completion a given theoretical work. Presumably every theorist believes that whatever level of abstraction they produce in their work is useful and necessary. One legal pragmatist suggested that the only way to decide how much abstraction is enough is to keep trying to construct theories to 'determine what level of generality works best' (Farber 1988: 1349). This is 'compelling' advice, Steven Smith (1990: 433) wryly observed in his review of pragmatism, 'and it will become significant just as soon as serious scholars begin to urge that theories be constructed on levels of generality that do not work best'.

B. Resort to Pragmatism for Constructive Proposals

With regard to the constructive uses of pragmatism in legal theory, four basic proposals have been proffered. In the discussion of Singer I have already mentioned one: 'The modern pragmatists' stress on conversation or dialogue . . .' (Radin 1990: 1708). There is nothing wrong with more talk, but that is the most one can say about the proposal. The three other proposals are traditionalism, attention to context, and taking the middle way.

Traditionalism is the centre-to-conservative take on pragmatism,[13] which suggests that change should occur slowly and incrementally, with respect for existing institutions. The argument is that traditions define who we are, they represent the inheritance of our culture, and they provide the very categories and beliefs with which we think. Accordingly, traditions are valuable and should be valued, within limits, for their own sake. In the legal context, traditionalism basically prescribes adherence to precedent and cautious institutional reform.

This view of the importance of tradition is not inconsistent with the pragmatism of James and Dewey,[14] though valuing traditions 'for their own sake' goes too far. The particular emphasis on tradition in pragmatism was that our thinking *cannot help* but be shaped by tradition-based ideas and beliefs. Remember that Dewey and James were social reformers who, as quoted earlier, had no patience for 'idealizing institutions as embodiments of eternal reason'. Dewey (1931: 139) directly addressed the danger in slavish adherence to longstanding rules:

Here is where the great practical evil of the doctrine of immutable and necessary antecedent rules comes in. It sanctifies the old; adherence to it in practice constantly widens the gap between current social conditions and the principles used by the courts. The effect is to breed irritation, disrespect for law, together with virtual alliance between the judiciary and entrenched interests that corre-

---

[13] A detailed discussion of traditionalists is contained in Chow (1992). The pre-eminent academic exponent of traditionalism is Anthony T. Kronman (see Kronman 1990).

[14] I should note that Anthony Kronman, a leading scholar of traditionalist pragmatism largely bases his views on the Burkean pragmatism, not that of Dewey and James. My objective is not to critique Kronman's analysis directly but to analyse the relationship between that kind of pragmatism and the philosophical pragmatism associated with James and Dewey.

spond most nearly to the conditions under which the rules of law were previously laid down.

Traditions should be valued, but only insofar as they do not erect barriers to our present social purposes. Any given set of traditions which so hinder us should be discarded without remorse. The crucial point, then, is to identify our social purposes in the instance at hand so we can determine whether to keep or discard the traditions at issue. And for this task, as for every substantive question, pragmatism offers no answers, especially when there are competing notions about our social purposes.

Next is attention to context, one of the more prominent and revealing themes of critical legal pragmatists.[15] Extrapolating from the pragmatic insights that thinking is always situated within a context, that experience is essential to knowledge, that a close eye must be kept on the facts, and that awareness of consequences is essential, critical scholars argue that contextual analysis is crucially important, that we need more of it in law. Moreover, critical feminists have asserted that this concern for 'concreteness, situatedness, contextuality, embeddedness' is what pragmatism shares with feminism (Radin 1990: 1707).

The call for attention to context is riven with paradox, as its promoters recognize (Minow and Spelman 1990: 1651), yet seemingly forget. If the 'pragmatist thesis is that human thought always and necessarily arises in a situated complex of beliefs' (Grey 1989: 801), if 'we are always in some context, as are the texts that we read, their authors and readers, our problems, and our efforts to achieve solutions' (Minow and Spelman 1990: 1065), as the legal pragmatists insist, then to urge attention to context is to say nothing, since we cannot help but be in a context and cannot help but see things through a contextual frame. Indeed, the notion of viewing matters 'acontextually' is inconceivable.

The suspicion that the general call for attention to context is vacuous is confirmed in a demonstration of how this advice works out in practice. In their article 'In Context', critical scholars Martha Minow and Elizabeth Spelman (1990) analysed the case of *Coy* v. *Iowa*,[16] in which the Supreme Court considered whether the Sixth Amendment's right to confrontation clause precludes the use of a screen to shield child

---

[15] Detailed discussions of context can be found in Minow and Spelman (1990); Wells (1990); Grey (1989: 793–805).
[16] *Coy* v. *Iowa*, 487 U.S. 1012 (1988).

witnesses from facing the accused in sex abuse cases. Minow and Spelman identified the following 'contexts' referred to by the Justices in their decision: Justice Scalia focused on the context of the text of the Constitution; Justice Blackmun, joined by Chief Justice Rehnquist, focused on the common law context, the historical context, and on the context in which state legislatures have passed these laws in the interest of protecting children; Justice O'Conner, joined by Justice White, focused somewhat on the context of the child, and on the context of the relationships between courts and legislatures and the relationship between the state and federal governments. The specific objection to the case raised by Minow and Spelman (p. 1645) is that greater attention should have been paid to 'the context of policy debates and agenda-setting,' a phrase which they fill in with a laundry list of other possible contexts that could also have been examined.

My point is that every single Justice, like Minow and Spelman, identified a context—they merely differed on which context should be the determinative one. Context just is; the proclamation that more context is needed, without more, suggests nothing. Buried in a footnote, Minow and Spelman (p. 1644, n. 160) admit as much: 'Although it may be tempting to find in "context" the closure needed for legal decision-making despite the indeterminacy of legal doctrine, context itself is at least as indeterminate, given the many layers and set of possible facts, time frames, and features that could be identified under the term context.' The key questions are which contexts are the crucial ones, and how should the considerations drawn from the various possible contexts be weighed against one another. As always, pragmatism offers no answer to these substantive issues. Furthermore, since these are the difficult questions that arise in every case every day in every court, without anyone ever specifically referring to the notion of context, there is no real point in interjecting the concept. It has no use value. By the pragmatic test of knowledge, it should be discarded.

As statements like the above acknowledgement reveal, these sophisticated critical scholars are aware of the objections I have raised. The value to the proposal for more context lies in advancing the critical political agenda. Critical scholars are aiming at two objectives, a narrow one and a broader one. Narrowly speaking, 'the call to context in the late twentieth century reflects a critical argument that prevailing legal and political norms have used the form of abstract, general, and universal prescriptions while neglecting the experiences and needs of women of all races and classes, people of color, and people without wealth' (Minow and Spelman 1990: 1632–3). Critical scholars have been propounding on this theme for some time now, long before pragmatism or context were mentioned. Hence references to context are partially a subterfuge, an attempt to get through the back door, under the prestige of pragmatism and the neutral-sounding notion of context, what couldn't be accomplished through direct argument. The problem with this strategy is that the call to context does not justify any particular emphasis on their concerns about race, gender and class. Arguments that these particular concerns should be taken into account must be pressed on their own terms, again having nothing to do with the concept of context.

The broader objective, though it is usually left implicit, is to nudge the legal system towards a more substantive justice stance. Substantive justice, in this usage, means doing what is 'right' in a given case, even if that goes against the weight of the applicable legal rules. A call to context implicitly achieves this objective because it brings in all sorts of considerations beyond just the rules themselves; the rules are thereby crowded into a corner where they become just one of many factors to be taken into account in making the decision. This effect is apparent in Catherine Wells' (1990: 1734) description: 'Contextual decisionmaking treats a case as an individual set of circumstances that requires resolution upon its own terms. Rather than fitting the facts to preconceived categories of legal significance, the decisionmaker focuses on the parties' own characterizations of what happened.' The general pragmatic insistence that consequences are important also tends to point in the direction of substantive justice, because it suggests that ends or outcomes are what matter, not just, and perhaps more so than, application of the rules. Substantive justice (in this 'do right' sense), it must be emphasized, is inevitably the product of values internalized by the decision-maker, which raises no problems in a homogeneous society but has troublesome implications in a pluralistic society.

The observation that the call for context, and resort to pragmatism generally, lean in the direction of more substantive justice, points again to the core problem with pragmatism in legal theory—its substantive emptiness. Here is an excellent summary of the approach prescribed by legal pragmatists:

Pragmatism in the sense that I find congenial means looking at problems concretely, experimentally, without illusions, with a full awareness of the limitations of human reason, with a sense of the 'localness' of human knowledge, the difficulty of translations between cultures, the unattainability of 'truth,' the consequent importance of keeping diverse paths of inquiry open, the dependence of inquiry on culture and social institutions, and above all the insistence that social thought and action be evaluated as instruments to valued human goals rather than as ends in themselves.

Most aspects of the above description can be found in the work of critical scholars who promote pragmatism, but this paragraph happened to be written by Richard Posner (1990a: 465), leader of the law and economics movement, the target of venomous attacks in CLS pieces.

This convergence should not be interpreted as a miraculous reconciliation of sworn foes, now embracing one another under the umbrella of pragmatism. They remain as far apart as ever.[17] The location of their vast disagreement can be found in just three words in the final sentence above: 'valued human goals'. What keeps them apart is they value different goals, and pragmatic philosophy lends support to no particular political position. This observation should give pause to critical scholars in their haste to pile on the pragmatism bandwagon. Richard Posner is a *judge*, and it would seem fair to speculate that there are many more judges with the political views of Posner than there are with the political views of Roberto Unger or Martha Minow. To make the call to context more concrete, critical scholars should imagine that the judge they are exhorting is Posner himself, who would eagerly endorse their suggestion to pay attention to context; and let's assume he would also undertake sincerely to consider such factors as race, gender, and class, and accept the invitation to de-emphasize the rules in the interest of doing substantive justice (doing what he thinks is right). Surely few critical scholars feel comfortable with this scenario—but that is where you end up with pragmatism in legal theory.

The final constructive proposal to come out of pragmatic legal theory is the suggestion to travel the middle path, to find the golden mean between traditionalist pragmatism and critical pragmatism (Chow 1992: 817–22). This is sound advice, as far as it goes, and it is probably often achieved in practice. From the radical reformist standpoint, however, it is unacceptable because it means a compromise which leaves intact the oppressive institutional structures. Moreover, the prob-

[17] One reviewer has suggested that in his text *The Problems of Jurisprudence* (1990), Posner has moved closer to CLS (see Levinson 1991). This book is indeed more explicitly skeptical of traditional legal ideas than any of Posner's previous work, though, as Levinson notes, it is not clear that this represents a change of position or merely a more explicit articulation. Regardless of this more explicit skepticism, however, there is no indication that Posner's substantive political position has changed, and he continues to urge the efficiency standard for judical decisions.

lems which divide us the most are not amenable to Solomonic solutions. What is the middle way between allowing a woman to choose an abortion or prohibiting abortions in the interest of protecting potential life?

C. Why Pragmatic Legal Theory; Implications for Socio-legal Studies

Among all of the uses of pragmatism in legal theory set forth above, only the first, negative use—the debunking of conceptualist/essentialist formalism—has any real vitality, though even this is of limited application since the Realists have already rooted out most of the extreme conceptualist/essentialist legal thought in the United States. This negative use of pragmatism is the most powerful because that is exactly what pragmatic philosophy was about. All of the other uses are for the most part banal or devoid of content. Richard Rorty (1990: 1813) has suggested that, while pragmatism was shocking when first introduced, it now sounds full of truisms because most of its insights have since been absorbed into American common sense.

That leaves the question of why pragmatism has gained so much attention in legal theory. Through the influence of his monumental work, *Philosophy and the Mirror of Nature* (1979), Rorty himself has been the seminal factor in the revival of pragmatism within philosophy (see Hall 1994), as well as within law. His pithy, irreverent anti-foundationalist attacks on the philosophical tradition were especially attractive to critical scholars, who sought to draft his thought in support of their assault on the legal tradition.[18] However, this infatuation with Rorty soon turned sour (see Singer 1989), owing mostly to Rorty's position that liberal democratic institutions—which are the specific targets of critical legal scholars—are well suited for Western societies. This split yet again demonstrates that the anti-foundationalism of pragmatism does not lead to any particular political vision.[19]

Beyond the influence of Rorty, the revival of pragmatism in law is connected to the longstanding battle between CLS and law and economics. The initial impetus for this conflict was in the opposing left-right political stances associated with these movements, respectively (though law and economics has since broadened to include practitioners on the centre and left). This natural political emnity is exacerbated

---

[18] For discussions of Rorty's relationship with critical legal scholars, see Weaver (1992); Baker (1992).

[19] See Bronner (1994: 292) (European admirers of pragmatism 'included Henri Bergson and Mussolini' as well as a number of conservative social theorists).

by the fact that 'both claim to be the rightful heirs to Legal Realism' (Horwitz 1992: 269–70). Law and economics absorbed the critical lessons of the Realists, and took up the consequentialist, instrumental, science-oriented aspects of constructive Realist thought, whereas CLS took up the politically progressive aspects, pressed the critique further, and discarded the social science. As Singer (1988: 540) asserts, 'we are still arguing about the legacy of legal realism'.

This sibling competition has helped boost the prominence of pragmatism in legal theory because both sides have claimed pragmatism as their own in an attempt to identify an even higher (in terms of prestige) source of authority than the Realists. At the same time, both have distanced themselves a bit from the Realists. In his book on pragmatic jurisprudence, Posner (1990a: 20) 'slights' (his word) Legal Realism because he has 'difficulty understanding what is original in it' that Holmes and Cardozo—the epitomes of pragmatic judges for Posner—had not said before; and he suggests that the relationship between law and economics and Legal Realism 'is equivocal' because many of its leading figures are economists 'who probably have never heard of legal realism' (p. 441). Similarly, in his recent historical account of Legal Realism, critical scholar Morton Horwitz (1992: 208–12) separates the 'good' Realists (critical ones) from the 'bad' Realists (social science ones); listed among the good Realists are Felix Cohen and John Dewey (pp. 183, 326 n. 88), while leading bad Realist is Karl Llewellyn; and in three superlative-laden pages Horwitz pays homage to Cardozo as the model pragmatist judge (pp. 190–2). It's as if the two schools were involved in an intricately choreographed dance, matching one another in synchrony as each furiously tries to sever its connection to the other and establish its position as first, favourite and true inheritor (initially of Realism, now of pragmatism).

An entirely different reason for the popularity of pragmatism may be just plain exhaustion. After weathering so much sharp criticism, from each other as well as from other schools, they have begun to retreat to less extreme positions—being a 'pragmatist' carries connotations of reasonableness. Contemporary CLS scholars have begun to 'de-emphasize the indeterminacy thesis in their work' (Minda 1993: 41); and most law and economics scholars (including Posner)[20] have given up earlier claims 'that efficiency should be regarded as the only legal norm' (Minda 1993: 37). After a lot of programmatic hot air, the deflation and

---

[20] See Posner (1990a: 387) ('we should be cautious in pushing wealth maximization').

domestication phase is well under way.[21] Ironically, considering that both CLS and law and economics have assumed quite extremist stances, a strong argument can be made that neither school has been consistent with the pragmatic abhorrence of dualistic extremes.

This debate between CLS and law and economics is of direct relevance to socio-legal studies because, as I mentioned in the preceding Chapter, the social scientific study of law is also a child of the Realists, and by implication the pragmatists. Socio-legal studies stands between its quarelling mates, with one foot in each camp. Most socio-legal scholars align themselves as progressives along with critical scholars, but they do social science nonetheless, no different from legal economists. A sign of the low status accorded to the field is that socio-legal studies is relegated to footnotes, or flatly ignored,[22] in legal theory discussions over the offspring of pragmatism and Legal Realism.

Despite remaining mostly on the sidelines, socio-legal studies has nevertheless been caught in the crossfire. Critical scholars have explicitly blamed the social science initiative of the Realists for the demise of Legal Realism, painting social scientists as dupes in the service of the status quo. This is how Horwitz (1992: 209–10) put it:

> In its constructive mode, Realism subordinated political and moral passion to social science expertise. In Llewellyn's famous phrase, Realism sought 'the temporary divorce of Is from Ought for purposes of study,' thus postponing the question of appropriate values while concentrating on developing a rich collection of social science studies about the way society actually worked. While Progressivism had initiated this distinctively modern emphasis on the legitimating role of expertise and professionalism, it was this strand of Realism that pushed the behavioral social sciences in directions that ultimately dulled the critical edge of Realism itself. Behavioral and value-free social science not only suppressed the moralism of early Progressive social science; it was also dependent on a completely naive view of social thought. . .
>
> But the question remains whether the turn to positivist social science was not also a political and moral failure because it not only suppressed the critical stand of Realism but also encouraged Realists to rely on a methodology that strongly tended to confer a privileged position on the status quo.

---

[21] See M. Tushnet (1991: 1537–44) (describing the assimilation of CLS into the legal academy).

[22] As Mark Tushnet (1991: 1542 n.102) observes, law and society studies have 'been unable to gain more than a toehold in the legal academy'. ('For example, the editors of The Yale Law Journal did not think it important to invite a contribution to this [centennial] issue from someone prominently associated with the law and society movement.')

This condemnation of the social science aspect of Legal Realism—coming from the folks socio-legal scholars stand in solidarity with—could not have been put in stronger terms, and must be responded to if there is to be a place for realistic socio-legal theory.

Horwitz mentions the critical scholars' hit list of the three evils of modern social science: positivism, behaviourism, and the fact-value distinction. Why these three aspects of social science are so reviled by critical scholars will be addressed in upcoming Sections. For the moment, it is important to point out in response to Horwitz's attempt to gerrymander the Realists and pragmatists in CLS's favour, that most of the Realists and pragmatists believed in substantial aspects of positivism, behaviourism, and the fact-value distinction. That is just how people—including the ones we now think of as enlightened—thought about social science in the heyday of Realism and pragmatism.

As Rorty (1979: 174–5) recognizes, Dewey adhered to a form of 'epistemological behaviourism' in his belief that knowledge should be understood in terms of what people do. Moreover, as Quine observes, Dewey's naturalistic view of language represents a behaviourist view of meaning. 'When we recognize with Dewey that "meaning . . . is primarily a property of behavior," we recognize that there are no meanings, nor likenesses nor distinctions of meaning, beyond what are implicit in people's dispositions to overt behavior. For naturalism the question whether two expressions are alike or unlike in meaning has no determinate answer, known or unknown, except insofar as the answer is settled in principle by people's speech dispositions, known or unknown' (statement of Quine, quoted in Murphy 1990: 84). Likewise, although Dewey and James's holistic views did reject a sharp fact-value distinction, they repeatedly used the two terms distinctly, especially in their discussions of the requirements of scientific inquiry. The interpenetration of fact and value is neither total nor viscious, and distinctions can and are routinely made both in everyday use and in science, though there are points—usually at the highest level of theory formation—at which it becomes impossible.

Similarly, Oliver Wendell Holmes (1897: 469), universally acclaimed to be the grandfather of both legal pragmatism and Legal Realism, quite positivistically opined that '[f]or the rational study of the law the black-letter man may be the man of the present, but the man of the future is the man of statistics and the master of economics.' Even worse, Felix Cohen, a hero among critical scholars for his unmatched flair at making formalist pretensions look foolish, positivistically proposed 'to substitute a realistic, rational scientific account of legal happenings for the classical theological jurisprudence of concepts' (1935: 820–1); and the functional approach he prescribed was essentially behaviouristic in his insistence that we apply 'statistical methods' to keep an eye on the 'actual facts of judicial behavior' (p. 833).

More examples can be offered but the point is clear: if you extract positivism, behaviourism, and the fact-value distinction from the Realists and pragmatists, you have removed central components of their beliefs, not errant misstatements which can be excised without loss. Ironically—irony abounds in all subjects infected by anti-foundationalism (see generally Rorty 1989)—Horwitz himself is skewered on the same dilemma. As a historian, he is a socio-legal scholar steeped in the social scientific tradition. He grapples with the problem in the Preface:

As one sees both theories and causes as more contingent, one's belief in one's own objectivity is also drawn into question. Is it just my story, with all the connotations of skepticism and subjectivity that the word 'story' implies? No; I still aspire to give the best possible explanation, but without the wish to suppress all difficulties by intoning pieties about what a terrible place the world would be without an objective account.

As a result, the book constantly wavers between, on the one hand, conventional efforts at historical explanation that continue to derive from nineteenth century models of objectivity, and, on the other hand, the recognition that modernism has challenged the objectivity of these forms in many different ways (Horwitz 1992: viii).

Consistent with his pragmatism and his refined historical instincts, Horwitz cannot give up his sense that there is truth in what he writes, that it does get to the facts, is not just a product of his values. Socio-legal studies needs the fact-value distinction. The question is how it can be understood with anti-foundationalism.

Grounding the Fact-value Distinction and the Pragmatic View of Science

Three themes of direct concern to socio-legal studies were woven into the above discussion of pragmatism in US legal theory. The first theme was to show that socio-legal studies sits smack in the centre of the historical-intellectual context of the legal theory discussion. The second theme was to hammer in the notion that nothing of a substantive political nature can be derived from philosophical pragmatism. These two themes are connected: the place of socio-legal studies in the entire mix is precisely that it matches the substantive emptiness of pragmatism.

The third theme has yet to be articulated, but the basis for it lay implicit in the pattern of instructive failures in the attempts to find a useful positive application of pragmatic philosophy in legal theory. It involves what I call, for lack of a better term, locating the 'ground'. By 'ground' I mean those conditions of our existence which we cannot alter by our recognition of them, conditions which are at once enabling and limiting. The interpretive turn in philosophy, especially, has brought us face to face with the conditions of our existence. Let me elaborate.

Each of the following are aspects of the ground: being situated within a context, looking at things contextually, having our thoughts shaped by a corpus of existing beliefs derived from our cultural tradition(s). For each of these examples it is equally nonsensical to suggest that we should not do it, as it would be to suggest that we should do it. Say I exhort you: 'be situated within a context.' No act need be taken, nor is it possible to imagine what kind of act could be taken. Now I give the opposite exhortation: 'remove yourself from any and all contexts.' No act can be taken, and it's impossible to even conceive how this instruction could be satisfied.

The second example is less obvious, but the same result obtains. Phenomenologists have taught, consistent with the assertions of Dewey and James, that mentality (thought, perception) inherently involves selective attention (see Flanagan 1991: 33–5; James 1890: Chapter XI). And while this selection process 'isolates' the object of perception from its environment, our very ability to see it as an object means we have already placed that object within a horizon of familiarity (Schutz 1962: 5–10).[23] This horizon of familiarity is, then, the context of the object which enables us to perceive it, conveyed primarily through language. That is why everything we perceive—from dogs and trees to a constitutional text—is in some kind of context, a context we project onto the object through our very perception of it. Stanley Fish (1980: 309) observed that even 'words are heard as already embedded in a context'. And a 'sentence is never apprehended independently of the context in which it is perceived, and therefore we never know a sentence except in the stabilized form a context has *already* conferred' (p. 283, emphasis in original). We fail to recognize that everything is perceived in a

---

[23] For an extended discussion of this subject see Tamanaha (1993a: 79–87).

context because the projection process is done subconsciously through internalized interpretive constructs.

So, if I direct you to 'see that text within a context,' there is nothing you can do because the very fact that you have seen it as a 'text' means you have already seen it within a context. For the same reason, you cannot comply with a request to 'see that text free from context.'

The same analysis applies to the example of having our thoughts shaped by our cultural tradition. Hans George Gadamer (1979: 108) demonstrated that '[U]nderstanding always implies a pre-understanding which is in turn pre-figured by the determinate tradition in which the interpreter lives and which shapes his prejudices.'[24] Or as Dewey put it, 'All knowing and effort to know starts from some belief, some received and asserted meaning which is a deposit of prior experience, personal and communal' (1925: 347). Thus, my instruction that you think within beliefs derived from your cultural tradition, like the instruction to think entirely free of your tradition, simply cannot be acted upon since your very ability to think presupposes the former and rules out the latter.

It is not accidental that these three examples have identical logical structures. All three comprise inseverable aspects of what is necessarily entailed in the fact that we are thinking, interpreting beings. Being situated is being situated in a cultural tradition or activity, and the contexts we see objects in (by projection) are the contexts our language, culture, and practices provide us with. What makes them a part of the 'ground' is the fact that each of these aspects are necessary to us as thinking, interpreting beings—they *enable* us to think, interpret, and do.

It is important to recognize that, while it is nonsensical to suggest that a person see things contextually or see them 'acontextually', or be influenced by tradition or be free of tradition, there was nothing nonsensical about the arguments by legal theorists to pay attention to context or to be tradition-bound. My critique was not that their prescriptions were absurd; rather, it was that pragmatic philosophy could not be enlisted in support because it focused on these aspects in their role as *necessary* conditions of our existence as thinking, interpreting beings—as the ground. The philosophical discussion is pitched at that level.

But these legal theorists were arguing, at least in the best formulations of their arguments, with feet planted firmly on the ground. The

---

[24] Gadamer laid out this thesis in Truth and Method (1991).

contextualists were in effect arguing that *given* the fact that we always see things contextually, there are certain contexts that bear particular attention. Traditionalists were arguing that, in situations where a conscious decision is involved, the prudent path to take is to remain close to existing precedent. They were, in other words, talking about explicitly thematized aspects of our contexts and traditions. That is normal social–political discourse in which we struggle over aspects of social life. In contrast, the ground is what enables social discourse to function; discussions about the ground itself—that is, reflections on the conditions of our existence as interpreting beings—don't refer to any particular contextual aspect or traditional aspect. They refer to context as such and thinking infused by tradition as such. Thus the very same phenomena are referred to, but at different levels.

This discussion is relevant to the fact-value distinction because precisely the same factors are involved. What has rendered the distinction problematic is our recognition that we inevitably see the world (the 'facts') from within a situated, tradition infused ('value' laden) perspective. Thus, it seems, facts simply cannot be perceived free from our values. Catherine Wells (1990: 1743) summarized the problem: 'it is clear that a sharp distinction between factual observations and normative judgments cannot be maintained. What we see and hear is filtered and interpreted within a cognitive framework that is constructed largely from our own individual temperament and prior experience.'

The logic is inescapable, but it seems to be saying something threatening only because it implicitly draws upon reference to what pragmatism emphatically denies: the divide between a perspective free, objective world of facts contrasted against the personal, subjective world of value; or the reverse divide constructed by the philosophers who erect a 'realm of values' (absolute, perspective free), 'constradistinguished from the realm of existence' (full of error and illusion) (Dewey 1925: 319, 336–8, 343–4). Both dichotomies refer to a standard which is free of the ground, free of our socially informed perspective, the very possibility of which is rejected outright by pragmatism. To even discuss the fact-value distinction in these terms is nonsensical. Scholars who dismiss the fact-value distinction on these grounds are frustrated objectivists, lashing out in disappointment at our inability to rise above the conditions of our existence.

When pragmatists draw the fact-value distinction, they do so *standing on the ground*, not in reference to a perspective-free versus perspective-bound contrast (Dewey 1925: 336–54). Dewey (p. 351) wrote:

Yet if man is within nature, not a little god outside, and is within as a mode of energy inseparably connected with other modes, interaction is the one inescapable trait of every human concern; thinking, even philosophic thinking, is not exempt. This interaction is subject to partiality because the human factor has bent and bias. But partiality is not obnoxious just because it is partial. . . . What is obnoxious in partiality is due to the illusion that there are states and acts which are not also interactions.

Given that we cannot perceive the world except from within a perspective, the fact-value distinction must be understood as arising out of our acting in the world, where both values (preferences, ideals, *oughts*) and facts (*is*) are naturalistically conceived as functionally distinct aspects of our experience (Dewey 1925: 340–6).

Basically, the separation between fact and value is the one drawn every day in common sense terms. The distinction exists because it is an indispensible tool in the pursuit of our projects, including survival: fact/*is* appraises the existing state of affairs; value/*ought* opens up a distance from the state of affairs which allows us to plan and set goals, and to render evaluative judgements over whether the situation meets with our satisfaction or desires. The distinction is unproblematic as long as we remain within a world view (a 'form of life' in Wittgenstein's terms) which applies the same standards to discern what counts as facts.

Postmoderns might be tempted to leap on this last observation to insist that their point is precisely that there are a plurality of such views, even within a single society like the United States, rendering it routinely impossible to provide a value-free account of the facts. But this response fails to appreciate what is meant by 'what counts as facts,' since there is widespread agreement about this regardless of divergent cultural views, and it fails to observe the distinction between *facts* (which can be adjudged 'true' or 'false') and what the facts *mean* (to which 'truth' does not apply, as I will take up in greater detail in the next Chapter). Consider, for example, the contrasting racial response to the acquittal of O. J. Simpson. A majority of blacks reacted with jubilation and a majority of whites with dismay. No doubt this disagreement is attributable to divergent cultural backgrounds and experiences; but this disagreement was over the *value* question of whether the verdict was right, and this value disagreement presupposed agreement about the *fact* that he was acquitted. While there was also disagreement along racial lines in beliefs about whether he *in fact* committed the murders, a disagreement which also reflects predispositions, this disagreement was a function of a lack of evidence; and again this disagreement presupposed agreement about the underlying facts, that is, two people were in fact killed by someone.

There is often disagreement about what the facts in any given instance might be, whether between people within or across cultural groups, disagreement which is related to evidence, or the quality of what Putnam (1990: viii–ix) calls the 'epistemic situation'. Nevertheless, there is widespread agreement about *what counts as facts*. To get beneath the use of value-laden terms, facts can be identified in bare descriptive terms, using alternative terminology when necessary. But the anti-scepticism of pragmatism would insist that the fact that we often make mistakes and often drape factual assertions in value-laden clothes does not lead to the denial of the possibility of drawing this distinction. The insistence of critical scholars and postmoderns that the fact/value distinction cannot be made is simply incorrect, since we do it every day on matters large and small, and it is integral to our ability to function.

Science has a role in relation to both fact and value. Science is the most highly developed system of inquiry we have for disclosing the empirical conditions—the facts—of our existence. But science also helps provide a mode for criticizing values, as Dewey and James argued, which is necessary because 'the organs of criticism [of common sense] are for the most part half-judgments, uncriticized products of custom, chance circumstance and vested interests' (Dewey 1925: 345; see also James 1975: 9). 'Practically then, in effect, knowledge, science, truth, is the method of criticizing beliefs' (Dewey 1925: 342). Knowing how the facts stand in relation to our objectives and beliefs helps us critically evaluate those objectives and beliefs. 'When the paths leading to the solution of moral problems are irremediably risky, then ethics is impossible without factual knowledge; when mere ethics of conviction has been surpassed, then experimental reflection on the consequences of one's own alternatives of action belongs to the very core of morality' (Joas 1993: 252, describing Mead's view of the role science has to play in relation to morality).

The postmodernist, or the objectivist, might respond to this analysis by insisting that the pragmatists' own argument indicates that even the scientist will see the 'facts' through tradition coloured (hence value-laden) lens. Once again, the initial pragmatist retort is 'yes, but so what'; there is no other way—to deny this critically important and routinely used distinction by reference to the impossible is arbitrary. The best we can do is insist, as Dewey and James repeatedly did, that scientists strive to maintain an attitude of disinterested and impartial inquiry and cultivate a sense of critical self-reflection.

As interpretive theorist Alfred Schutz argued (1962: 245–59), the social sciences are themselves traditions of thought and practices into which scientists are indoctrinated. These traditions and schools of thought do reflect values, but not necessarily values at play in the social arena studied. There is a substantial difference between the instrumental (achieve objectives) cognitive orientation which governs many of our activities in everyday life, and the open cognitive interest (aimed at knowing or understanding) that governs scientific exploration.[25] In addition, research methodologies are designed to lessen the influence of non-scientific factors, even if they are not entirely successful. Most important, we can and do subject the products of scientists to testing under public and objectively existing conditions (the reality posited *ab initio*). To ask for anything more is to yearn for the Absolute.

Weak as they may sound in contrast to the comfort of the Absolute, these constraints regularly allow us to distinguish the facts from the partiality of the scientific investigator, and to separate the facts from the framework in which they are presented. Peter Just, in the example cited in the previous Chapter, was able to use Laura Nader's own ethnographic data as well as a comparison with other similar situations to critique her attempt to bend the facts toward her predisposition to see Christian based anti-hegemonic strategies among Zapotec practices. I turned to the facts of Felix Cohen's writings to contest Morton Horwitz's politically inspired attempt to deny that Cohen was a promoter of the positivistic social science initiative of the Realists. As every scientist knows, the facts regularly resist our attempts to mold them to our purposes, though often it takes feedback from others to be persuaded, which is why the existence of a community of investigators dedicated to the impartial and disinterested pursuit of knowledge is essential to the process.

Presumably both Nader and Horwitz would insist that any diligent investigator, regardless of ideological predisposition, would have been able to uncover the same empirical occurences or events they recite (granting that there might well be a dispute over how these facts should be interpreted or what they mean). That is the standard social science strives toward and it is met with frequency. When this standard is met, the account is true to the facts. Just because there are other ways to

[25] For an in depth elaboration and critique of Schutz's views, see Tamanaha, (1993a: 87–94).

approach the same situation—other facts to draw out or emphasize or place in a different light through the application of a different framework—does not mean the facts are any less true, only that there are other possible facts their accounts do not relate. What it does suggest is that social science, either in a given work or among the group of scientists, should strive to recover as many perspectives on a given situation as possible.

Note also that pursuant to the pragmatic understanding of the fact-value distinction and the notion of truth, we can use the terms true, false, and fact without enclosing them in quotation marks, or attaching conditions or embarassed asides about the problems with positivism and objectivity that these terms supposedly invoke. Such problems arise only if you start with the presupposition that truth and fact refer to the absolute in the philosophical sense critiqued by pragmatism and anti-foundationalism. Wittgenstein (1958: 48) observed: 'Philosophy may in no way interfere with the actual use of language: it can in the end only describe it. For it cannot give it any foundation either. It leaves everything as it is.' Under the pragmatic view, the only problems with the application of these terms is one of agreement with the sentences in which they are used and the empirical reality to which they refer, which are difficult problems to be sure. Verification, use value, and successful resistance to rigorous attempts at falsification provide the only assurances we can have—or need—when we invoke these terms, because that is exactly how they function in practice.

These pragmatist-based assertions about social science and the fact-value distinction run directly contrary to the new and influential school of 'post-empiricist' socio-legal studies. As expressed by Austin Sarat (1990), post-empiricist social scientists insist that their work is not just politics, but they have discarded modernist claims that social science involves producing knowledge which can be tested in terms of 'validity and reliability'. Post-empiricists attempt this precarious balance because they are unwilling to give up the belief that doing science involves something distinct, yet they are under pressure from postmodernism, and are egged on by 'critical empiricists' who taunt the post-empiricists with charges of residual scientism and encourage them to embrace the inevitability of politics (see Trubek and Esser 1989). In the post-empiricist view, social scientists are inevitably trapped in their different 'backgrounds and biographies': 'The procedures [used] to make observations are neither neutral nor universal and are not so powerful as to be able to produce consistency in spite of differences in the race, class, gender, and history of observers' (Sarat 1990: 164). For their epistemology, in place of validity, reliability and the stance of neutrality in the production and testing of knowledge, all of which they reject (pp. 159–66), the post-empiricists suggest that 'the ultimate arbiter of what counts . . . is the research community itself' (p. 161).

According to pragmatist tenets, the post-empiricists have given up far too much. Validity and reliability are not just essential to science, they are integral to empirical knowledge as such. Information that is neither valid nor reliable is of limited use. And an attitude of probing neutrality is essential if the inquiry is to be more than a replication of what the investigator already (perhaps erroneously) believes. Finally, the ultimate test of knowledge cannot be defined as agreement within so narrow a community. Agreement must, in the first instance, be with the facts of the matter, as determined by the 'community' defined in the *widest* possible terms. Agreement with regard to what counts as facts, can, as I have argued, extend beyond our backgrounds and biographies to produce consistency despite race, class, gender and even culture (although there may still be differences with regard to what these facts mean, as will be addressed in the next Chapter).

The final objection to the understanding of social science I have presented will come from the sophisticated anti-foundationalist who insists that all of James's and Dewey's talk about the scientific method no longer has any plausibility because later philosophers have conclusively demonstrated that there is no distinct scientific method. Identifying where the new pragmatists part with the old, Rorty (1990: 1813–14) says, 'we have all read Kuhn, Hanson, Toumlin, and Feyerabend, and have thereby become suspicious of the term "scientific method". New pragmatists wish that Dewey, Sidney Hook, and Ernest Nagel had not insisted on using this term as a catchphrase, since we are unable to provide anything distinctive for it to denote.'

This objection is devastating only if Dewey and James did see the scientific method as something distinct, but their descriptions of the scientific method recognize that it evolved out of the same method of inquiry applied by ordinary craftsmen (Dewey 1925: 107). The essence to the method lies in an *attitude* which involves detached and impartial inquiry (which does not rule out having an opinion based on faith or insight to guide the inquiry), close attention to the facts, and experimentation and testing. This is a 'method' in only the loosest possible sense, and they were quite generous in not limiting it to just scientists. Judging from comments like the following, which he made in support of granting scientific status to anthropology and history, Dewey (1925: 135) had no illusions about the method of inquiry he touted: 'There is superstitious awe reflected in the current estimate of science. If we could free ourselves from a somewhat abject emotion, it would be clear enough that what makes any proposition scientific is its power to yield understanding, insight, intellectual at-homeness, in connection with any existential state of affairs, by filling events with coherent and tested meanings.'

The new pragmatists and philosophers of science were focused on the question what makes scientific reasoning distinct. Those in the scientific profession have an interest in perpetuating the idea that there is such a distinction because it would confer a measure of authority on their work. But the classical pragmatists were focused on the best and most reliable ways to acquire knowledge, regardless of whether we call it science. Social theorist Hans Joas (1993: 256) made a similar point:

By conceiving of science as the type of systematized solution of cognitive action problems, pragmatism makes evident the practical foundation of all science. Neither a specific system of propositions, nor a method that can be described univocally, but rather the relatively most successful procedure for solving specific problems of cognition—that is what science is.

So the issue is not whether the method of inquiry proposed by Dewey and James is distinctively scientific, but whether it is useful and productive in the accumulation of knowledge. On that score there can be no doubt.

This conclusion does not, it must be emphasized, suggest that science is not distinct, only that the scientific method of inquiry is not unique or exclusive to science and therefore cannot be the source of the distinction. What makes science distinct is that it consists of communities of persons trained in the various scientific traditions, engaging in various scientific practices, talking about the same subjects using the same language and bodies of ideas, supported by various science-oriented academic, research or government institutions, and so forth. Science is distinct because as a product of historically contingent social organization it has taken on separate qualities that define it as a shared pursuit.

This is a social theory of science. Realistic socio-legal theory sees science in these terms, and law also, as upcoming Chapters will articulate.

The bottom line of the foregoing discussion may seem disappointingly ordinary, even passé. It leaves us precisely where we stood before. Nothing changed because philosophical pragmatism leaves the world unchanged. As Stanley Fish (1990: 1464) pointed out, 'if the pragmatist account of things is right, then everyone has always been a pragmatist anyway.' All pragmatism does is help wean us from our illusions.

The most profound lesson to take from the pragmatists is based upon their example rather than on the content of their theory. The core postmodern insights were contained in pragmatic philosophy, yet their reaction to these insights is the opposite of the postmodern's. Postmodernism is imbued with a deep skepticism and sense of doubt, and the absence of objectivity is construed to be destabilizing, as if we have really lost something in a way that threatens our grip on the world or the coherence of our activities. The only things we have lost are our illusions; postmodernism too leaves the world untouched. A hundred years ago the pragmatists gave up the very same illusions but saw that as a liberation more so than a loss because they set out their anti-foundationalist ideas in the context of an overarching belief that we—collectively—contribute to and create reality through our action in the world. The core difference is in attitude.

Social life consists of three basic elements: 1) behaviour and 2) meaning, 3) manifested within a material context. A pragmatic approach fastens upon these elements as the basis and builds up from there. In common sense terms this means carefully watching what people do, figuring out why they are doing it, and trying to grasp how it all comes together.

3 Behaviourism and Interpretivism in Complement

Typical of philosophical pragmatism, much of the emphasis in the preceding Chapter was negative, clearing the underbrush to make room for realistic socio-legal studies. The positivism versus interpretivism debate is the last piece of dried bramble to sweep away. As I indicated at the outset, the social sciences have for the past few decades been involved in a struggle to absorb the interpretive challenge to positivism. To repeat briefly, the positivistic view is premised upon the notion of a unified science, with the natural sciences providing the model for the social sciences. Under this view, the function of social science is to explain social behaviour through the formulation of causal laws of behaviour which allow for reliable prediction. Interpretivists, in contrast, argue that the social sciences are distinct from the natural sciences because the former focus on thinking, interpreting, meaningfully oriented subjects, subjects who construct the social world through shared meaning, in contrast to the insensate objects studies by natural science. According to interpretivism, the objective of the social sciences should be to come to an interpretive understanding of social behaviour by exploring the meaning that infuses and gives rise to complexes of social action. Both kinds of works are represented in socio-legal studies, although the older approaches tended to be positivist while the newer approaches are increasingly interpretivist.

In the early phase of the social science debate the issues were framed in either-positivism-or-interpretivism terms. More recent discussions reflect a general recognition that both approaches have their uses, and that most of the various paradigms contained within these two approaches provide an interesting and informative perspective on the world.[1] The issues now are about finding ways of linkage.[2]

The pragmatic reaction to this state of affairs should be obvious: apply whichever approach or combination of approaches proves to be useful and informative. While this advice would seem uncontroversial,

---

[1] For a collection of works written by representatives of most of the competing schools, see Giddens and Turner, eds. (1987); see also Wilson (1983: 10) (arguing that the many competing schools in social science are its strength).

[2] See generally Alexander et al., eds. (1987).

it is not easily accomplished. Positivism and interpretivism have been articulated in opposition to one another, and their more extreme formulations deny legitimacy to the other. This emnity is especially acute in socio-legal studies, where critical scholars have demonized positivism in the course of championing interpretivism.

Two warring camps which jealously demand fidelity to their side alone are another example of what the pragmatists condemned as forcing an impoverished choice between extremes. In this Chapter I will show how positivism—in particular, the behaviourist version—and interpretivism complement one another, indicating the strengths and weakness of each and revealing how the weaknesses of one are set off by the strengths of the other.

Rehabilitating Behaviorism

A. The Critical View of Positivism.

As David Trubek (1984: 615) observed, 'a major theme in CLS is the hostility to what the CLS scholars call "positivism", and especially to behaviourism, which they consider to be the worst example of positivism. Trubek lists four basic objections: 1) it is thought to necessarily entail determinism; 2) it is reductionist by identifying factors external to social actors while ignoring the meaning underlying the actions; 3) positivism/behaviourism is politically conservative because it, in effect, only reveals existing patterns of behaviour and thereby serves to reify them; and 4) positivism pretends to 'lead to objective and value neutral knowledge' which 'hides an implicit and conservative political message' (pp. 616–18).

The first objection, as Trubek observes, is based upon confusing a methodology for obtaining knowledge with a metaphysical theory. There is no necessary connection between positivism and determinism, though many positivists have interpreted their results in deterministic terms. The second objection—reductionism—is correct for those versions of positivism which deny the very existence or causal influence of meaning, though it is less applicable to behaviourist approaches which merely 'bracket' (refuse to consider) meaning in the course of studying patterns of behaviour. However, neither version merits an outright rejection of positivist/behaviourist approaches, only recognition that they don't tell the whole story. I have already addressed the issue of value neutrality cited in the fourth objection.

That leaves the third objection, that positivist or behaviourist social science is conservative in nature and perpetuates the status quo, and the fourth objection that it hides a conservative political message. To put it bluntly, these claims are flatly wrong. As noted above, Dewey and James believed that science has an inherently critical capacity because it provides a way to test our ideas and beliefs. A science which focuses on behaviour—the core meaning of behaviourism—tells us the facts about what people are actually doing, people in society as well as the people who make up legal institutions. If matters are as bad as critical scholars claim, only carefully conducted research into the facts can establish this, but by Trubek's own acknowledgment (p. 616) CLS scholars do scant empirical research and rarely cite empirical studies. Wilful abstention from acquiring information, regardless of whether the source of this information is behaviourist studies, cannot be squared with a self-declared 'key tenet' of critical scholars: 'belief in the liberating and transformative value of the truth' (p. 596).

The CLS charge of conservativism is particularly inapt considering that the current generation of socio-legal scholars, including positivists, are overwhelmingly left oriented, and if anything hostile to the status quo. For example, Donald Black, a prominent legal sociologist, is the most uncompromising positivist working in the field today, but he is also more totally critical of the law than many critical scholars. Black has argued that 'discrimination [in law] is ubiquitous' and cannot be eliminated (1989: 21–2), that the rule of law can 'never' be achieved in reality (p. 57), that law is actually a 'cause' of crime (p. 80), and that the solution to these problems is simply to reduce or abolish law, since law itself cannot effectively be reformed (pp. 73–88). Moreover, beginning in the late 1950s and continuing up through the present, many of the political scientists who study judicial decision-making have been positivistic behaviourists, as I will recount in Chapter Seven, yet most expressly adhered to and have tried to produce support for the Realist's critical views about law. As these examples demonstrate, nothing inherent to positivism leads to an endorsement of the status quo.

The source of this caricatured view of positivist science is readily identifiable. It's a generational article of faith among the radical left. A history of the CLS movement written by John Henry Schlegel (1984) reveals that participants in the formation of CLS were born in the 1930s and 1940s. During their college years in the 1960s, positivism did have these connotations. B. F. Skinner's methodological behaviourism, which suggested that human behaviour was based upon operant conditioning and thus predictive laws of behaviour could be formulated without reference to what people were thinking, was reductionist and determinist. And Alvin Gouldner's book, *The Coming Crisis of Western Sociology* (cited in CLS literature), published in 1970 at the heart of the civil rights struggle and the Vietnam war, powerfully argued that social science of the day, dominated by Parsons' structural-functional analysis of social order and research projects designed to enhance management and administrative efficiency, was conservative in character. Finally, 'Critical Theory' of the Frankurt School (from which CLS takes its name),[3] which was prominent among the radical left in the 1960s and 1970s, was hostile to all 'positivisms', and charged American social science with promoting conformism and contributing to the decay of mass culture (see Joas 1993: 79–83). Leaving aside the question of whether these characterizations were fair, in view of the fact that social science departments might well be the last bastion of Marxism today[4] (along with a scattering of jungle-based guerilla movements), things have changed dramatically since then.

B. *An Interpretive Critique of Behaviourism*

Much of the popular denigration of positivism operates at an abstract level which leads too easily to blanket condemnations. An examination of the work of Black and his collaborator M. P. Baumgartner will reveal both the weaknesses and strengths of positivism. They formulate their approach in classic positivist terms: behaviouristic legal sociology involves the explanation and prediction of the behaviour of law through the formulation of causal laws based upon the observation of empirical regularities (see Black 1972, 1976). 'It is therefore unnecessary—and possibly misleading—to invoke the conscious experiences of officials in order to account for their conduct' (Baumgartner 1992: 130). They claim that the 'sociological laws' of legal behaviour Black has identified 'are general and unchanging. They apply throughout history, in all locations, at all stages of a legal system, and in the handling of all kinds of crime' (ibid.). This universality of application is precisely why the regularities they identify qualify as causal 'laws', and also why they purportedly cannot be altered despite efforts at reform.

---

[3] As Roger Cotterrell (1995: 204–17) argues, the relationship between CLS and Critical Theory is ambiguous. Despite references to Continental Critical theorists, the theory itself is seldom explicitly engaged.

[4] For a discussion of how the left has come to be a 'dominant force' in American Universities, see Duxbury (1995: 428–50).

Several of the more important 'laws' Black has formulated include: law varies inversely with other social control; law varies directly with relational distance (the greater the intimacy between people the less law); law varies directly with stratification; law varies directly with social status; law varies directly with respectability; downward law is greater than upward law (Black 1976, 1989). The basic thrust of these 'laws' of legal behaviour is that the more other forms of social control are present, the less law there is, and vice versa; and the cumulative effect of law and other forms of social control is to protect the interests of the high status, respectable members of society, while oppressing and ignoring the interests of the low status, downtrodden members of society. In support of these 'laws' of legal behaviour, Black cites a wealth of material which ranges from anthropological studies of primitive society to statistical studies of modern courts and police behaviour.

It is a formidable portrait, vast in scope and confidently presented. Armed with the interpretive critique of positivism of the last thirty years, however, it is relatively easy to identify weak points. Positivism gets off the ground by placing phenomena into categories and then quantifying them. Both moves implicate serious difficulties. Categorization is a problem because social reality is gloriously complex and chaotic, filled with phenomena and variations of phenomena in shades and degrees that do not come in categorical boxes. Even the question of what law is, taken up in the next Chapter, has been debated for ages without resolution; but Black must answer this question before he can claim to have formulated universally applicable 'laws' about law.

Black (1976: 2) adroitly solves this problem at the outset of his analysis by stipulating that 'law is governmental social control'. This allows him to avoid engaging in the debate, but the problem (silently) crops up every time he resorts to studies of law in primitive societies because anthropologists have used several different definitions of law, a fact which Black ignores despite his heavy reliance on anthropological studies. This point can be illustrated by going through his exposition and randomly substituting the terms 'governmental social control' whenever the term 'law' is present. He asserts (1976: 90), for example, that: 'The Paiutes of Utah and Nevada had [governmental social control] during the rabbit hunt—a headman whose authority was limited to that occasion.' Questions immediately arise about whether the phenomenon identified can be considered governmental social control, or can be placed in the same category with the law of Germany or Georgia (or indeed, as Black (1995: 843) claims, with law 'throughout the world and across history, including classical India, Imperial China, medieval Europe, colonial Africa, and modern Japan'), questions which are suppressed in the presentation because after Black defines law in terms of governmental social control he rarely uses this definition, referring throughout his work simply to 'law'.

Hence, the first problem positivists face is categorizing the objects to be studied, or the dependent and independent variables at issue, in a way which insures that the same discrete phenomena are being observed. The tactic adopted by Black to deal with this problem, a common tactic for positivist studies, is to formulate an abstract category or box, then squeeze reality into that box. While this is a defensible tactic, what is indefensible is the tendency to then think that the box is reality. The box is just a box, and the implications that can be taken from studies of boxes depends upon their sturdiness and the selectiveness of those who squeeze in their contents; the bigger the box—like governmental social control—the less reliable they are, and the more they contain items that are closer in nature to things left outside the box. Equally important, some of the things left out have an impact on the operation of the things inside, though they are invisible to the gaze of the scientist peering into the box.

The second problem is that positivism depends upon quantification to generate statistical data. But how do we quantify law? Without specifically addressing this issue, Black stipulates that law is a quantitative variable, and he provides a list of what involves 'more' law and 'less' law. Here is a sampling of his list:

A decision in behalf of the plaintiff is more law than a decision in behalf of the defendant, and conviction is more than acquittal. The more compensation awarded, the more law . . . If a government provides treatment for a deviant, such as hospitalization or rehabilitation, this is also more law. The same applies to mediation or arbitration of a dispute. If a decision is against the plaintiff and he appeals, this is more law, and a reversal in his behalf is more as well. But if a defendant wins a reversal, this is less law . . . (Black 1976: 3).

This list illustrates two problems which dog positivists in the course of quantification. First, contortions occur in the effort to reduce qualitative differences (winning or losing) into quantitative ones (more or less), contortions which can result in distortions.[5]

---

[5] For example, Howard (1968) demonstrated how quantitative studies of judicial decisions are distorting because they flatten aspects like intensity for a particular position and differing reasons for taking this position. See also Tanenhaus (1966).

Secondly, there are a multitude of different ways to quantify the same phenomena, each as defensible as any other. Why is more compensation—which is often a function of the injury—more law? Is a one week trial that ends in a large award more law than a six month trial which results in no compensation but an injunction? Why is an appeal by a losing plaintiff more law? (And what about an appeal by a losing defendant?) And if the plaintiff loses the appeal, does that mean less law and how much less (less than the increase caused by the appeal itself, or still more than would have occured had there been no appeal?)? Couldn't the quantity of law be better measured by calculating the amount of time and resources actually expended in legal pursuits by legal actors? There are innumerable questions of this kind, which Black has not begun to address.

Most positivist studies create a scale, thoughtfully but arbitrarily selected (internally consistent once formulated), in relation to which specific numerical quantities are assigned and then compared. Again there is nothing objectionable about this procedure, as long as it is understood that the findings are relative to the scale, and a function of decisions made in the course of quantification. Behaviourist studies of judicial decision-making, discussed in Chapter Seven, apply a scaling system of this kind, and despite the limitations are able to provide useful information. Black, in contrast, does not even attempt to identify specific quantities. Had he done so it would have exposed the impossibility of coming up with a scale which could flatten out all the different phenomena involved such that they could be assigned numerical figures along a single scale, and would have revealed the ultimate arbitrariness and contestability of his designations regarding the quantity attached to a given phenomenon. Black wisely remained at the level of vague generalities regarding 'more' and 'less', though this raises serious doubts about whether his theory is falsifiable or rigourous. As David Frankford (1995: 94 n. 26) remarked, 'It is odd that someone who claims that quantification is the *sine qua non* of scientific inquiry relies on little quantitative evidence and uses no form of quantitative method.'

These difficulties with categorization and quantification, which are ever present though not aways so problematic, force the conclusion that positivists substantially construct the facts they purport to find. They construct the boxes they study, which determines the selected cut of social complexity to be observed, and they construct the measuring system which produces their figures. If different categories or different methods of quantification are applied, different patterns or regularities would emerge or be 'found'.

Another objection raised by interpretivists is that positivists continually violate their self-declared abstention from considering the meaning of the social actors (Hunt 1983: 22). As Black (1995: 849) put it: 'my work . . . contains no psychology whatsoever and entirely eliminates the individual from its formulations . . . Consider, for example, the principle stated earlier: Law varies directly with relational distance. It contains no assumptions, assertions, or implications about the human mind or even human beings as such.' His sociology is 'pure': 'It ignores what people think and feel. It ignores their goals and preferences. It ignores their intentions.' (p. 866) Positivists adhere to these methodological restrictions because it emulates the natural science model of the observation and measurement of 'a concrete empirical referent', safe from subjectivity and meaning (Black 1972: 1092).

The problem with these claims is that they are impossible to achieve. Although it is possible to ignore the meaningful explanations of the people involved when formulating predictive 'laws' regarding their behaviour, it is not possible to eliminate entirely subjective meaning because the preliminary stage of identifying what falls in or out of—what qualifies as—a given pattern of behaviour requires resort to meaning-based distinctions.[6] Black and Baumgartner repeatedly use terms like 'intimacy', 'respectability', 'attractiveness', all of which necessarily rely upon judgements about the meaning for the people involved. For example, in elaborating his above cited principle about 'relational distance', Black (1995: 854) asserts that a 'distant case (between strangers) attracts more law than a close case (between intimates) . . .' Unless we measure 'distance' and 'closeness' solely in terms of factors like geographical proximity or repetitiveness of interaction—which is absurd because there are people we are intimate with who live far away and people we interact with daily who are basically strangers—we must take into account what people think and feel. There is no other way to talk about intimacy. Behaviourism is thus parasitic upon meaning, regardless of claims otherwise.

A further interpretivist objection is that the regularities identified, and the 'laws' constructed thereupon, cannot be a 'causal explanation' of the behaviour, as behaviourists claim. The explanations are to be found in the meaningful intentional states of the people involved. For

---

[6] Mark Cooney (1986: 264), a defender of Black's form of analysis, concedes that behaviourism 'invariably has a psychological dimension' in the sense I set out.

example, when postulating the 'law' that people high on the respectability scale do better before law than people low on the scale, Baumgartner (1992: 136) observes that:

Officials of all kinds take aggressive action more often against accused individuals who have previously been in trouble with the law, for example, than against those who are first time violators. Thus, the police are more likely to arrest people with prior records, when they know about them, and to pursue the cases against them vigorously. One study concluded that 'nothing makes [the police] more enthusiastic about a case than to find out the assailant has other charges against him or a prison record.' Another study found that the police are sensitive not only to the existence of a prior record but to the precise nature of the earlier misbehavior. They distinguish various categories of offenders, including 'fresh meat' (first time violators), 'dirt bags' (continual petty thieves and fighters), 'pukes' (those who have served prison time for felonies), and 'animals' (those believed to lack all morals and to be indiscriminately violent). As the seriousness of a citizen's previous misconduct goes up in police eyes, so does the importance of vigorous legal control.

Baumgartner cites this as evidence of the dramatic point that law, as a consequence of sociological forces, systematically discriminates against people with poor reputations.

The obvious retort to this argument is that the legal actors assuredly are discriminating, but intentionally and for quite rational reasons—they are allocating their limited energy and resources towards dealing with the relatively greater threat presented by serious repeat offenders. Indeed we would question their behaviour if they were not discriminating in this way. This instrumental orientation of the actors is what 'explains' their behaviour, but a positivistic science which rules out consideration of meaning is blind to it, leaving only an inexplicable pattern of discrimination which is then pointed to as evidence that law treats people unfairly.

Interpretivists also object to the very possibility that there can be universal, invariant laws of social behaviour beyond those imposed by our physical and instinctual nature. The problem is that humans are thinking, interpreting beings who collectively define themselves. As we change our self-definitions, who we are changes, and our behaviour changes, obviating any so-called 'laws' which were based on ealier patterns of behaviour (Taylor 1979: 69–70). This effect can be seen by following historical changes over time.

According to Black and Baumgartner, the 'relational distance' principle—the greater the intimacy between the parties involved, the more 'indifferent and lenient' legal officials will be—is one of the 'most powerful and best documented' laws of legal behaviour (Baumgartner 1992: 131). 'Police officers, for example, are less likely to recognize disputes between intimates as crimes, and less likely to arrest offenders in such matters; prosecutors are less likely to press charges; grand juries are less likely to indict; judges and trial juries are less likely to convict; and judges are less likely to sentence harshly' (p. 131).

Again, there is a meaningful explanation for this pattern. In many places, and implicit within Black's own definition, law (and culture) developed along lines which recognized the public-private distinction, exerting authority over the former but not the latter. Family relations were considered the epitome of the private, thus beyond the purview of the law—acts of violence between intimates often were not deemed to be even illegal. As cultural attitudes changed, law began to criminalize these acts, but there continued to be strong residual beliefs about the sanctity of the family along with the concomitant sentiment that law should be a last resort in such matters. These situations were seen (by police, prosecutors, judges, and juries) in a more forgiving light, by contrast to the directly threatening and less understandable violence between strangers. Another contributing factor, as feminist jurisprudence insists, is that the law has been male-dominated, and thus has tended to treat leniently violence among intimates, which is largely perpetrated by males. These ideas and beliefs explain the pattern observed.

More to the point, these beliefs have in fact changed over time, resulting in greater legal intervention into intimate relationships. In the past several decades there has been an almost complete abolishment of the interspousal immunity doctrine in the US, and substantial cutbacks on the parental immunity doctrine, which has resulted in an increased number of lawsuits between family members. There have also been changes in criminal law. In a study of domestic violence in Hawaii, to cite one example, Sally Engle Merry (1994) has confirmed a 'sharp increase' in the prosecution of spousal abuse cases in the past decade directly attributable to a new attitude among police, prosecutors and judges that domestic violence will no longer be tolerated. Similarly, there have been increasing legal efforts at dealing with child abuse, albeit often tragically ineffective. Finally, women have begun to enter the law at every level, exposing the ways in which the law has operated to project and protect male interests. These developments demonstrate that the patterns identified by Black and Baumgartner are only regularities that reflect existing behaviour shaped by prevailing attitudes and beliefs, which can and do change; they are not sociological 'laws' that govern behaviour.

This last observation also discloses why the regularities identified by positivism do not necessarily entail determinism. There are regularities in behaviour because people in a community who are similarly socialized often have shared ideas, beliefs and reasoning patterns, and operate under similar constraining conditions (like scarcity and the need for food and shelter). Socialization, the imprinting of cultural knowledge and beliefs in individuals, is where sociological factors come into play and is why sociological analysis is a necessary component to any attempt to explain behaviour. These factors shape and set limits on our attitudes and understandings and therefore on our available range of possible actions (though they also enable our actions). Choice ordinarily operates within the scope of these factors, but the realm of possibilities can always be expanded through self-reflective questioning of existing beliefs or through leaps of imagination, or by contesting or altering the surrounding material constraining conditions. Regularities in our behaviour, therefore, in no way imply that we must or will always maintain the same patterns.

Black repeatedly asserts that his 'laws' 'predict *and explain*' the behaviour of law. The regularities that Black identifies may have predictive power (reliable across a number of cases, though less so in any given case), but they have no explanatory power. To the contrary, it is the regularities themselves that call for explanation. Assuming law varies with relational distance, the obvious question is: why? On this issue Black is completely silent. The explanation cannot be found in all the confirming instances of this regularity, for that is circular. *Invariable* regularities can serve as an 'explanation' in the natural sciences because their laws do not allow a single disconfirming instance, and because as far as science can tell the regularities observed—in a natural world apparently devoid of agency and teleology—just *are*, they stand on their own bottom. Not so for the social world, which is full of exceptions to (deviations from) regularities in behaviour, where regularities change, and where purposeful behaviour is ubiquitous. The explanation for the regularities in behaviour Black has identified must be found in the complex of meaningful ideas and beliefs which generate the behaviour observed.

Finally, interpretivists object to the positivist tendency to, in the name of science, assign a higher degree of reality to 'structures' or 'functions' than to the individuals whose meaningful actions they reflect. Black (1995: 968–70) also succumbed to this: 'I pursued accepted ideals of science: generality, simplicity, and the rest of it. But my strategy had consequences I never expected: It stripped humanity itself. It reduced human behavior to its simplest expression. It left nothing but social life . . . I assassinated the person.' The abject dismissal of positivism is understandable considering this kind of hyperbole (spouted by Professor Black, not by social life). It is a perfect example of what the pragmatists condemned—theorists gazing into their abstract construction and persuading themselves that it *is* reality. Structures and functions, habitus, autopoiesis, figurations, the semi-autonomous social field, practices, and the like, are all just analytical constructs, heuristic devices, ways of framing the field for the purposes of study. Without such devices analysis could not proceed, but they are not more real than the people who construct them or the people whose behaviour they purport to reflect or explain.

C. The Merits of Behaviourism

Despite the above objections, which do not vitiate positivist studies but do suggest that they must be read with caution, positivism has valuable strengths. Ignoring the meaningful orientation of actors is a useful self-imposed blinder because it frees the observer from being bound by what the actors think they are doing, focusing instead on their actions. This allows us to test whether people are in fact doing what they believe they are doing or claim to be doing. It was for this reason that the Legal Realists as well as the classical social scientists who studied law, including Bronislaw Malinowski, Eugen Ehrlich and Adamson Hoebel, above all emphasized the close observation of actual behaviour (as I will recount in the next Chapter).

Another benefit of positivist studies is they are able to accumulate data across a large number of instances of behaviour. We need not describe the results in terms of 'laws' to appreciate the significance of information that, for example, blacks who kill whites have a high risk of receiving the death penalty while whites who kill blacks have almost no risk (Black 1989: 10), or that Republican judges are relatively more severe in criminal cases than Democratic judges (Nagel 1969: 227–36), or that legal institutions have often appeared to treat the wealthy more favourably than the poor.

It is essential to observe matters on a grand scale, using analytical devices like 'structures' or 'figurations', because social reality is more than just the accumulation of individual meanings and behaviours. And what if, in fact, 'laws' of social behaviour do exist and can be demonstrated? This possibility should not be absolutely ruled out in advance. At the very least, the information learned in the search is useful even if the answers prove to be negative. Regardless of their ultimate correctness, Black's 'laws' of legal behaviour are intriguing.

Finally, behaviourism, in the sense of keeping an eye on patterns of behaviour (including speech behaviour), has an undeniable advantage over interpretivism: what it focuses on is directly observable in a way that meaning is not. There is a fact of the matter to behaviour; whereas meaning is more elusive. Interpretivism is actually parasitic upon behaviourism, for it is only through observing behaviour that meaning can be discerned, as the pragmatists recognized. And disputes over meaning (over the proper interpretation) can only be settled through continued observations about behaviour, over longer periods of time or broader in scope, or through comparing behaviour in different contexts. Interpretivism needs behaviourism. The interpretivist tendency to scorn behaviourism is ill-conceived.

A duly chastened positivism—one that acknowledges that its very methodology shapes the objects it observes, that there could have been other ways to categorize the object or other methods of quantification, that it does to a degree draw from meaning-based distinctions made by the actors, that the explanations it provides are one sided and need to be supplemented or tested by consideration of the actors meaningful orientations, that the structures and functions it identifies through patterns of behaviour are not more real than the messy reality they have been abstracted from, that it is highly contestable whether the regularities identified are 'laws' in a causal, deterministic sense—can still contribute essential information to the understanding and analysis of social life.

Interpretivists might insist that these concessions leave very little of the original positivist project. That is correct. With the exception of a few extremists like Black, social scientists today have generally come to recognize that this project could not be met without the exhorbitant cost of eliminating consideration of much of what is interesting and important in social life, and few feel the need to make such claims or set such standards for their activities. There is still a good deal of information to be learned from positivist methodologies, which are consistent with pragmatic injunctions about the acquisition of knowledge through close, impartial observation and testing, and this is all the justification it needs.

The Limits of Interpretivism

Interpretivism has all the momentum in socio-legal studies today. It is the favoured social science of critical scholars (Trubek 1984: 600–5), and underlies the currently popular themes of ideology critique and social constructionism (on ideology see Special Issue: Law and Ideology 1988; on social constructionism see Mertz 1994). In view of the long-standing dominance of positivism, the infatuation with interpretivism of the past ten years is surely merited, but interpretivism also has its own partialities and defects, many of which are the flip side of the strengths of behaviourism. An obvious such defect is that because interpretivism focuses on meaning-oriented behaviour, it cannot easily take account of the unintentional consequences of behaviour, nor can it systematically provide for the structures which shape the constraining conditions within which social action takes place (Habermas 1988: 173–4). Interpretivism inclines heavily towards micro-analyses of meaningful behaviour, losing sight of the macro aspects that determine the available range of choices. Interpretivism also cannot adequately deal with issues of material power, that is, power which is not immediatly a function of ideas but of who has raw possession of or access to resources.

To encourage caution in the embrace of interpretivism, I will discuss in order six difficulties with present socio-legal uses: 1) the social construction thesis cannot give critical scholars what they want from it; 2) beyond the initial shock of recognition the thesis loses its power; 3) the value of certain kinds of interpretive studies is questionable; 4) there is an increased danger of political bias; 5) there are deep and complex problems about the notion of meaning that have yet to be resolved; and 6) there are unresolved problems involving the concept of ideology. The first four issues will be dealt with in the next Part below; those surrounding meaning will be dealt with separately in the Part that follows; and those dealing with ideology in the Part thereafter.

A. Four Difficulties for Socio-Legal Studies

The first problem can be found in Trubek's (1984) argument for why critical scholars find the interpretive approach so important:

Critical scholars see social order as maintained by a system of beliefs. The belief systems that structure action and maintain order in capitalist societies present as eternal and necessary what is only the transitory and arbitrary interests of a dominant elite. This commonly accepted body of ideas justifies the unequal and unjust power of the dominant group. These systems of ideas are reifications, presenting as essential, necessary, and objective what is contingent, arbitrary and subjective. Furthermore, they are hegemonic, that is, they serve to legitimate interests of the dominant class alone (p. 606).

. . . .

Reifications distort what we really are as human beings. They alienate us from what is fundamental in ourselves (p. 608).

. . . .

For the Critical scholar, this world [as it seems to be] is a dream, and the task of scholarship is not simply to understand the dream, but also to awaken the dreamers (p. 618).

According to the tenets of interpretivism, critical scholars cannot get what they want out of the social construction thesis because it goes all the way to the 'ground'. As meaningfully oriented interpreting beings, there is nothing beneath systems of ideas; there is no bedrock 'what we really are as human beings,' other than base physical instincts and needs. What is fundamental in us are just those desires, ideas and beliefs we hold dear. Every system of ideas is as 'contingent, arbitrary, and subjective' as any other (though 'intersubjective' is a better word than 'subjective', since systems of ideas are generated by and shared among social groups); hence these charges are inapt; they have no sting. Consequently—to borrow Trubek's metaphor—any dreamer who thinks they have awakened will merely be dreaming that they are awake. The mistake, as Rorty (1991: 239–40) articulated, is that the radical left 'think that deep thinking is required to get down to this deep level, and that only there, when all the superstructural appearances have been undercut, can things be seen as they really are.' There is no *there* to get to, only other ideas and beliefs.

This conclusion leads to the second difficulty. The first time one hears the social construction thesis it is a revelation. The impact is profound the very first time one reads a convincing demonstration that 'legal facts are made not born, are socially constructed . . . by everything from evidence rules, courtroom etiquette, and law reporting traditions, to advocacy techniques, the rhetoric of judges, and the scholasticisms of law school education' (Geertz 1983: 173). But once you *get* it, really understand the point, then every additional demonstration is superfluous, because most everything in social life is constructed in precisely the same way—that's what the social construction of reality means—reality is socially constructed through-and-through. So now what?

The critical faith is that once people absorb this insight, the givenness of things—reification—dissolves and we can then remake reality into the way we think things should be. The error in this idealistic faith is that the givenness of things is not an illusion but a social fact, a social fact that exists by virtue of the entrenched beliefs and activities of everyone in the social arena whose actions reproduce (construct) this fact on an ongoing basis. These beliefs and activities are not clothes people can shed at will; they form the very (socially constructed) identities of those involved. Imagine the futility of instructing the Bosnian Serbs, Croats and Muslims, or the Tutsis and Hutus of Rwanda, or the Palestinians and Israelis, that their social identities and historical hatreds are socially constructed, so it's absurd that they continue to kill one another. Considered in these concrete terms, the social construction thesis is revealed to have a superficial, overly intellectualized quality.

People can throw off or renounce aspects of their beliefs. However, the instigating factor in such an event is not hearing the social construction thesis itself, but in deciding that the old beliefs should no longer be accepted because the cost is too high or a new belief is preferable. When such moments occur in a radical way for individuals, it is called an epiphany, for societies it is a revolution. For both of these events, the social construction thesis is irrelevant—the battle over what beliefs should be held is what counts. Thus, if we want to change things, to achieve social reform, we must still persuade others to adopt the new set of beliefs (just as contingent, arbitrary, and intersubjective) by convincing them that the old ideas are not in their interest but the new ones are. That is the age-old task of political persuasion, and neither interpretivism nor the social construction thesis alter this process one whit.[7]

Interpretivism and the social construction thesis were developed in the context of social science as new ways to gain insight into the social world. However, for all the reasons stated earlier, they address the ground, the enabling yet limiting conditions of our existence which we cannot alter by our recognition of them. Perhaps the only implication they have beyond informing us of the conditions of our existence comes in the hope expressed by Rorty that if we were all aware that our dearest ideas and beliefs have no absolute foundation, we might be more

---

[7] Stanley Fish (1989: 394–5) has repeatedly made this point: 'To put the matter baldly, already-in-place interpretive constructs are a condition of our consciousness . . . Nor is it the case that the hold our interpretive constructs have on us will be loosened simply because we have been alerted to it by [Critical scholars]. To think otherwise is to fall into the characteristically left error of assuming that an insight into the source of our convictions (they come from culture, not from God) will render them less compelling.'

tolerant toward others with different ideas and beliefs, resulting in an overall dimunition of extremism. This is, of course, a quintessentially modern, Enlightenment hope.

The third difficulty for interpretive studies is the questionable value of the information produced. Interpretivism is especially enlightening when it is applied to situations to demonstrate that the people involved have contrasting or bypassing meanings but are oblivious to that fact— the interaction proceeds despite a breakdown in communication (see e.g. Tamanaha 1993a). And it is enlightening when applied to the study of alien cultures, as in traditional anthropology, where the differences in meaning and ways of thinking between the subjects and the observers/readers are so great that there is much to be learned from being exposed to another way of being. The situation differs, however, when interpretive techniques are applied at home, as is the recent trend in socio-legal studies, because there is an increased danger that the information provided will be already known or banal.

Examples of this can be found in Patricia Ewick's and Susan Silbey's (1995) recent article, 'Subversive Stories and Hegemonic Tales: Toward a Sociology of Narrative', touting the use of narratives in socio-legal studies, and setting out its theoretical elements. Ewick and Silbey assert that 'storytelling is strategic. Narrators tell tales in order to achieve some goal or advance some interest' (p. 208). To establish this point in a legal context, they recite a study by James Holstein:

Holstein describes the strategic use of legal interrogation by both district attorneys and public defenders to impede or facilitate the development of narratives by defendants in involuntary commitment hearings. In direct examination defense counsel employs specific techniques to help organize the narratives of patients in ways that demonstrate their mental competence. For instance, the public defender asks questions to elicit brief, direct answers. The logic of the interaction and the adequacy of the answers is largely organized by counsel so as to make the patient/witness appear coherent and responsive. Whenever a patient/witness begins to say anything that could be construed as 'crazy,' the public defender quickly intervenes to change the subject. By contrast, district attorneys use techinques of cross-examination in such hearings to produce narrative incompetence. Among these various techniques, district attorneys in these hearings organize incompetence by orchestrating questions so as to violate conventional narrative lines. For instance, they ask in rapid sequence a series of unrelated questions which, even when answered appropriately, give the appearance of talk that is discontinuous, multifocused, and incoherent. Finally, although district attorneys limit the length of appropriate and reasonable answers given by witnesses, they will refrain from interrupting what they refer to as 'crazy talk.' At that point, long, rambling uninterrupted narratives are allowed, even validated and encouraged. The district attorneys Holstein studied refer to this strategy as 'letting the patients hang themselves.'

Thus, with these various strategies, lawyers elicit talk that indicates either mental competence or incompetence. The type and sequence of questions they pose, the rules of elicitation they observe (or knowingly violate), are strategically chosen to demonstrate their legal argument (pp. 209–10).

This account of the tactics of defence counsel and district attorney clearly reveals that everyone involved, including the patients (at least the competent ones), and certainly the judge, know exactly what is going on: the defence attorney is trying to make their 'witness' appear sane, and the district attorney trying to make the 'patient' appear incompetent, through techniques as subtle as the label applied to refer to the person. The entire account, and the point it makes—narratives are strategic—seems entirely obvious, not just to the participants but to anyone who pauses to think about it. Social science, and academia more generally, should strive to produce knowledge which, if not new, is at least 'nonobvious' or adds to the body of knowledge in some way (cf. Farber and Sherry 1993: 848).

When applied to particular subcommunities with unique ways of approaching the law, or to odd situations in which the legal actors engage in counter-intuitive activities, there is still much to be learned from applying interpretivism to home. Interpretive studies of the everyday aspects of law or legal activities, however, run the risk of producing insights obvious to the participants, useful mainly, if at all, for the edification of the social scientists themselves. Moreover, modern print and visual journalism are likewise engaged in story-telling, are often better at it, and reach a much wider audience. If general consciousness raising as a means to social transformation is the goal, as is often asserted, interpretive socio-legal scholarship seems futile by comparison.

The difficulty with politics in interpretive social science, the fourth difficulty, is a function of the obscurity of meaning, exacerbated by the internal dynamics in today's socio-legal community. There is an observable fact of the matter to behaviour, which can serve as a test for behaviouristic studies. Presumably many different social scientists can duplicate the same study, or construct others, to come up with confirming or refuting reports of behaviour. The check for interpretations is also behaviour, but behaviour is underdeterminative in relation to meaning. Often the same behaviour can give rise to several different interpretations. Further complicating this problem is the 'interpreter effect': interpretations are 'in large part a function of the vocabulary and the theoretical presuppositions of the investigator' (Smelser 1992: 17). As interpretive anthropologist Clifford Geertz (1973: 29) observed, interpretations are 'essentially contestable'.

These conditions led philosopher Charles Taylor (1979: 66) to conclude that there is no way to test a given interpretation other than by resort to more interpretations—'[A] hermeneutic science cannot but rely upon insight.' The quality of the studies produced by interpretive social science are thus directly dependent upon the ability of the scientist to observe in an impartial way, to be self-critical about predispositions to see things that support existing beliefs or political positions, and to be open to the possibility that the outcome of the study may be the opposite of what one would like to find.

These are difficult though not impossible demands. But there is no chance they will be met by critical scholars who argue that interpretive socio-legal studies should assume an 'oppositional consciousness' and evince 'loyalty to subordinate persons and groups,' and who accuse social scientists who take a disinterested stance of 'actively collaborating' in the social order they claim to observe (Silbey 1991: 814). This critical approach requires 'that the observer become [an] advocate' (Harrington and Yngvesson 1990: 147). There is nothing left of the scientific attitude in this formulation—the cognitive orientation of the socio-legal scholar is instrumental, identical to that of social actors in the pursuit of their projects, rather than an open cognitive interest oriented towards knowing or understanding. Only the earnestness of its proponents serves to distinguish this stance from unabashed politics.

B. The Complexity of Meaning in Interpretive Social Science

The fifth difficulty is complexity with the notion of meaning. Lawyers, who cannot agree on the comparatively simple question of how to decide what a statute means, are familiar with the mystery of meaning. It is beyond my capacity and the scope of this work to delve deeply in its nature, so I will limit the discussion to the issues meaning poses for interpretive social scientists. Several hurdles have already been mentioned: meaning cannot be directly observed; behaviour is underdeterminative in relation to meaning; the interpreter effect influences interpretations of meaning; and there is no final or conclusive way to confirm assertions of meaning. The following discussion will focus on the considerations surrounding meaning in two distinguishable senses that have been applied in interpretive social science: meaning for the actors, and the meaning of events or complexes of action. Interpretive socio-legal scholars have not always recognized the distinction between these two senses, or the unresolved puzzles that accompany each.

1. Meaning for the Actors

Meaning *for* the particular individual or group of individuals whose actions are being observed is the first sense. Alfred Schutz (1967: 45–138), who has developed the most sophisticated phenomenological account of interpretive social science, identified two senses of this first kind of meaning: meaning in the 'primordial' sense and meaning as experienced between social actors. Meaning in the primordial sense is meaning within the consciousness of an individual. Meaning in this sense exists when the individual reflects upon lived experience and constitutes it as meaningful. It depends upon the kind of attention the person gives it and the moment at which the reflection occurs. 'The specific meaning of a lived experience . . . consists in the ordering of this lived experience within the total context of experiences that is present at hand' (p. 78). Schutz emphasized that many experiences are not reflected upon in this manner and thus do not have meaning in this sense.

Schutz argued that it is absurd to think that a scientist could recover meaning in the primordial sense, because it would require that the scientist live through all the conscious states and intentional acts which constituted the experience of the actor, and give them exactly the same degree of attention. To satisfy these requirements the stream of consciousness of the scientist would have to coincide with that of the actor, 'which is the same as saying that I should have to *be* the other person' (p. 99, emphasis in original).

Social scientists can, however, recover meaning as experienced between social actors. This is the level of meaning at which individuals interacting in the social world understand one another. All acts by the other are understood by the observer only in terms of the observer's own lived experiences. 'He interprets the other person's subjective meaning as if it were his own. In the process he draws upon his whole knowledge of the speaker, especially the latter's ways and habits of expressing himself . . . The same process goes on in the mind of the speaker' (p. 127).

This process goes on beneath awareness unless there is a disturbance. It works because the meaning which informs each participant is intersubjective—that is, derived from the shared language and social group in which they are socialized. Schutz asserted that the intersubjective meaning social actors draw upon largely consists of social recipies or typifications, through which behaviour is standardized in socially shared patterns of meaning and conduct.

The key for the interpretive social scientist, then, is to understand these intersubjective typifications, to understand the form of life within which the actions take place. This is what Clifford Geertz called the public context of meaning. 'The ethnographer does not, and in my opinion largely cannot, perceive what his informants perceive. What he perceives, and that uncertainly enough, is what they perceive 'with'— or 'by means of, ' or 'through' . . . or whatever the word should be' (Geertz 1983: 58). 'The trick is to figure out what the devil they think they are up to' (p. 58).

Schutz's account should sound familiar to socio-legal scholars. In many respects it is similar to, though far more elaborated than, Geertz's influential work in interpretive anthropology.[8] Both suggested that the task of the social scientist is to use the paradigms or perspectives derived from their scientific tradition ('second level' or 'experience far' constructs) to render the meaning for the social actors being studied ('first level' or 'experience near' constructs) (Schutz 1962: 5–7, 63; Geertz 1983: 57). As a check on the scientist, Schutz (1962: 44) asserted that the scientist's interpretations should 'be understandable for the actor himself as well as for his fellow-men in terms of common-sense interpretation of everyday life'.

Though their work has provided a solid foundation for interpretive studies, two major limitations stand out. The first limitation is that their focus on intersubjective or public meaning tends to obscure the ways in which there are different meanings at play in a social arena. John D. Thompson (1990: 135) criticized Geertz for his emphasis 'on *the* meaning rather than the divergent and conflicting meanings that cultural phenomena may have for individuals situated in different circumstances and endowed with differing resources and opportunities' (emphasis in original). As I argued earlier, the most informative interpretive studies are those which disclose all the divergent meanings for social actors in a complex of action.

The second limitation is that neither theorist has adequately considered a series of related questions raised by their work. The first question is whether and under what circumstances the analyst can insist that

---

[8] A more detailed elaboration of Schutz's ideas and their parallels with Geertz's can be found in Tamanaha (1993a: 79–101).

the meaning offered by the social actor is not in fact the social actor's meaning. Can the analyst tell the actors that they are wrong about what they believe their meaning to be? If yes, on what authority? And by what standards are such disputes to be resolved? If after initial resistance the actor is persuaded to accept the analysts' meaning, does that indicate that the analyst was correct, or that the persuasive power of the analyst changed the meaning for the actor? If the actor continues to refuse to accept the analyst's meaning following attempts at persuasion, does that mean the analyst was wrong? Do actors, in other words, have epistemological authority with regard to meaning for them?

A related but distinct issue is whether and under what circumstances the analyst can say that the meaning for the actor is the product of false consciousness. In this scenario the analyst and the actor agree about what the meaning for the actor is, but the analyst goes on to assert that the actor should have some other meaning, that this meaning is the product of an ideologically induced delusion. Implicit in this assertion is that there is a meaning which is not the product of a delusion, and that the analyst knows what that true or correct meaning is.

These questions must be grappled with by critical socio-legal scholars, in particular, because, as I will show in greater detail in Chapter Six, they regularly assert that social actors are deluded about the nature of their own activities, or suffer from false consciousness. Joel Handler (1992: 342–3) has argued, for example, that the consciousness of disadvantaged people has been manipulated. According to Handler, this can be seen in the attitudes of the recipients of public assistance who feel that it is appropriate to impose certain corresponding obligations on people who receive a minimum level of support, who believe that there is no entitlement to such support without return responsibilities. 'To the extent that the applicant for assistance has internalized these values . . . then the dominant group has prevented even the conception of the grievance' (p. 343).

False consciousness arguments of this nature disable the actor from contesting the analyst. Any response the actors might give—that they find it important for their own sense of dignity that there be some responsibility attached to receipt of the assistance—is invalidated at the outset because the reasons given are themselves the product of the ideologically induced adoption of values that benefit the elite (i.e. that personal dignity should be seen in such terms). Although Handler makes his argument as an advocate for the disadvantaged, it has a condescending quality which condemns an entire population to delusion while the analyst alone sees the light. Handler (p. 344) recognizes, in passing, that there are troubling questions raised by his assertions: '[H]ow do we know whether the consent is genuine or manipulated? How does the researcher . . . avoid imputing her values, the social construction of meaning, to the quiescent?' If critical socio-legal scholars continue to press such claims, these questions must be taken seriously.

Extrapolating from Schutz's analysis and the pragmatists' assertions about the limited scope of truth in the realm of meaning, several answers can be proffered. There is a matter of fact to meaning in the primordial sense, although we have access to this only through meaning in the sense between social actors. When a person reflects upon their experience and forms an understanding about it in the way suggested by Schutz, that is the meaning of the experience for that person at that particular moment of reflection. The social scientist who insists that this person has a different meaning will be wrong. Keep in mind, however, that the meaning for a person of a given experience can change because it depends upon the moment of reflection (a later reflection can even give meaning to an experience which was not meaningful at the time), which in turn is shaped by the particular attention given and all the experiences lived since the previous moment of reflection. Thus, if the scientist persuades the person that they should adopt a different meaning, then that will be the meaning at that latter moment of reflection.

A similar analysis applies to meaning as experienced between social actors in a given complex of action. The operative meaning as between the actors at the time of interaction (or across a series of interactions) is a question of fact, keeping in mind that it may also be a fact that unbeknownst to the actors involved they had divergent meanings, or even no meanings.

The matter-of-factness of meanings for the actors are thus timebound, contingent upon attention, context and lived experience. Assertions about meaning in this sense can be true or false, and the best guides to the proper determination is close observation of behaviour, and asking the participants themselves, although there are no certain verification procedures (reports from the actors may be faulty or duplicitous). But there is no true meaning outside of or rising above these particular moments of experienced factual meaning. As Dewey (1925: 332) stated, 'a large part of our life is carried on in a realm of meanings to which truth and falsity as such are irrelevant.'

If this is correct, analysts should stop proclaiming that the meanings actors attach to their actions are wrong, or are the product of ideologically induced delusion, since both claims erroneously presuppose that there is a true meaning. Instead the analyst should argue that the actor would be better off if they attached the meaning suggested by the analyst, and the argument must be pressed by concretely demonstrating how the actor would benefit from adopting this proposed meaning. This is a harder argument to make because the analyst cannot bypass or dismiss the beliefs of the actors as deluded; the case for correctness must be made on the merits.

2. Meaning of Social Events or Situations

The second sense in which meaning is used in the social sciences is not meaning for the actors involved, but meaning of the social event, or situation, or complex of actions or beliefs studied. This meaning may be a function of or influenced by the meaning of the actors involved, but the two senses of meaning remain distinct. The 'meaning' of the French Revolution, for example, is not determined by the individual meanings for the antagonists involved. The 'meaning' of the acquittal of O. J. Simpson is not determined by the meanings for the jurors who set him free, or the lawyers who participated in the case. As Paul Ricouer (1979: 80–8) observed, action becomes detached from the actor and has consequences of its own.

By its nature, meaning in this sense is relative to the person interpreting, the context in which the event is placed and the context from which it is examined. There is no 'meaning-in-itself' of the French Revolution or the Simpson trial. Social events, to put it in starker terms, have no built-in or inherent meaning; there is no truth or falsity with regard to the meaning of events; there is no fact of the matter to this kind of meaning—the facts of the matter are the behaviour of, and individual meanings for, the actors involved. The meaning of a given championship football game may differ for each fan watching (if they attach a meaning), and will certainly differ from the meaning attributed by the owner of the team, or from a sociologist who studies the game as an example of mass behaviour, or from the meaning as seen by a football historian, and all of these meanings will be sharply different from the meaning of the players while they are playing (many will be doing, not reflecting on meaning), or the meaning for them after the game is over.

Because of this democracy of meaning, interpretive social scientists must proceed with caution when making assertions about the meaning of social events or situations or complexes of action. Attempts have been made to formalize the field of study to make it more solid. Ricouer (1979) drew an analogy between the interpretation of social action and the interpretation of texts to argue that interpretive social science can study situations which have undergone a kind of 'objectification'; the event can then be seen at a distance from the psychological-social-historical conditions of its production, allowing the internal structure and content of the action to be analysed. The cost of this abstracting procedure is that it severs the ties the event had with the surrounding circumstances which gave rise to it, while little is gained in terms of making it more amenable to 'scientific' interpretation.

No amount of methodological restrictions can alter the fact that there is no fact-of-the-matter to the meaning attributed to social events or situations. It's not just that there are many ways and levels at which to frame the event to be studied; the interests and background of the interpreter in shaping the meaning found—the interpreter effect—cannot be entirely repressed. Echoing Dewey, Hans Georg Gadamer (1979;1991) asserted that understanding always implies a pre-understanding which is a function of the 'prejudices' of the interpreter. 'Both the interpreter and the part of the tradition he is interested in contain their own horizon; the task consists, however, not in placing oneself within the latter, but in widening one's own horizon so that it can integrate the other' (Bleicher 1980: 112). The interpreter's horizon is thus a necessary aspect of the interpretation. A neo-Marxist social scientist will interpret a given social event in an entirely different way from a functionalist.

Nevertheless, interpretations can still be evaluated as right or wrong, or better or worse. Interpretations which are inconsistent with the behaviour observed are highly suspect; this includes interpretations which arbitrarily fail to consider integral aspects of the behaviour, or which point to abberational or unusual behaviour as support for a thesis which purports to describe the meaning of the whole. Also suspect are interpretations that have little or no connection to the meanings for the actors involved. The social construction of reality thesis says, after all, that our meaningful actions construct reality. Aside from testing interpretations against the behaviour of and meaning for the actors, the best way to evaluate interpretations is to compare them against other interpretations on various criteria, such as which has better explanatory power and predictive capacity.

An interpretation which is mostly a projection of the desires or prejudices of the social scientist is a bad interpretation. The interpretation must be 'adequate to the object', to the social event or activity which is being interpreted. The only way to achieve this is to approach the study with an open attitude oriented toward understanding.

However, there is an irreducible aspect of political views involved in the attribution of meaning to social events. Thus I would not assert here, as I have earlier in relation to studies of matters of fact, that it is harmful to bring a political perspective to this task. Without some such perspective no interpretation at all about the meaning of a social event could be ventured. An alternative, of course, is to choose to abstain from offering these kinds of interpretations. Social scientists should not be so precluded, however. This is the arena in which the clash of visions about the nature of society take place, and social scientists have as much to contribute to this debate as anyone. What the scientist cannot claim is that there is anything distinctively scientific about the interpretation he or she espouses. Interpretations of the meaning of social events by social scientists should be evaluated by the same standards applied to all such interpretations: the degree to which it fits the behaviour and meaning for the persons involved (fits the facts), and the extent to which the political vision underlying the interpretation is an attractive one.

The two senses of meaning articulated above can be illustrated through a return to Nader's study of the Zapotec, and her assertion that their 'harmony ideology' was a form of Christian-based resistance against the encroachment of outside power. If she meant that this was the *meaning for* the Zapotec, which is an assertion of fact, it would seem that there was questionable support in the sense that they apparently did not articulate or understand this ideodology in such terms. If she meant that this was the *meaning of* their way of interacting, an assertion for which there is no fact of the matter, then the question is whether this interpretation seems like the right way to understand the situation: is it 'adequate' to what was going on and is it an informative way of viewing the situation? The critique pressed by Just is that it was not 'adequate' to the situation, but was instead a projection by Nader of her own concerns. He made this determination by contrasting Nader's interpretation against what the Zapotec thought they were doing (the meaning for the Zapotec), and by comparing the behaviour and meaning for the Zapotec with similar situations around the world in which Nader's interpretation had no application. According to Just, Nader's interpretation was wrong, or at least a bad one, and it is entirely appropriate to render this kind of evaluation. We must, of course, subject Just's interpretation to the same tests.

The transformative power of meaning adds a significant twist to this analysis. Assume that initially the meaning for the Zapotec was not the meaning attributed by Nader, and that they were exposed to Nader's interpretation and came to accept that as their meaning. Then, in fact, Nader's meaning would become the meaning for the Zapotec, and by virtue of this change in meaning the situation, including their behaviour, would change. That's why it is essential to evaluate the political attractiveness of interpretations.

C. *The Complexity of the Notion of Ideology*

One of the dominant themes in interpretive socio-legal work, alluded to by Trubek in the earlier quote, is the exposure or defrocking of legal ideology—'ideology critique'. Here is a representative view of law and ideology, taken from the Introduction to a special issue of the Law and Society Review dedicated to the subject:

> In studies of law and ideology, the power of law resides in part in its capacity to inscribe the arbitrary and cultural features of social life with the aura of the natural and inevitable. All of the articles in this issue illustrate the power of law associated with the capacity to forge authoritative understandings of social relationships. In addition to the ability to 'naturalize' what is conditional and arbitrary legal ideologies can also be powerful as they conceal, falsify, or distort. It is not the immutable natural reality assumed by positive science that is concealed, however, but alternative social constructions forged from diverse experiences and competing visions. By rejecting alternative interpretations, legal ideologies are powerful to the extent that they deny that they are themselves constructions (Special Issue Editors 1988: 633).

At the heart of this passage lies a crucial adjustment in the concept of ideology. Consistent with its Marxist heritage, the 'most pervasive' understanding in the social sciences 'reduces ideology to false beliefs' (Special Issue Editors 1988: 630). But as I argued earlier, and as this passage implicitly recognizes, the charge of false consciousness carries with it a deeply problematic notion of truth (cf. Cotterrell 1995: 7–14; Hunt 1985: 18–19), one inconsistent with the general body of interpretivist ideas.

In lieu of false consciousness, the modified version of legal ideology articulated above sees the 'falsity' instead in the claim of law (or legal rules or categories), and the cultural features it reflects or ratifies, to 'naturalness' or inevitability, denying their own arbitrariness and foreclosing the possibility of alternative constructions. The flaw in this charge is that it fails to appreciate the universal nature of the social construction thesis. If reality is socially constructed (see Berger and Luckmann 1966), as the thesis asserts, then each and every construction is as arbitrary and conditional as any other; and each and every entrenched construction takes on the aura of the 'natural and inevitable'; and each and every prevailing construction forges authoritative understandings of social relationships. Moreover, no single social construction carries a sign which announces that it is merely a construction. If these characteristics are what make law and its exercise of power 'ideological', then virtually everything in social life is subject to the same charge.

When the false consciousness claim is truly given up, it is not clear that the notion of ideology contains a distinctive, analytically rigourous core. Socio-legal theorists have of late begun to grapple with articulating a servicable concept of ideology, but these efforts merely reinforce the suspicion that it would be prudent to de-emphasize ideology, as I will now argue.

Roger Cotterrell (1995: 10–11) articulated ideology in the following terms:

Legal ideology consists of currents of 'common sense,' taken-for-granted understanding, and belief that are informed and sustained by legal doctrine and which, in turn, reinforce it and are to some extent expressed in it. It comprises the more general structures of values and cognitive ideas that legal doctrine presupposes or invokes. Legal ideology includes, for example, currents of understanding and belief about property and contract, punishment and compensation, obligation and responsibility, authority and personality, individual freedom and social bonds, justice and order, among other matters. It also includes beliefs and assumptions about the nature of law itself and about its inevitable and appropriate functions.
. . . .
Ideological thought assumes its own completeness and its unassailable integrity; it purports to offer a total picture, a full and true understanding within its sphere of concern. Ideology presents itself as a comprehensive perspective, a self-evidently correct understanding, not subject to doubts, caveats and revision. Its evaluations are absolutely and obviously justified.

This formulation is rather similar to the old anthropological concept of culture, and more specifically to the concept of legal culture articulated by Lawrence Friedman (1969, 1975), among others, twenty-five years ago, which was set out in terms of the various attitudes and beliefs about law which characterize a given legal system or tradition. Cotterrell's version is a 'neutral' conception of ideology: 'Neutral conceptions are those which purport to characterize phenomena as ideology or ideological without implying that these phenomena are necessarily misleading, illusory, or aligned with the interests of any particular group' (Thompson 1990: 53). ' "Ideology", according to this general formulation, may be regarded as the interwoven systems of thought and modes of experience which are conditioned by social circumstances and shared by groups of individuals' (p. 48).

The problem with Cotterrell's description is that it is far from apparent that comprehensive, self-assured views about law exist in the strong terms he paints. Perhaps only the long defunct Formalist picture of law presented itself in this manner. Furthermore, it is highly questionable whether there is any single taken-for-granted understanding about law. Cotterrell (1995: 13) weakly acknowledges, and attempts to pre-empt, this objection when he suggests that we 'envisage ideology not as unified but as a complex interweaving of ideological currents of thought in any given social context, often with incompatibilities and tensions between them'.

David Trubek and John Esser (1990: 175–6) also recognize this problem, and offer the following version of legal ideology: 'There are a number of "legal ideologies". These include the elite production called legal doctrine and everyday understandings about law. Hence, when we speak of legal ideology, we mean views held in society about the nature and function of law.' Trubek and Esser immediately add, however, that views held in society about law are 'strongly influenced' by the ' "official" story the legal system tells about itself' (p. 176). In contrast to Cotterrell, Trubek and Esser hold to a 'critical' conception of ideology: 'Critical conceptions are those which convey a negative, critical or pejorative sense. Unlike neutral conceptions, critical conceptions imply that the phenomena characterized as ideology or ideological are misleading, illusory or one-sided; and the very characterization of phenomena as ideology carries with it an implict criticism or condmenation of them' (Thompson 1990: 52). This pejorative version is constructed around the notion of hegemony, or 'dominant ideology', 'a notion that implies "benefit" for the dominant classes and quiescence of the subordinated classes' (Smelser 1992: 15). Legal ideology is involved in 'the production and reproduction of hegemony' (Hunt 1985: 31).

Socio-legal scholars Patricia Ewick and Susan Silbey (1995: 212 n.10) have attempted to distinguish the often associated terms, ideology and hegemony:

Here the concept of hegemony is defined in terms of its relationship to the taken-for-granted everyday world . . . We identify the hegemonic as 'the order of signs, practices, relations and distinctions, images and epistemologies—drawn from a historically situated cultural field—that come to be taken-for-granted as the natural and received shape of the world and everything that inhabits it . . . But where there is an articulated set of meanings, values, and beliefs where there is active contest over meanings, values, and beliefs, we shall use the term *ideology*. The ideological is that part of the meaning system that does not go without saying. Any struggle is ideological to the extent in which it 'involves an effort to control the cultural terms in which the world is ordered and, within it, power legitimized.' (emphasis in original) (citations omitted).

Ewick's and Silby's concept of ideology appears to be directly contrary Cotterrell's. For Cotterrell ideology is the taken-for-granted; for Ewick and Silbey the taken for granted is hegemony—ideology is that which does not go without saying. Ideology, for Ewick and Silby, involves a political battle of world views.

This brief sampling of the treatment of the concept of ideology within the socio-legal community, among theorists who otherwise agree on a great deal, reveals that the concept is seen in various ways: as the taken-for-granted, or not the taken-for-granted; a singular ideology comprised of a complex interweave of different currents, or a plurality of ideologies; in the service of the reproduction of hegemony, or involved in a contest to become hegemonic; in pejorative terms (concealing or distorting in the service of the dominant class) or in neutral terms (a complex of ideas and beliefs).

My point is not just to repeat the acknowledged fact that there is a great deal of confusion surrounding the concept of legal ideology. It is to illustrate that there are two basic alternatives in the socio-legal literature, the first with questionable value and the second used in questionable ways. The neutral conception is difficult to distinguish from the concept of legal culture, and no good reasons have been given for exchanging the notion of culture, with all of its attendant confusions, for the even more uncertain and connotation-laden concept of ideology.

More problematic, the pejorative conception exploits the theoretical inconsistencies identified above to operate in a manner strongly reminiscent of a discredited form of functional analysis. Ideology, in this view, is squarely defined in functional terms: ideology is 'an essential element in the process of legitimation and hence in the reproduction of the prevailing social relations' (Hunt 1985: 17). Serving this function makes ideology what it is. Ideas and beliefs which do not serve this function are cultural beliefs, or something else, but not 'ideology'.

Because this functional aspect is built in by definition, once something has been dubbed an 'ideology' we cannot ask whether it is involved in the process of legitimation or the reproduction of domination. That has been presupposed in the initial designation. This would be less problematic if the existence of the function were established prior to branding something with the label ideology. But almost invariably the label is attached first—as in the blanket condemnation 'legal ideology'. Only at that point does the search for the function fulfilling aspects begin. That is precisely the point at which the abuse occurs, for it is all too easy to rationalize most everything, or its opposite, as operating in the service of a function.

An example can be found in the exchange over the Marxist view of law as superstructure. If law served the interests of the dominant class, it was asked, why is it that law often appears to act as a restraint on, against the interests of, the dominant class? The response is that the law and legal rights may act against the short-term interests of the dominant class, but only as an ingenious way of preserving its long term interests—give a little to make everything look fair, while concealing the overarching inequities (see Horwitz 1977a). Another example is the argument that legal rules and judgments apparently in favour of labour against capital actually operate against the interest of labour, because they serve to pacify and co-op labour into going along with a fundamentally inequitable order (see Klare 1978). And the same argument has been played out with regard to fundamental rights (see Delgado 1987; Horwitz 1988).

Once we are convinced that a given function is being served, it becomes a matter of exercising imagination to come up with an explanation to demonstrate that a disconfirming example is in fact further proof of the strength of the functional connection. Ideology critique is highly susceptible to this form of analysis. Consider this passage from the editors of the special issue on Law and Ideology (1988: 634): 'The power of legal ideologies and law itself derives not only from its constitutive effects, but from internal contradictions, paradoxes, and impurities as well. Whereas some might see such contradictions, paradoxes, and impurities as weakening the power of law to intrude on and successfully order social life, these apparent weaknesses make law available for innumerable uses and provide an extraordinarily wide arc for its compass.' So, we are told, what might have appeared to be a weakness, a reason to question law's ideological power (how can it serve and perpetuate domination if it is internally conflicted?), is in fact the source of its extraordinary strength. This is where the theoretical inconsistencies surrounding the concept come into play. One the one hand, it is the very coherence and universality of ideology that gives it power; on the other hand, the internal conflicts and tensions give it power. It is difficult to avoid the suspicion that no matter what the evidence, the convinced analyst will always be able to impose a construction that confirms the ideological function of law.

Recall that interpretivism suggests that it is helpful, if not necessary, to consider the meaning for the social actors involved in a given complex of interaction, since their meaningful ideas and beliefs collectively construct social reality. Ideology critique attempts to get behind that, suggesting that there is a deeper meaning which operates unbeknownst to the actors, including the elite actors, such that the oppressed are in fact tightening their own chains even as they think they are doing what they desire in their own interest, and the elite are oppressing others even as they strive to act in a fair and principled manner—legal ideology operates 'to mystify *both* dominators and dominated' (Kennedy 1979: 210). Ideology critique wants to break free of meaning for the social actors, to occupy the supra-realm of social teleology, rendering individuals, their meaningful actions, almost irrelevant, mere puppets playing out the dynamics of class relations. Without the checks provided by the behaviour of and meaning for the social actors, however, we are left with nothing to test the theories of these socio-legal scholars against, no way to be rigourous.

Domination is a real phenomenon which *must* be studied, but the very concept implies an element of intention. And like all intention-generated phenomena, it should be amenable to observation and demonstration, both with relation to behaviour and meaning (through behaviour). Too often, however, the concept of ideology, combined with the rationalization it licenses, is applied to *serve as* the demonstration. That must not suffice as proof in socio-legal studies. The study of intentional domination and its effects, and the study and disclosure of how bodies of beliefs operate to the disadvantage of some and advantage of others in ways not openly apparent, can in combination virtually cover the field now covered by ideology critique without ever mentioning the term.

Behaviourism and Interpretivism Together

Since behaviour and meaning are inseparable aspects of human interaction, it would seem obvious that social science must pay attention to both. Scientific positivism is responsible for dividing the two and discarding meaning. Only now are we recovering from this error, committed in the name of a scientistic fetish for methodology and causal laws. The danger now is a perpetuation of this error by going too far in the embrace of interpretivism, discarding behaviourism. The rhetoric of critical scholars against behaviourism is overblown, and threatens to continue a divide within socio-legal studies which is gradually being overcome in the philosophy of social science and the social sciences generally.

In this exploration of the two streams of thought I have emphasized the weaknesses of both to demonstate that each needs the other. Each either presupposes the other, or is ultimately grounded in the other, or must refer to the other as means of verification. Max Weber, who is credited with being the founder of interpretive sociology (despite his positivist inclinations), endorsed simultaneous use of both: 'On the one hand he recognized explanation in terms of causality and statistical correlations . . . On the other hand there was explanation by means of the attempt to understand the motivations of actors' (Wilson 1983: 119). Instead of successfully bringing the two sides together, he has been simultaneously praised and criticized by both.

It's time to declare a truce and explore the ways in which these approaches are complementary rather than conflicting. No doubt there will always be dismissive extremists on both sides, but that need not slow the progress toward reuniting in social science what social science alone tore asunder, to its own detriment. A realistic socio-legal theory takes this approach. It views the social arena as consisting of people behaving in meaningful ways. The focus of inquiry is on what are they doing and what they and others think they are doing. With this guiding perspective, I will now turn to the starting point for a social scientific approach to law: what is law?

4 An Analytical Map of the Concept of Law

An intractable puzzle brought almost to a standstill the development of theory in the social scientific study of law from the 1950s through the 1970s. The debate over a social scientific concept of law was the central focus of theoretical discussion during this period. The puzzle lie in the fact that the debate seemed incapable of resolution. There appeared to be almost as many concepts of law as there were theorists, with no apparent means to determine which concept, if any, was the correct one.

Legal philosophers have also long been exercised by the question of what law is, as H. L. A. Hart noted on the very first page of *The Concept of Law* (1961). But a lack of agreement has not been as debilitating. Legal philosophers, especially those in the positivist tradition, have the luxury of focusing on state law. Many social scientists, in contrast, consider state law to be an unacceptable starting point because it does not comprise a scientific category, and more so because application of the state law model would result in the conclusion that many societies (historically speaking) did not have law. Especially for legal anthropologists, this smacked of Western ethnocentrism.

This mix of scientism and concern about ethnocentrism resulted in analytical gridlock. Scientists who declared—at the outset of the inquiry—that, '[n]o society is without law' (Moore 1978: 215), were inevitably led to identify a different concept of law from those scientists who believed that whether or not particular societies have law should be an empirical question, one that can be answered in the negative.

After decades of heated exchanges, with no apparent progress, scholars in the field became frustrated with the issue. The debate over *what is law?* was characterized as 'endless wrangling' which operated 'to the hindrance of more fruitful endeavors' (Moore 1978: 224); as 'arid and unproductive' (Comaroff and Roberts 1981: 4); as a 'sterile' or 'barren topic' (Hamnett 1977: 4); as a waste of 'floods of ink' (Mair 1962: 19); as an exercise which has 'not borne much fruit' (Nader 1965: 5); and 'like the quest for the Holy Grail' (Hoebel 1954: 18). By the mid-1970's, the general consensus was that 'for the time being, at least, it seems clear that we must displace law from the center of our conceptual focus as we attempt to build social theory' (Abel 1973: 224).

Giving up on the issue, however, was costly. It has often been observed that socio-legal studies suffer from under-developed theory. Without agreement on the threshhold question *what is law?*, the precise object or field to be studied by 'legal' anthropology and 'legal' sociology could not easily be identified,[1] and no foundation existed upon which to construct theory. Although there has been a revival of theory in the field in the past ten years—owing mostly to the application of new social theories like interpretivism and autopoiesis to the study of law—the underlying problems with the conceptualization of law remained, concealed beneath the surface yet exerting an influence.

A second consequence was that the lack of resolution created a state of licence, permitting all sorts of claims to be made in the name of a scientific concept of law. Legal pluralists, for example, have recently made assertions to the effect that they alone hold to an objective, scientific concept of law, that social life is filled with a complex of competing legal orders, and that those who believe that 'law' is linked to the state are suffering from ideological delusion (see Tamanaha 1993b). Another example, from an entirely different perspective, can be found in the growing chorus of claims by social theorists that law is increasingly penetrating all aspects of life, that the life world is becoming juridified or colonized by the law. Without first knowing what law is, however, it is not easy to make sense of, or respond to, these kinds of claims.

Finally, and most important, when the participants involved quit the debate without having come to an understanding of what led to the impasse to begin with, they failed to uncover the lessons hidden within the impasse itself. There were important reasons why the debate could not be resolved, reasons which tell a great deal.

This Chapter will revisit the debate, not as an end in itself, but as a means to get beyond it in a more satisfactory way, and to uncover what remained concealed. I will survey the dominant social scientific concepts of law, categorize them, and map the relations between these categories. In the course of drawing this map the logic underlying the impasse will be made evident, though I will not stop there. My overarching objective will be to draw out the many implications of the map, which range from insights about the concept of law to the sources of

---

[1] A number of other social science disciplines study law, including economic analysis, history, political science and psychology. However, only legal anthropology and legal sociology have specifically grappled with the question of a concept of law, and the discussion herein will therefore be limited to these two fields.

social order. The end-product of this mapping exercise will be a foundation for the social theory of law I set out in the next Chapter.

Maps are valuable because they simplify. A map true to every detail would be identical with the terrain covered, and hence superfluous. A distorted or overly simplified map, however, is either misleading or provides no guidance at all. This map will straddle the line between too much and too little by highlighting the important features, then filling in the local detail as they relate to these features.

Two Fundamental Categories of the Concept of Law

Although many different concepts of law have been proffered in the social sciences, there is general agreement on the basic alternatives. Usually these are viewed as discrete, self-standing options. Instead, I will show that at the highest level of inclusiveness these concepts can be placed into one of two fundamental catgories. The first category sees law in terms of actual patterns of behaviour; the second category sees law in terms of the state law model.

A. First Category: Law Abstracted from Patterns of Behaviour

Eugen Ehrlich and Bronislaw Malinowski are giants in the field of social scientific approaches to law. Ehrlich has been called the 'inventor' of sociology of law as well as the 'founder' of sociological jurisprudence (Ziegert 1980: 76; Schur 1968: 37). And Malinowski's *Crime and Custom in Savage Society* is the single most influential text in the anthropology of law, as well as one of the most widely read texts in anthropology generally (Hamnet 1977: 6). Despite the fact that they worked under markedly different circumstances—Ehrlich as a law professor in a relatively poor, distant part of what was then Austria, Malinowski as a pioneering field researcher among the Trobriand of Melanesia—their concepts of law substantially overlap. The central insight of both analysts was that law consists of and can be found in the regularized conduct or actual patterns of behaviour in a community, association, or society (cf. Pospisil 1971: 28–31).

This view of law led them to reject the notion that law is connected to the state. Ehrlich (1975: 24) asserted:

It is not an essential element of the concept of law that it be created by the State, nor that it constitute the basis for the decisions of the courts or other tribunals, nor that it be the basis of a legal compulsion consequent upon such a division. A fourth element remains, and that will have to be the point of departure, i.e. the law is an ordering.

Malinowksi (1926: 14) made the same point when he contested the belief that law consists of 'central authority, codes, courts, and constables,' and insisted that law does 'not consist in any independent institutions' (ibid.); rather law represents 'an aspect of their tribal life' (ibid.).

Ehrlich believed that society largely consists of social associations at various levels—the family, corporations, business associations or communities, professions, clubs, a school or factory, a farm, the state, and so forth. 'A social association is a plurality of human beings who, in their relations with one another, recognize certain rules of conduct as binding, and, generally at least, actually regulate their conduct according to them' (Ehrlich 1975: 39). The 'living law' consists of the spontaneously generated inner ordering of these associations. The legal rules of this inner ordering consist of 'rules of conduct'—customary practices which govern the behaviour of persons in the association. Ehrlich (1975: 85, 501) emphasized time and again that the investigator finds the law through direct observation of 'concrete usages'. 'The living law is the law which dominates life itself even though it has not been posited in legal propositions . . . [It] is not the part of the content of the document that the courts recognize as binding when they decide a legal controversy, but only that part which the parties actually observe in life' (p. 497).

Because Malinowski studied a relatively homogeneous and undifferentiated tribal society, he did not focus directly on associations as such. Nonetheless, he saw law in much the same way. For Malinowski (1926: 66), legal rules consist of 'a class of binding rules which control most aspects of tribal life, which regulate personal relations between kinsman, clansmen and tribesmen, settle economic relations, the exercise of power and of magic, the status of husband and wife and of their respective families.' Like Ehrlich, Malinowski emphasized that law can be found in actual usages; and his methodological prescription for the scientific investigator of law was remarkably similar to Ehrlich's: 'we are demanding a new line of anthropological field-work: the study by direct observation of the rules of custom as they function in actual life' (p. 125).

Thus Ehrlich and Malinowski viewed law in essentially the same manner—as the actually followed body of rules which govern the behaviour of members of a social group. They also identified the same basic 'binding mechanism' supporting the law. Both acknowledged the significance of sanction, but denied sanction the place of primary importance. As Malinowski (p. 67) put it, '[t[he binding forces of Melanesian civil law are to be found in the concatenation of the obligations, in the fact that they are arranged into chains of mutual services, a give and take extending over long periods of time and covering wide aspects of interest and activity.' Or as Ehrlich (1975: 64) summarized, '[a] man therefore conducts himself according to law, chiefly because this is made imperative by his social relations.' Ehrlich and Malinowski both believed that (in additon to simple habit) people followed the law largely due to positive inducement—it was in their interest to do so— rather than from fear of sanction. And in another convergence, both specifically emphasized the role of reciprocity as a major aspect of this positive inducement (Ehrlich 1975: 78; Malinowski 1926: 52).

In view of the substantial overlap in approach, it is inevitable that their concepts of law would have shared flaws, and would be subject to the same criticisms. In particular, Ehrlich and Malinowski were confronted with a devilishly difficult problem: how to distinguish specifically legal norms from the many other kinds of norms operative in social life. Legal Realist Felix Cohen (1960: 187) observed that 'under Ehrlich's terminology, law itself merges with religion, ethical custom, morality, decorum, tact, fashion, and etiquette.' Both Ehrlich and Malinowski asserted that it was important to make the distinction (Ehrlich 1975: 164–70; Malinoski 1926: 50, 54). Malinowski, however, offered no specific criteria, and it appears that he ultimately abandoned the attempt (Schapera 1957: 153). Ehrlich (1975: 165) suggested that the characteristic feature of the legal norm is *opinio necessitatis*; that is, within the group the legal norm is felt to be 'of great importance, of basic significance' (pp. 167–8). Obviously this criterion is difficult to apply and is incapable of providing a reliable distinction between legal and non-legal norms.

This has proven to be a dauntingly serious defect, one that prompted most socio-legal scholars to look elsewhere for a concept of law. One commentator even suggested that Ehrlich's notion of the inner ordering of associations 'was quite similar to what anthropologists now mean by "culture pattern" ' (Schur 1968: 37). Similarly, legal anthropologist Sally Falk Moore (1978: 220) concluded that 'the conception of law that Malinowski propounded was so broad that it was virtually indistinguishable from the study of the obligatory aspect of all social relationships.' Despite this flaw, the concept of law articulated by Ehrlich and

Malinowski has proven surprisingly resilient, [2] and has been resurrected in a number of different forms, which I will mention briefly.

The notion of customary law, which Ehrlich drew heavily from when devising his concept of living law, shares the same basic elements and the same problem. There are many different formulations of customary law. Ian Hamnett's (1975: 14) definition is representative of the version I am referring to: '[c]ustomary law can be regarded as a set of norms which the actors in a social situation abstract from practice and which they invest with binding authority.' Identical to Ehrlich and Malinowski's concept, this version of customary law is based upon an abstraction from the actual practices of a group. Analysts of customary law who adopt this version face the perennial problem of trying to distinguish those customs which are 'legal' from those which are not.

Other prominent examples are Marc Galanter's (1981: 17–18) concept of 'indigenous law', which he defines in terms of 'concrete patterns of social ordering'; Moore's (1978: 54–81) concept of the spontaneous rule-bound order of the 'semi-autonomous social field';[3] and the dominant notion of law postulated within the legal pluralism paradigm.[4] Each of these concepts, in one form or another, focuses on the actual regularized behaviour within groups, and all of them are plagued by an inability to identify the distinctively legal (Tamanaha 1993b: 205–7). Sally Engle Merry's (1988: 870) objection to the concept of legal pluralism bears this out: 'calling all forms of ordering that are not state law by the name law confounds the analysis.'

The struggle to identify the distinctively legal gave rise to many of the concepts of law in the next category.

---

[2] I have limited the discussion to social scientists of this century, mostly because they are the most influential, but also because social scientific approaches to law 'officially' originated at the beginning of this century (see Pound 1959b: 186–7). However, the view of law herein attributed to Malinowski and Ehrlich has antecedents, especially in the historical school of Savigny (who Ehrlich acknowledges) and the 'social-psychological' school of Gierke and Jellinek (Pound 1959a: 312–20).

[3] Moore does not herself apply the term 'law' to the rules she identifies, but others, especially legal pluralists, have interpreted her to this effect (see Griffiths 1986: 38).

[4] Legal pluralists are a diverse group with internal disagreement, and many have not identified the concept of law they adhere to. This assertion is based upon the concept of law set out in an influential and widely cited article about legal pluralism by John Griffiths (1986).

B. Second Category: State Law Model of Rules and Institutions

The most influential concept of law applied in the social sciences is the view that law consists of institutionalized norm enforcement (cf. Feeley 1976: 498). Max Weber and Adamson Hoebel have produced the most often cited versions of this concept, set out respectively below:

The term 'guaranteed law' shall be understood to mean that there exists a 'coercive apparatus,' i.e., that there are one or more persons whose special task is to hold themselves ready to apply specially provided means of coercion (legal coercion) for the purpose of norm enforcement (Rheinstein 1954: 13).

A social norm is legal if its neglect or infraction is regularly met, in threat or in fact, by the application of physical force by an individual or group possessing the socially recognized privilege of so acting (Hoebel 1954: 28).

These definitions immediately solved the problem faced by Ehrlich and Malinowski. The test for law is based upon the severity (coercion/force) and nature (publically approved and executed) of the sanction imposed upon infraction. Legal norms are only those norms that, when violated, are enforced by publically administered sanctions. All other norms are moral, political, custom or manners, but not law.

Although the state is not mentioned in either definition, there is a close link between this concept of law and the state law model. The element of socially privileged staff or coercive apparatus is a reference to state bureaucratic legal institutions, stripped of their connection to the state.[5] Norm enforcement is the presumed function of state legal institutions: what courts and police do is visit a sanction, on behalf of the public, upon the violations of norms. This implicit though direct link to the state law model should not be surprising. Weber was trained as a lawyer (Kronman 1983: 189–93), and Hoebel (1954: 22) credited his concept of law to 'contemporary jurisprudence', citing Hohfeld, Llewellyn, Cardozo, and Holmes.

A related version of this concept of law, also popular among socio-legal scholars, was that put forth by Paul Bohannan. The test Bohannan (1967: 47) used to distinguish legal from non-legal norms was simply affirmative recognition by the legal institution:

---

[5] Edwin Schur (1968: 75) recognized that 'Weber's approach is clearly quite positivistic (his definition is not unlike that of Austin) [except that] he simply refers to a specialized staff, rather than to 'the state' or 'the sovereign'.

Customs are norms or rules (more or less strict, and with greater or less support of moral, ethical, or even physical coercion) about the ways in which people must behave if social institutions are to perform their tasks and society is to endure . . . Some customs, in some societies, are reinstitutionalized at another level: they are restated for the more precise purposes of legal institutions. When this happens, therefore, law may be regarded as a custom that has been restated in order to make it amenable to the activities of the legal institutions.

Legal institutions are those institutions which settle disputes or counteract violations of rules. This concept of law borrowed from H. L. A. Hart's positivist legal philosophy built around state law. Bohannan's notion of the reinstitutionalization of norms was related to Hart's idea of secondary rules of recognition (Hart 1961: 89–96).

Despite the fact that these concepts appeared to capture general intuitions about the nature of law (at least for those who accepted that law need not be linked to the state), and they avoided the dilemma that led to the rejection of Malinowski's and Ehrlich's concepts, they were not acceptable to the group of social scientists who held to the belief that law is a fundamental social process that exists in all societies. Pre-state societies that lacked an overarching political organization often did not use institutions to enforce norms. Under the criteria suggested above, these societies would not have law.

Dissatisfaction with the implications of these sorts of 'pedigree' tests for law resulted in a slight shift in focus. Since all societies had disputes, and these disputes had to be resolved in some manner, dispute processing became the subject (see Abel 1973). However, an insistent old problem again arose: how to distinguish legal from political or other forms of dispute processing. Initially, attempts were made to base the distinction on the structure of the institution and on the role played by norms—legal dispute processing institutions involved an authoritative third-party decision-maker and decisions were based upon on the application of norms, whereas political dispute processing institutions did not involve a third party and the outcome was determined by power. But these distinctions were later softened or abandoned as untenable (see Gulliver 1973). From our post-formalist vantage point, it seems that the line between legal and political is a slippery one.

The focus on dispute processing institutions, as with all concepts of law in this category, was also a product of the state law model. A widely held assumption is that the primary function of courts is to resolve disputes (Gibbs 1982: 95); and a functional description of how state courts are typically constituted and operate results in the institutionalized, third-party, rule-oriented adjudicator model.

Again, as with the preceeding concepts, a focus on dispute institutions was unsatisfactory for those whose starting presupposition was that all societies have law. It appears that a number of small-scale pre-state societies did not use institutions to respond to disputes, and those that did treated rules in a variety of ways. In certain societies a compromise was arranged without the presence of a third party, or rules did not seem to play a primary role, or contests, self-help or retribution were the reponses to disputes.

A clear pattern can thus be found in the above concepts of law, and in their reception or rejection. All of these concepts got away from equating law with state law by identifying a function that state law plays and by providing a functional description of how state legal institutions are constituted and operate. No matter how we try to define law, it seems we are continually forced back to the state law model of institutions and norms.

Scholars who are committed to the proposition that all societies have law must reject any notion of law based upon the state law model, in whatever form, because state law was a contingent development that could not be found everywhere, even when described in functional terms. It has proven impossible, however, to come up with an acceptable notion of law that is not ultimately derived from the state law model. State law is the currently dominant paradigm for law. This shared cultural paradigm informs social scientists' intuitions of the nature of law, and it is the underlying source from which these scientists abstract when they strive to produce a scientific concept of law, even when they explicitly set out to escape the state law model (Tamanaha 1993b: 201).

There is no way out from this conceptual box except to stop talking about law—and that's exactly what many socio-legal scholars, legal anthropologists in particular, did. Various aspects of 'order' and 'dispute' became the objects of study, and 'the word "law" is rarely used in many of these works' (Roberts 1979: 198). A striking example of the resultant anomalies can be found in Simon Robert's text *Order and Dispute: An Introduction to Legal Anthropology* (1979: 9), which states in the Preface that 'Despite the sub-title, it must be said that this is not a book about law,' and dedicates an entire chapter to explaining 'Why Not Law.' These scholars were mistaken, however, to the extent that they believed that the shift to order and dispute involved a complete 'rejection of a legal mould' (p. 198). After all, they continued to work in the self-described field of 'legal' anthropology, and they selected 'order' and 'dispute' due to the pervasive belief that what law does is maintain order and respond to disputes.[6] For the purposes of this Chapter, the main point is they proferred no new concepts of law.

The preceding discussion applies more so to legal anthropologists than legal sociologists. Anti-ethnocentrism and the study of non-state societies, which decisively shaped the anthropological debate, have not been primary concerns of legal sociologists. Closely linked in origin to sociological jurisprudence, legal sociology developed along a path which mostly entailed the application of sociological techniques to the study of different aspects of state law and its relation to society. Thus, the issue *what is law?* was not of especially burning moment. Nonetheless, legal sociologists were influenced by scientism, and this led to the formulation of a concept of law in scientific terms apart from the State.

Roscoe Pound's concept of law as social control through the application of force by a politically organized society—also an influential view among earlier legal anthropologists—was and remains (with certain variations) the dominant concept of law in legal sociology. Pound (1942: 25) saw a close, almost inseverable connection between state law and social control:

Today social control is primarily the function of the state and is exercised through law. Its ultimate effectiveness depends upon the application of force exercised by bodies and agencies and officials set up or chosen for that purpose. It operates chiefly through law, that is, through the systematic and orderly application of force by the appointed agents.

Pound's view of law is represented today in the work of Donald Black, who sets his analysis in a more sophisticated scientific framework. Black (1972: 1092) believes that 'science can know only phenomena and never essences'; he concluded that 'the quest for the one correct concept of law or for anything else 'distinctively legal' is therefore inherently unscientific' (p. 1092). From this standpoint the question *what is law?* was not an analytical one; rather, it was just a matter of designating the phenomenon to be studied by legal sociologists. Thus

---

[6] In an important respect a number of legal anthroplogists did significantly depart from the state law model. Influenced by interactional social theory, (certain) adherents of what is called the process approach changed their focus from dispute processing institutions (from how society responds to disputes), to look at the process of disputing itself, at the disputants and their constraints and motivations, and at why disputes erupt (see Krygier 1980: 46–7).

Black (1976: 2) simply stipulated that 'law is governmental social control,' thereby sidestepping the entire debate. This move nicely immunized Black from conceptual criticism, though not from objections about application or use value.

A related sociological concept of law started with institutionalized social control, but placed special emphasis on the presence of formalized rules or doctrines. As Philip Selznick (1969: 7; 1968) put it, '[w]e should see law as endemic in all institutions that rely for social control on formal authority and rule-making.' According to this view, the characteristic which distinguishes law is 'legality', a particular orientation pursuant to which rules form restraints or limitations on decisions or actions. This concept of law—which was derived from the 'rule of law' ideology that has shaped the Western legal tradition—was applicable beyond the state to many private institutions, yet was still able to distinguish those that are rule-bound (and hence legal) from those that are not.

A final concept of law in the social sciences, adhered to mainly by Marxists but also taken for granted by many sociological researchers in the trenches, was the view that law must be seen in terms of state power (Cotterrell 1984: 41). According to this perspective—as the mass of lawyers, legislators, and judges would attest to without hesitation—law is state law.

Behaviourism, the Gap Problem, and New Approaches

To begin the task of mapping the relations between the above two categories, it is important to note what they had in common, and how they differ from more recent approaches to the concept of law. Virtually all of the scientists who proferred the above concepts of law adhered to one or another version of behaviourism. As I emphasized, both Ehrlich and Malinowski focused on patterns of actual behaviour. Hoebel (1954: 23) called his own method 'legal behaviourism', and declared that the 'anthropological approach to law is flatly behaviouristic' (p. 5).

Their shared orientation to the observation of actual behaviour must not obscure a crucial difference between the two categories of the concept of law: they identified and settled upon different realms of behaviour as their object of focus when locating 'law'. For the first category, the relevant behaviour was that of people within the community or social group; whereas for the second category the relevant behaviour was that of the legal actors or the legal institutions themselves.

Despite this difference, proponents in both categories shared the same basic objective in their focus on actual behaviour: to distinguish the *real* law from that which merely was claimed to be law. Ehrlich saw patterns of social behaviour as the real law of the community, not the unknown or ignored legal norms set forth in the civil code; Malinowski was concerned to separate the real law from the often unreliable statements of rules made by informants, and believed 'the only way to discover the discrepancy between the ideal of law and its realization, between the orthodox version and the practice of actual life, is to play close and extended attention to the latter' (Krygier 1980: 40). With a similar purpose, Hoebel (1954: 22–3) included the element of 'regularity' of enforcement (which was derived from Holmes' prediction theory of law) in his concept of law to identify and separate the real law from among the many norms espoused but not acted upon by legal institutions. Pound and the Legal Realists urged the very same focus on the actual behaviour of legal institutions for the same reason.

These observations point to another notable similarity between the two categories of the concept of law, though again with a significant difference. Both categories relate to what is known as the 'gap problem'. For a time the gap problem was 'the central issue for studies about law' (Abel 1976: 189). Curiously, it is seldom recognized that there are two distinct versions of the gap problem. One version is the gap between state legal rules (or the rules cited as binding by non-state 'legal' institutions) and *what people in the community actually do*, the rules they actually follow in the course of social life. Many of the concepts of law in the first category highlighted this first gap. A second version is the gap between state legal rules (or the rules cited as binding by non-state 'legal' institutions) and *what the legal institutions actually do*, which norms they in fact enforce and how they do so, regardless of what they claim. Many of the concepts of law in the second category highlighted this second gap.

Their role in relation to the gap problem reveals the special power of behaviour oriented approaches to law, regardless of which category they fall into—they have an inherently critical edge. They serve as checks or reminders that the rules we espouse are one matter, but how people in a group actually behave, or what legal actors actually do, are an entirely different matter. Although behaviourism has lapsed into disfavour with the modern turn to interpretation, this valuable quality must not be forgotten.

The distinguishing characteristic of the handful of novel social scientific concepts of law that have been elaborated in recent years is precisely their departure from the earlier focus on behaviour, towards a greater emphasis on meaning or on the symbolic realm. Niklas Luhmann's autopoiesis, for example, views law as 'a system of meaning' (King 1993: 226), not as a set of institutions. Law is present whenever someone communicates, or even thinks, in legal terms. This approach to the concept of law opens up entirely new realms of inquiry. Its radically different look, however, should not create the impression that two categories of the concept of law I have identified have been surpassed or overcome. To identify law as a system of meaning still requires that we be able to distinguish this system from, say, the economic system or the political system, which requires that we identify criteria for what law is.

Luhmann's concept of law is openly parasitic upon the state law model, because autopoiesis defines law in terms of 'the law's unique *binary code of lawful/unlawful, legal/illegal*' (King 1993: 223, emphasis in original). 'Any act or utterance that codes social acts according to this binary code of lawful/unlawful may be regarded as part of the legal system, no matter where it was made and no matter who made it' (ibid.). But the very ability to say (or think) that something involves 'lawful/unlawful' or 'legal/illegal' presupposes the existence of law—presupposes that there is an existing source which generates this binary code such that it can be invoked (acted, uttered, or thought). For Luhmann, as I will demonstrate in a later Part, that source is either state law or non-state 'law' (defined as institutional norm enforcement) dictates about lawfulness and legality.

What this new concept of law—and others like it—does is alter the dimension referred to in the second category, away from the former flat orientation to just behaviour, in the direction of the more complex dimensions of meaning and communication. But it is still firmly anchored in the second category. Indeed, for the present, at least until the meaning of law dramatically changes, anyone who wishes to formulate a social scientific concept of law will necessarily produce some variation of one or both of the two categories of the concept of law, because these categories take up the two sides of the same fundamental belief about law.

Born of the Same Fundamental Belief

Both categories were born out of the single article of faith that has dominated our understanding of law at least since Hobbes threatened that life without law would be 'solitary, poor, nasty, brutish, and short'. That is: *law maintains social order*. Regardless of the many sharp disagreements which divided the scholars in the debate over the concept of law, there was universal agreement on the point that law is the primary mechanism of social control which preserves the normative order of society (cf. Pospisil 1971: 24). Sharing this baseline, the two categories of the concept of law identified opposite starting points.

Ehrlich and Malinowski were explicit about their belief that what law did—the function of law—was maintain social order (see Malinowski 1942; Ehrlich 1922). And in an often quoted phrase, Malinowski (1934: xiii) observed that law should be defined 'by function and not by form'. Malinowski studied a society that had no state law; Ehrlich was struck by the irrelevant and often alien rules contained in the Austrian Civil Code. Life in the societies they studied was nonetheless quite orderly, and it appeared that people engaged in their affairs with hardly a thought about institutionally enforced sanctions. Thus they examined social life, identified what they found to be the source of order, and appended to that source the label 'law'. The syllogistic-like chain of reasoning involved operates like this: the function of law is to maintain social order; social order can be found in regularized patterns of actual behaviour; the binding mechanism maintaining these patterns of behaviour is the complex of social obligations (i.e. reciprocity); *ipso facto*, legal norms are the norms abstracted from actual patterns of behaviour and the mechanism of law resides in the social relations themselves. The defining characteristic of the concepts in the first category was they took seriously law's *claims* to be or represent or embody the normative order of society.

In contrast, all of the concepts of law in the second category were derived from the state law model alone, applying functional analysis at different levels to eliminate the trappings of the state. Institutionalized norm enforcement was a functional description of what the state legal apparatus (legislature, courts, and police) presumably does; institutionalized dispute processing was a functional description that isolated upon just the court (which is the primary organ of law in the Anglo-American legal tradition). Taken one step further—to render explicit the implicit reasoning involved—the presumed function of enforcing norms is to maintain the normative cohesion of society; the presumed function of resolving disputes is to restore peace in society, thereby maintaining order. The defining characteristic of the concepts in the second category was they took for granted that the state law model was the epitome of law, and they assumed that institutional norm enforcement or dispute processing played the dominant role in maintaining order in society.

That is the explanation for how these competing categories of the concept of law came about. The key aspect to the concepts in the first category was that their proponents worked their way up from the context of achieved social order. The key aspect to the concepts in the second category was that the scholars involved started and stayed with the state law model, redescribed in functional terms.

In effect, each category staked out a position directly critical of the other: the first category said to the second, 'you are wrong if you believe the source of normative order in society is to be found in the activities of coercive institutions'; the second said to the first, 'what you are talking about is not what we mean by law because it brings in all of social life, not matching our intuitions about what law is, and rendering it impossible to identify the distinctively legal.'

Each side was essentially correct in their critique of the other. The problem lay not in what they were saying, but in the belief they shared. They can be reconciled only by giving up this belief. If 'law' means the publicly approved, institutional enforcement of norms (which is the scientific abstraction of the common meaning of law today), then 'law' (meant as such) is not the only or even the primary generative mechanism of normative order in society.

Functional Analysis Cannot Answer *What is Law?*

As the above description indicates, proponents of both categories of the concept of law applied functional analysis. A great deal of confusion exists, however, because the label functionalism encompasses several different kinds of analysis. I will distinguish two basic versions of functionalism.

The first kind is Functionalism (with a capital F) from the field of sociology. Durkheim is the acknowledged progenitor of this version. Its basic postulate is that society should be viewed as an organism with interdependent parts. Each part satisfies an essential function that contributes to the survival of the whole. Malinowski was one of the pioneers and most extreme theorists of Functional analysis (see Malinowski 1944),[7] though Functionalism is not limited to the first category of the

---

[7] For a critique of Malinowski's version of functionalism see Merton (1968: 84–6). An influential critique of functionalism generally and Malinowski in particular can be found in Hempel (1965).

concept of law. Talcott Parsons and Niklas Luhmann, whose views of law fit the second category, have been important Functionalist theorists (see Parsons 1980; Luhmann 1985).

For our purposes the relevant aspect of Functionalism is the fact that the role and nature of law are determined *a priori*, by virtue of the function it is deemed to serve in the context of the overall social system. Under Functionalism, the characteristics of law are not specific to any actual legal system; rather, they are analytically specified according to a given theorist's abstract construction of the elements of a social system (as such) and its functional needs. Almost invariably, Functionalism holds that the function of law is to maintain order in society (Wilkinson 1981: 61). Functionalism has thus built into its systems analysis the problematic shared belief about law I identified in the preceding Part.

The second kind I will label Functional Realism, following Hoebel (1954: 5), to recognize the lead role Pound and the Legal Realists played in formulating it. As Felix Cohen (1960: 33–94) described it, Functional Realism was a product of different influences in philosophy and the sciences, including logical positivism and pragmatism. It amounts to a general eschewing of meaningless concepts and questions and metaphysical entities ('transcendental nonsense'). According to Functional Realism, the significance of all things are determined by their actual consequences. Pound (1959a: 349) described it as 'asking not merely what law is and how it has come to be but what (in all its senses) it does, how it does it, and how it may be made to do it better.' This consequentialist approach led many Functional Realists to adopt Holmes' definition of law: 'The prophesies of what the courts will do in fact, and nothing more pretentious, are what I mean by law' (Holmes 1897: 461; Cohen 1960: 61–5). Functional Realism is best understood not as a coherent theory, but as a reaction to obscurantist conceptualizing, combined with a faith in scientific observation. The basic point is an admonition to pay close attention to reality, which led to the earlier described emphasis on the observation of actual behaviour.

Contrary to the belief of its adherents, Functional Realism, and indeed all forms of functional analysis, are incapable of answering the question, *What is Law?* The answer must always be given or assumed. Observe Holmes' definition of law as what a *court* does; to start with a court is to presuppose that a court is the locus of law. In essence, Functional Realism says: *law is what law does*.[8] But to find out what law

[8] Llewellyn (1930) put it thus: 'What these officials [judges, sheriffs, jailers, lawyers] do about disputes is, to my mind, the law itself.'

does (its function), we must first posit that which is doing (the object whose function we are examining)—we must presuppose what law is.

We could instead start by positing the function (maintain social order) and work backwards to locate the object (law), just as Ehrlich and Malinowski did. This reverse analysis would work, however, only if a single object alone served the posited function. Otherwise we would be left with a choice among several objects which contribute to maintaining social order with no function-based criteria by which to identify *the* object at issue, precisely the problem Malinowski and Ehrlich could not surmount. Any attempt to locate criteria for law—for the distinctively 'legal'—necessarily presupposes what law is, for only by already knowing what law is can we identify its distinctive characteristics. Hence the inevitable resort to the state law model, which provides our current paradigm for 'law'.

In response to sharp criticism (of Malinowski in particular) about the logic of functional analysis applied to social systems, later Functionalist theory disavowed the notion that a single object alone serves a given function, and acknowledged the existence of functional equivalents or alternatives (Merton 1968: 86–91). Thus the problem I have identified is endemic to functionalist thought.

The point bears repeating: functional analysis of whatever variety is incapable of providing an answer to the question, *What is Law?* 'Law' must be posited *before* functional analysis can be engaged to inquire what it does, how it does it, and what its consequences are; we can instead posit the function—maintain social order—but then we must still come up with criteria to distinguish the distinctively 'legal' phenomena from among the other kinds of phenomena (including culture, reciprocity, and language) which serve this function; which means, again, we must already know what law is. Whichever way we begin, we either end up with the state law model (which leads to the conclusion that certain societies did not have law) or we stop talking about 'law'. And therein lies the logic that led to the impasse in the debate over the concept of law.

Existing in Tension

Although the two categories of the concept of law are in agreement on several core aspects—the belief that law maintains social order, resort to functional analysis, an orientation to the scientific observation of actual behaviour—they exist in tension with one another. The first sign of this tension is that each category stakes out a position directly critical of the other, as described earlier. There are three further signs.

For one, these categories are *competitors*. Several of the concepts of law in the second category were reactions to the inability of Malinowski and Ehrlich to isolate satisfactorily the distinctively legal. The two categories cannot easily be combined, because application of the criteria used in the second category would eliminate much of what Ehrlich and Malinowksi (especially) would want to call law.

Another sign of this tension is evident in the *polemical thrust* directed by the first category against the second. I have already mentioned Ehrlich's attack on codification. Customary law has always existed in tension with state law, especially with its connotations of pre-existing state law and being closer to the people. Galanter offered indigenous law by way of contrast to state law. And legal pluralists are among the most vociferous critics of the perceived hegemonic impulses of state law. Although these polemics were mostly directed at state law, Malinowski's insistence on the irrelevance of institutions extends the polemical opposition of the first category to the second category as a whole.

A third sign of tension consists in the *contrasting objects* they centred upon. The first category was oriented toward the behaviour of people in social groups or society, the second category toward the behaviour of legal actors within legal institutions. The first category focused on regular or routine behaviour, the second category on institutionalized reactions to disruptions of this routine. The first category saw the binding mechanism of law in the complex of social relations, the second category in the institutionalized imposition of sanctions.

These signs of tension indicate that the relationship between the two categories of the concept of law is an uneasy one. Yet they are mixed together all the time. Look at the very first entry for 'law' in Webster's (1981) Dictionary:

1(a) a binding custom or practice of a community: a rule or mode of conduct or action that is prescribed or formally recognized as binding by a supreme controlling authority or is made obligatory by a sanction (as an edict, decree, rescript, order, ordinance, statute, resolution, rule, judicial decision, or usage) made, recognized, or enforced by the controlling authority.

The part before the colon refers to the first category, for custom and practice always involves what people actually do; the part after the colon refers to the second category, the state law model of law. But we now know there is no automatic correspondence between the two, and if anything the relationship is often one of antagonism.

Although the dictionary can be excused for a lack of subtlety, even sophisticated legal theorists have used concepts of law from both categories at the same time, not recognizing their incongruity, as I will show in the upcoming discussion of Luhmann's concept of law. The belief that these two categories are internally connected or otherwise strongly correlated runs deep—it is a product of the faith that law represents the consensual normative order of society.

A Brief Excursus on the Concept of Social Control

A prominent feature of the discussion thus far is the persistence with which the terms social order and social control keep popping up. Law is thoroughly understood in terms of these notions. Thus a brief excursion into the sociological literature on social control—the modern scientific terminology we apply to the old problem of social order (Janowitz 1978: 30)—will help identify the boundaries of the map.

Much of the background discussion can be avoided at the outset by observing that, despite the close association between ideas about law and about social control, there is general consensus on the point that law is distinct from social control—the relationship between the two is not one of identity or equivalence. Law (at least state law) performs many functions besides social control, including, *inter alia*, enabling or facilitative, performative, status conferring, defining, legitimative, integrative, distributive, power conferring, and symbolic (see Nader and Yngvesson 1973: 908–9; Feeley 1976: 503–8); and there are many forms of social control besides law. For various reasons we have often lost sight of both halves of this non-identity. A functional definition of law as social control tends to obscure any other functions law may perform (Krygier 1980: 38–9); and the continuing influence of Hobbes' dicta, combined with a law-centred perspective, misled many to believe that law was 'the only important mechanism' of social control (Coser 1982: 14).[9] Sociological studies have helped loosen the grip of this view, though a strong residual belief in it remains.

'The study of social control has traditionally been a central aspect of the sociological enterprise' (Horwitz 1990: 1). As is standard fare in the

---

[9] Coser (1982: 14) added that early sociological investigators have taught us that among the various mechanisms of social control, law 'is one of many, and possibly not even the most important one'.

social sciences, a number of different meanings have been attached to the term, and it has gone through various phases of development. Fortunately, just two basic senses of the term have been dominant throughout.

According to Morris Janowitz (1978: 20), in an influential formulation, the 'classical' sense of social control referred to the 'capacity of a society to regulate itself'. Janowitz asserted that this meaning dominated from the inception of the sociological discussion of the concept, at the early part of this century, until it was replaced in the 1930's by a narrower meaning of social control as 'the processes of developing conformity' (p. 20). Janowitz argued that the classical sense retained its vitality during this period, and has recently begun to re-emerge, sometimes under the rubric of 'social regulation'. Donald Black offered a slightly different chronology, but used the same two basic meanings. For Black (1984: 4) the early meaning of social control referred 'broadly to virtually all of the human practices and arrangements that contribute to social order and, in particular, that influence people to conform;' whereas the more recent meaning 'refers more narrowly to how people define and respond to deviant behaviour' (p. 5).

These two senses of social control resulted in alternative emphases. Those (mostly social psychologists) who saw social control as the process of developing conformity to social practices identified socialization as the primary mechanism of social control (Coser 1982: 14–19). Education, in particular, but also the family, television, advertising, music, and so forth, are the means by which attitudes and values are inculated in members of a community or society. Internalization by individuals of shared cultural orientations determines many of the customary patterns of behaviour that prevail within a group (Roucek 1978: 4–5). This form of social control has been characterized as internal control: whereby 'the individual himself is motivated to conform in his behaviour (conscience, conditioning processes, attitudes, indoctrination, socialization)' (p. 12).

Those who instead saw social control as societal responses to deviance tended to emphasize the role of rules and institutions, and the presence of compulsion as a means to insure conformity (p. 12–13). Many studies were conducted on state institutions, such as the police, juvenile courts, mental hospitals, and reformatories. The degree of coercion or repression involved was often a central focus for these works (Horwitz 1990: 4–5). This form of social control has been characterized as external control: controls 'imposed from without' (Roucek 1978: 12).

The parallels between these two versions of social control and the two categories of the concept of law I set out earlier are plainly evident. Internal control matches up with the first category (regularized patterns of behaviour), and external control with the second category (institutionalized norm enforcement or dispute processing). The basic difference is that in both instances the sociological approach to social control casts a broader net.

Ehrlich and Malinowski were well aware of the overarching influence of socialization. They both recognized the significance of education in generating conformity (Ehrlich 1975: 78; Schapera 1957: 142–43), and Malinowki even discussed 'cultural determinism' (Schapera 1957: 143). Trying to get at 'law', Ehrlich and Malinowski narrowed their focus to the considerable space for alternative courses of action left open by socialization. Likewise, although the response to deviance branch of social control overwhelmingly focused on state institutions, sociological studies have also been done on informal forms of coercive social control. These differences aside, the parallel remains a strong one.

The two categories I have identified appear to reflect a basic (albeit not always recognized) divide that runs through the legal as well as sociological literature: the consensus/coercion dichotomy (see Hunt 1993: 58–89).[10] Recent efforts to break down this dichotomy, especially those which highlight the phenomenon of coercively generated consensus, alter the dichotomy from a sharp one to a matter of degree, but do not eliminate it entirely.

Luhmann's Attempt to Overcome the Divide

An examination of Niklas Luhmann's concept of law, which appears to fall into both categories at once, will help test whether the divide is as sturdy as it seems. Luhmann articulated his concept of law in his earlier work, but carried over the basic elements of this concept when he shifted to autopoietic analysis.

Luhmann (1985: 82, emphasis in original) defined law as the '*structure of a social system which depends upon the congruent generalisation of normative behavioral expectations*'. He asserted that the function of law is to limit or resolve incongruencies of expectation which arise in every society in the course of interaction between people. 'Law is in no way primarily a coercive order, but rather a facilitation of expectation' (p. 78). These

---

[10] Hunt argued that this dichotomy exists *within* each theorist's concept of law. I have shown that it also exists at the most general level across concepts of law as well.

expectations are based upon generalized norms, and incongruencies arise when the generalizations break down or when people act against the generalized norm. Luhmann (p. 83) stated:

> We are not returning to the popular thesis that there have been societies without law either in the history of mankind or even in crosscultural comparisons of the present (namely, those which do not have a coercive state apparatus). Rather, our functional concept of law makes it clear that law fulfills a necessary function in every meaningfully constituted society and must therefore always exist. The development of law is not to be understood as the step from the pre-legal to legal forms of societies, but as a gradual differentiation and functional independence of law.

Thus, according to Luhmann, law is not primarily coercive and exists in all societies (thereby falling into the first category), and law evolves as society does to become institutionalized (thereby falling into the second category).

Luhmann (p. 81) recognized the problems with his concept of law. He asserted that the 'areas of custom and law are by no means equivalent, although the precise delimitation can only be made at a concrete and empirical level'. However, he offered no criteria upon which to make the delimitation. He (p. 81) went on to admit: '[i]t is more difficult to establish a clear delineation between law, language and its accessories (e.g. rules of spelling). Although it may be intuitively clear that law is not identical with language, it takes some reflection to find the crucial point of difference.'

Needless to say, this is the Malinowski/Ehrlich problem with a vengeance. Like Malinowski and Ehrlich, he was unable to distinguish law from custom; and just as their concepts appeared to encompass even 'culture patterns' or 'the obligatory aspects of all social relationships,' Luhmann's concept cannot clearly be distinguished from language! The inability of functional analysis to make such distinctions, as I established earlier, is inevitable whenever functional alternatives are present, and results in a totalizing impulse (swallowing up all of the other functional alternatives) that cannot be contained.

Although Luhmann (p. 83) suggested a few ways to distinguish law from language, in the end he pointed to the development of legal institutions as an 'important step . . . which permits a clearer separation between law and language, truth, art, and rational practice.' Luhmann thus shifted to the second category of the concept of law to solve his problems with locating the distinctively legal. Thereafter, Luhmann's discussion is almost entirely related to law in its differentiated form.

As the flow of his argument reveals, when struggling through the problem in the course of a few pages of analysis, Luhmann actually replicated the debate over the concept of law. The answer to whether he successfully straddled the two categories of the concept of law rests upon how we interpret his evolutionary sequence. According to Luhmann's description, prior to the differentiation of society and the emergence of a differentiated law, there was a kind of primordial soup in which law, custom, and language (among others) all served the function of stabilizing behavioural expectations, and could not be sharply distinguished from one another.

An alternative interpretation is this: if they all served the same function, and if there were no clearly identifiable criteria by which to distinguish among them, then there was no distinction to be made in the primordial period. There was no 'law' which underwent a continuous evolutionary development from the very beginning of the existence of social groups. There was primordial soup before differentiation, and something else after. With the differentiation of society, the emergence of institutions, and the separation of public and private realms, entirely new social phenomena arose.

The only apparent reason for Luhmann to insist that law exists even when it has no separate identity was to preserve the coherence of his *a priori* constructed Functionalist paradigm, which built law in as an inherent part of a social system. Social analysts can legitimately maintain that all societies (including undifferentiated ones) require mechanisms to co-ordinate normative expectations. The dubious move is the separate assertion that what fills this function is, by definition, 'law'. Without this additional assertion, however, Luhmann cannot claim that all societies or social systems have 'law'.

Luhmann straddled the divide in the only way possible, by altering midstream what he meant by 'law', applying the first category meaning to societies lacking in differentiation and the second category to those with differentiation. However, this shift in meaning is not a satisfactory solution to his problem because even after the emergence of 'legal' institutions, language and custom (as well as other factors) still substantially contributed to maintaining 'the congruent generalization of normative behavioral expectations', and therefore must still be considered 'law' consistent with Luhmann's explicit, non-coercion based definition of law, which he did not give up when shifting to the focus on institutions. Under Luhmann's analysis, after differentiation, society contains two fundamentally distinct phenomena going by the label 'law', one non-coercive and the other coercive. Besides creating an ambiguity at the core of his theory, this simultaneous usage is affirmatively and perhaps dangerously misleading insofar as it analytically clothes a coercive phenomenon within a non-coercive one. Any successful attempt to overcome the two categories must be consistent in the meaning it applies to the term 'law'.

The divide is a resilient one. Indeed, the forms of 'law' identified by these categories regularly coexist in the social arena, both temporally and spatially, with different scopes of application, belying any suggestion that they are related to one another through evolutionary descent.

Outline of the Map, Legal Versus Social Scientific Perspectives

A preliminary outline of the map can now be provided. Although I began the map focused on social scientific concepts of law, it turns out that the territory covered by the map is actually that of social order. The two categories of the concept of law stand as prominent features set at opposing corners of this shared terrain.

The first category is located squarely upon regularized conduct, what people actually do, the patterns of behaviour they engage in on a routine basis; it sits on a base which at its broadest includes socialization. The second category is centred upon publicly organized institutional reactions to disruptions of regularized conduct; it sits on a base that broadly includes non-institutional (i.e. shaming, ostracism) reactions as well. The line where these two respective bases meet is a fuzzy one, drawn where positive inducement and negative sanction tend to support and feed into one another, where external and internal control intermingle, where coercion has a role in generating consensus.

A general action sequence is involved, which can be divided into three phases—routine conduct, disruption, and social reaction to disruption—with the first category of the concept of law applicable to the first phase and the second category to the third phase. The table opposite should help clarify matters.

The table makes abundantly clear that the two categories are thoroughly distinct in nature. What shapes routine conduct is an entirely different matter from what happens when society responds to the disruption of routine conduct.

Neither state law nor institutionalized norm enforcement or dispute processessing (the second category) *of themselves* directly result in or gen-

Concept of Law	Phase	'Legal' Mechanism	Sociological Studies	Sociological Mechanism	Effective Moment
First category— lived norms	Patterned or regular conduct	Complex of social obligations	Internal control— conformity	Socialization	Proactive (shaping conduct)
Second category— enforced norms	Social reaction to disruption of regular conduct	Institutionally imposed sanction	External control— response to deviance	Coercive application of power	Reactive (following disruptive conduct)

erate regularized patterns of behaviour (the first category).[11] The former is not the underlying operative mechanism of the latter. Institutionalized norm enforcement can give rise to regularized behaviour only if it is incorporated into the socialization process or if it becomes a part of the complex of social obligations or calculations leading to the behaviour. There must be an intimate internal link between the two categories if what comes after (institutionalized response to breach) is to have a role in shaping what came before (routine conduct).

This link will be elaborated upon in a moment. First I should note the very different look the above table presents from the lawyer's typical view of law. According to the widely held legal positivist view of law, as articulated most ably by H. L. A. Hart, legal norms are all those norms legitimately recognized as such by legal actors, including code provisions promulgated in advance of enforcement activities. Thus many a lawyer reader will deny that state law has only a reactive presence.

The response to this objection is that the lawyer reader is correct within the self-understanding of law as articulated by legal positivism, an understanding which is essential to those who are functionaries within a given legal system. However, many of the social scientific concepts were set up in opposition to legal positivism, with the express purpose of identifying and separating out those legal norms actually lived by members of the community, or actually enforced or applied by legal institutions, from among those 'paper only' legal norms merely declared as such but not reflected in social behaviour or regularly enforced by

---

[11] An institution itself consists of the patterned behaviour of those whose complex of actions make up the institution. What is meant here, however, is the influence of institutional enforcement in generating compliant behaviour in society at large.

legal institutions. These approaches deny the label 'law' to unobserved or unenforced norms because they have no role in the maintenance of social order. According to legal positivism, however, as long as the rule of recognition is satisfied, even paper only norms are entirely valid legal norms.

Social scientific concepts of law carve up the world of norms quite differently from legal positivism, to the extent that state law norms have no special status when viewed from the scientific perspective. Those norms actually lived by members of the community (regardless of whether they are codified in state law) fall into the first category, and are effective proactively since they lead to behaviour; those norms regularly enforced by legal institutions fall into the second category, and are reactive since enforcement actions are seldom undertaken prior to a breach.

The contrast between the legal positivist and the social scientific point of view is critically important. They operate in different realms of activity—legal versus social scientific. Both views are entirely legitimate when kept within their respective boundaries, and neither view has authority over the other. Untold confusion has resulted in socio-legal studies from the failure to recognize the activity-based and activity-bound validity of both views, the most recent manifestation of which are assertions by legal pluralists that the lawyer's view of law is the product of ideological delusion, and inferior to the scientific view of law.

Two Theses About the Link Between the Two Categories

Building upon norms, two separate theses provide the link between the two categories: a thesis about the source of legal norms, and a thesis about social engineering through law.

The first thesis about the connection between the two categories of the concept of law holds that institutionally enforced norms (the second category) are derived from actually lived norms (the first category), that lived social rules are the source of enforced legal rules.[12] This view of the source of legal norms can be traced at least as far back as Savigny's argument that legal rules reflect the legal consciousness of the people,

[12] Lived social rules are also 'law', according to the first category. To avoid confusion, however, since both categories claim the label 'law', I will now refer to first category rules as social rules and second category rules as legal rules. This terminology has been adopted because it more closely matches the understanding of readers, not because I intend to deny the claim of the first category to the label 'law', although it does reveal that confusion easily arises in relation to the first category's application of the term law.

and it is consistent with the self-understanding of the Anglo-American common law tradition that common law rules gradually developed out of existing social practices that were recognized by courts.

Ehrlich, who extensively cited Savigny, and promoted the common law system as the ideal one, exemplified this thesis in his assertion that rules for decision (rules applied by courts) often are—and should be—derived from rules of conduct (actually lived rules) (1975: 121–36). Indeed, his major criticism of codification was that the act of codification, combined with the tendency toward abstraction exhibited by codifiers, freezes rules for decision while rules for conduct continue to develop, thus resulting over time in a growing gap between the living law and state law.

An even more direct claim that legal rules are derived from social rules can be found in Hoebel's and Bohannan's concepts of law. Hoebel began by asserting, 'A social rule is legal if . . .,' and Bohannan asserted that 'law may be regarded as a custom that has been restated' for the purposes of the legal institution. Thus the thesis of the social origin of enforced legal norms applies equally to state law as well as to non-state institutions of norm enforcement or dispute processing.

A critical link between the two categories is provided by this thesis. If the norms applied by state law or by institutionalized norm enforcement are derived from actually lived norms, then the rules applied at the reactive stage of institutional enforcement will directly correspond to the rules which shape behaviour at the proactive stage. Strictly speaking, however, it is not the actual influence of the legal rules but the fact of correspondence to lived social rules which matters. Enforcement of the legal rules does not itself generate the routine behaviour, as the Legal Realists recognized,[13] though legal endorsement of the social rules may be a reinforcing factor in their continued socialization.

This initially plausible thesis is weakened—at least with regard to state law—when we recognize that the history of legal development around the world substantially consists of the transplantation of norms and institutions from one society to another, either through natural diffusion, colonial imposition or voluntary borrowing (see Watson 1974).

---

[13] See Llewellyn (1962: 401–2). ('Law observance, so called, to be generally effective requires that folkways in conformity with the purposes of the law concerned shall have been first developed. It is the folkways, not the law, which are known; it is the folkways, not the law, which our present scheme of things offers some guaranty of people learning and following.')

Furthermore, legal institutions often formulate or mold norms to fit the internal demands of legal discourse, sometimes rendering them unrecognizable in relation to lived social norms. Neither the alien origin of norms nor their legalistic phrasing, however, are the final determinative factors, since the key for the second category is how they are actually enforced. Judges applying the mix of available rules often come up with an outcome that matches prevailing social norms regardless of what the legal norms actually say. But this does not solve the further problem that many societies or groups consist of different subcommunities each with their own bodies of sometimes competing norms. Therefore, even assuming that judges' decisions match lived social rules, the outcomes may still conflict with other (competing) bodies of lived social rules.

Finally, many actually enforced legal rules—like the annual reporting requirements imposed upon corporations, or jursidictional requirements for courts—have nothing to do with actually lived social norms, but rather exist for a multitude of other social purposes, or are generated by the needs of legal discourse itself. Many enforced legal rules relate to and are solely the product of other legal rules, or are concerned with expressing (or limiting) the power and authority of the state and its apparatus, and have no connection in origin or application to social behaviour.

Thus the first thesis is contingent upon several factors, each of which is fraught with difficulties, as is reflected by the pervasive presence of the gap problem. Commercial transactions are the one area where there often is a match between lived social norms (actually followed business practices) and the norms enforced by legal institutions, in Ehrlich's time as well as our own. This is in part because legal actors have more often paid attention to prevailing business practices (as with the Uniform Commercial Code), and in part because the particular content of the rules governing transactions is often less important than the fact that everyone follows the same format. Thus business practices are more easily modified to meet changes in the law. Gaps exist even here, however, as Stuart Macaulay (1963) showed in his study of the non-contractual relations in business.

The second thesis about the connection between these two categories is the reverse of the first thesis. This thesis holds that law instrumentally shapes routine behaviour in virtue of its authority as law, or due to the fear of sanction that supports the law—legal rules thereby create new lived social rules.

When social engineering through law is successful, two different mechanisms are involved. In the short term it operates by altering the complex of social obligations (usually by changing the perceived costs or benefits attached to existing courses of action); in the long term, if the new pattern of behaviour is established, it operates through continued socialization of the behaviour reflected in (now) lived social rules.

The problem with this thesis is that attempts at social engineering through law have a notable failure rate.[14] A threshold barrier is communication of the legal rules. In a truism that is repeated as often as it is forgotten: 'most of us are vastly ignorant of the law, and are continually violating or disregarding the law.' (Cohen 1960: 87). Lest you forget: 'we do not know what the law is' (Llewellyn 1962: 401), at least not much beyond the bare minimum that we should pay our taxes, and shouldn't steal from or physically harm others. Even the fact that a given set of legal rules are enforced does not of itself assure that they are widely known. 'It is certain that law does not secure obedience except in so far as it is known' (Cohen 1960: 87).[15] Generally speaking, people know something about the law only if they have a specific reason to know, and often this knowledge is acquired after the relevant behaviour has occured; indeed, often those most knowledgeable about the law (i.e. recidivists, tax advisors) use their knowledge to avoid the law.

Another problem is that prevailing social rules resist the new behaviour required by the law, as Sally Falk Moore demonstrated in her notion of the semi-autonomous social field. In these situations the enforced legal rules must compete with existing social rules which have the marked advantage of being the rules already actually followed. Aside from the symbolic authority which attaches to law, and in the absence of positive inducements, law has only the threat of sanction to secure compliance. But as Ehrlich (1975: 21) observed, in most everyday behaviour 'the thought of complusion by the courts does not even enter the minds of men.'[16]

---

[14] The most dramatic example of this failure can be found in the law and development movement, which urged law as a means to alter social relations and lead the way to development in developing countries (see Trubek and Galanter 1974).

[15] For an elaboration of this point, see Seidman (1972). It must be emphasized that this ignorance is not limited to lay people. As a former public defender, and then state attorney general, I seldom knew in advance what the law was in any given case. At most I had general ideas about the possibly applicable rules, and I knew where to look to find the law.

[16] See also Llewellyn (1962: 401). ('Rarely, very rarely, we check conduct, or embark on conduct, or modify conduct, with a conscious eye to the law.')

A third problem is that, with regard to both state law and non-state institutions, legal rules are often articulated only after the fact, in the course of the institutional response to the dispute. 'It is on such occasions [after break down] that existing values and norms are likely to be articulated and, in the course of debate, consciously or unconsciously reformulated to accommodate the situation which has arisen' (Roberts 1979: 43). Rules articulated (or reformulated) later cannot govern behaviour which comes before. Although the newly articulated rules can influence later behaviour, the populace will have good reason to be suspicious of reliance upon such rules.

Yet another problem with this second thesis comes from the typical form of legal norms. At least with regard to state law, a large proportion of enforced legal norms do not prescribe an affirmative course of routine conduct, and many of those that do have a facilitative or enabling function rather than a social control function. For example, a statute that punishes murder does not give rise to any routine patterns of conduct. A nimble retort might be that not killing is itself a pattern of behaviour. But the point remains that—except in a nightmarish (and short lived) community where people are socialized to routinely kill— the negative statute did not give rise to this non-behaviour; rather, it never occurs to most people to kill to begin with, and thus the statute itself is irrelevant.

A final problem with this thesis is that it assumes a commitment as well as capacity on the part of the law announcer, the law enforcer, and the law applier (roles that can be distributed or held by one person or group) to effectuate the content of the rules. Many legal rules are proclaimed for mostly symbolic purposes, with no intention on the part of legal actors to enforce the paraded norms. And on many occasions, even when the commitment exists, legal institutions simply lack the power to enforce the rules. Because they are not actually enforced, these norms would not qualify under the second category of the concept of law anyway, but it is important to be reminded of these reasons when addressing the failure of law to give rise to lived social norms.

These objections should not be interpreted to indicate that legal rules do not influence behaviour. They most assuredly do in a myriad of ways, often unanticipated by the promulgators of the rules. Frustratingly for the law issuers, newly enforced legal rules often give rise to actual patterns of behaviour which are designed by the participants to get around the legal rules so that pre-existing patterns of behaviour can continue in substance or effect. These objections more narrowly suggest that, for a variety of reasons, it is quite a formidable task for enforced legal norms (the second category) directly and intentionally to result in corresponding lived social norms (the first category).

Many of the above points can be expeditiously illustrated by the recent US Supreme Court case *Bowers* v. *Hardwick*.[17] A Georgia statute prohibited sodomy, defined as 'any sexual act involving the sex organs of one person and the mouth or anus of another'. Obviously this prohibition, which reflected the moral views of a part of the community, was not consistent with the sexual behaviour of many Georgians, especially but not limited to homosexuals. Prior to the publicity engendered by the case, probably few people were aware of the existence of the prohibition, which Georgia officials did not actively enforce. The decision enforcing the legal rule undoubtedly had little if any effect on reducing the incidence of sodomy, though perhaps more people thereafter closed their curtains.

The conclusion from an examination of these two theses is that the link between the two categories of the concept of law is a complex and often tenuous one. No doubt, with regard to specific systems or contexts, many points of correspondence can be found. The objective of the foregoing analysis was not to deny that the link exists, but to suggest that the link is much more problematic than is usually assumed. The common belief that law represents the consensual normative order of society seduces us into taking for granted that there is a link between lived social norms and the norms enforced by legal institutions. Often that is not the case.

This conclusion exposes a flaw in the concepts of law formulated by Hoebel and Bohannan, and others who defined law as social norms enforced by legal institutions or as reinstitutionalized custom—in effect they analytically merged lived social norms and enforced legal norms,[18] thereby removing from scrutiny the uncertain relationship between the two.

---

[17] 478 U.S. 186 (1986).
[18] In their defence it might be said that they were defining non-state 'law' and legal institutions, and in such instances there is an internal connection between social norms and legal norms, at least more so than with regard to state law. The problem with this response is, first, if indeed differences exist they must be established through investigation; and secondly, they cannot be investigated unless the two are kept analytically separate to begin with.

A Concept of Law Based upon the Union of Both Categories

The final step in drawing the map is to consider the implications of formulating a single concept of law out of the union of both categories of the concept of law. The preceding Part focused on the *empirical* links between the two categories. Here I will explore what results when they are joined on a *conceptual* level, by formulating a concept of law which includes only those norms that are actually enforced by publicly approved coercive institutions, *and* only when the norms so enforced are also reflected in the actual social behaviour of the group.[19]

This joinder is quite instructive. Because the scopes of application of the two categories are not co-extensive, joining them sharply narrows the band of what qualifies for the label 'law'. This narrowing comes on top of the fact that each category, in its own way, already restricts the use of the label 'law' on behavioural grounds, banning non-lived or non-enforced rules from being considered 'law'. One consequence of this scientific approach was to remove ideals from the domain of law—as reflected in the Realist's controversial stance that they must set aside the *ought*, at least temporarily, while scientifically investigating what *is*.

The immediately beneficial effect of joining the two categories is it dramatically restricts the scope of the first category of the concept of law, eliminating most of the many lived social norms it encompasses which we do not normally think of as 'legal'. But there is a price to pay: the claim that all societies have law must be given up, for the same old reason that some societies did not use publicly approved institutions to enforce norms. This explains why the coherence of Luhmann's concept of law, which referred to both categories, could not be saved by being interpreted as a union of the two categories rather than as an unacknowledged shift in meaning from the first category to the second—his Functionalist framework prohibited him from granting the possibility that certain societies lacked law.

The joinder drastically cuts back on the second category of the concept of law in an even more revealing way. Earlier I asserted that many enforced legal norms have no relation to actually lived social norms. The examples are legion. Consider standard tax codes filled with a

---

[19] Responding to an earlier draft of this chapter, Gordon Woodman suggested this union as a suitable scientific definition for law. Letter of 19 August 1994. A similar kind of joinder has occasionally been proposed by legal theorists. Joseph Raz (1979: 58–90) argued that Hans Kelsen required a degree of efficacy (that is, behaviour had to conform to it) for a state legal norm to be valid.

complex body of rules. Some of these rules are designed to shape routine behaviour, like the hefty tax imposed on cigarettes to reduce smoking or the tax on petrol to inhibit driving. But many other tax rules have the purpose of raising revenue or redistributing income. These latter rules cannot be considered to give rise to any lived social rules, except in the limited sense (involving only a handful of the total body of tax rules) that people file their tax returns and pay the amount due by the legally designated day. Another example involves laws governing marriage. Many of these legal rules also do not give rise to lived social rules; rather their primary effect is to create a new status recognized in law, to which a variety of consequences are attached. The same can be said of the massive volume of legal rules that apply to corporations, many of which do not even refer to social behaviour. Their most dramatic effect is to grant life (or at least existence) to entirely new entities.

These kinds of phenomena and the rules which produce them form a substantial bulk of what law—state law, and often non-state 'legal' institutions and rules as well—actually does. However, they would all be excluded if a scientific concept of law were based upon the union of the two categories of the concept of law, because they have nothing to do with lived social rules and would thus fail to satisfy the requirements of the first category.

This implication of the union is particularly revealing insofar as it again raises a crucial limitation of the scientific concepts of law in both categories. They were constructed around the notion of social order. This orientation resulted in an emphasis on various aspects of the control of social behaviour. When the focus was on simple societies, perhaps this emphasis was appropriate. But only a part of the activities of state legal institutions—largely the part dealing with criminal law—fall within this limited focus.

The social order lens thus artifically constricted the scope of scientific inquiry into law and legal phenomena. Law today does much more than social control. With the increasing differentiation of society and the internal development of state law, social control based concepts of law lacked the analytical capacity to keep up with the change.

Reading the Map, and the 'Centrality of Law' Thesis

Assuming social order is largely comprised of regularized patterns of behaviour, the foregoing analysis suggests that in general all forms of institutionalized norm enforcement or dispute processing (including state law) play a relatively small role in generating social order, at least in comparison to the influence of socialization, habit, and the complex of social obligations. This disproportion is simply a reflection of the greater degree to which internal control influences most behaviour relative to external control—the greater degree to which we do things because we want to, not because we are forced to by sanction or fear of sanction.

It would appear that the map is not divided into territories of equal size. The base upon which the first category of the concept of law sits extends to three corners of the map, with the base of the second category left to occupy the last remaining corner. A map of this sort can be drawn for entire societies or for communities or groups, whenever institutionalized norm enforcement is present. Different societies or communities, and the same society under different circumstances, differ with regard to the relative proportion of these bases. But most long term stable communities should have a far greater proportion of the first category to the second.[20] Perhaps only totalitarian societies would have this proportion reversed.

If correct, this conclusion sits in apparent conflict with an influential thesis about the modern condition currently sweeping through the community of socio-legal scholars. Alan Hunt (1993: 12–13) summarized this thesis:

In a variety of different expressions contemporary social theory points to the thesis that the law continues to occupy an increasingly central and organizing place, whether for good or ill, in advanced capitalist democracies . . . For such diverse figures as Weber, Poulantzas, Habermas, and Luhmann are to be found distinct, but related, versions of a thesis that state law has been an increasingly central feature of modernity. Whether expressed as the advance of legal rationality, the centrality of the 'juridico-political instance,' the process of 'juridification,' or as the 'positivization' of a self-referential legal system, these are all variants of what I call the centrality of law thesis. Another very popular version of this general thesis is that of 'legalization' that makes the general point

---

[20] These observations should not be mistaken for Donald Black's (1976: 62) thesis that law is inversely related to other means of social control. My observations about the relative proportions between the first and second categories need not remain in inverse relation. For example, it is easily conceivable that a society with a high degree of other social control might also have an ambitious, strong arm leader who expands the power and activity of legal institutions to achieve his own pursuit of power in the name of society. In this situation there would be a high degree of the second category, without any compensating reduction in the first. There is no cap on the total quantum of coercive and non-coercive forms of social control operative in a given society.

that legal regulation penetrates more pervasively into social life (citations omitted).

The 'centrality of law' thesis described by Hunt applies to the second category of the concept of law, specifically to state law.

Hunt's description combines several different theses under one name. If the thesis is that state bureaucratic legal institutions are increasing in size and specialization, along with the number of legal professionals and the volume of law books, and that law has increasingly become rationalized as Weber described, and positivized and autonomous (at least relatively) as Luhmann describes, there is much evidence to support it. Note, however, that these observations relate primarily to changes in state law itself. The material growth of law and its continued internal development, which accompanies the growth and differentiation of society, says nothing about a relative increase in the actual reach of law.

If the thesis is that the coercive activities of state legal institutions (second category of the concept of law) have taken over from and increased in proportion relative to non-coercive sources of social behaviour (first category of the concept of law)—that the iron grip of law is closing ever in upon us—as Habermas' notion of juridification and Hunt's final sentence appear to indicate, it is highly questionable. People still generally do not know what the law is, and still give hardly a thought to it when engaging in routine behaviour. And application of the coercive power of the state legal apparatus remains a marginal phenomenon relative to the mass of social interaction. As Hunt (p. 327) cautioned, '[i]t remains important, because of the inflated self-aggrandisement of legal discourses, to chip away at the myth of legalism and not to assume that law makes much difference to lived relations.'

The latter version of the centrality of law thesis is especially dubious when one considers a phenomenon that has emerged in cities around the world, from Washington DC to Paris: the almost total impotence of the state legal apparatus within certain urban pockets surrendered to the control of gangs or local warlords, or simply left to a state of anarchy. The beleaguered residents of these abandoned regions would not likely be persuaded that their social life was being colonized by state law. Moreover, statistics have shown a sharp increase (among the wealthy) of expenditures on private security, such that by 1990 'twice as much money was spent on private as on public police' (Thurow 1996: 264), which suggests the possibility that a relative decrease in governmental social control has occurred.

The mistake lies in taking the undeniable explosion of legal forms, and the increasing adoption by private institutions of legal procedures like due process requirements, for an intensification of law's interference in our everyday lives. These changes are part and parcel of the rationalization of society along the trajectory identified by Weber. The increase in legal forms is a reflection of the modern penchant for typifying transactions and for intercourse in writing. To be sure, this penchant is substantially driven by the fact that law prefers and imposes typification (especially for substantial or commercial transactions), and recognizes and often requires the written form. However, the essential resulting change is that we increasingly conduct and embody our transactions in a regularized format. This standardization of transactions—which is made necessary by their ever-increasing volume as population expands—is more a process of rationalization (in terms of efficiency and uniformity) than legalization. And the legalization it entails is largely facilitative in nature rather than oppressive.[21] For the most part legal institutions and legal rules are passive, lying in wait until sought out and invoked by users, which can hardly be characterized as an intrusion or penetration by law itself.

A positivist view of law leads us to see these changes as involving an expansion of law. From within the legal positivist perspective this is correct, and would be irrefutably confirmed by a glance at shelves overflowing with codes and legal regulations. But a social scientific view of law, with its focus on observation of the behaviour of legal institutions, suggests that a real tightening of the iron grip of law would involve an actual increase in the application of the power of the state legal apparatus into the everyday lives of citizens, as has occurred and continues to occur in totalitarian societies.

Those who fear that law is increasingly penetrating the life world are perhaps also swayed by the astonishing expansion of law in the cultural arena, from daily news coverage of sensational or important cases, to popular novels and television programs, like LA Law, to the O. J. Simpson trial—broadcast live and watched by millions. This is the age of the symbolic ascendance of law. Ordinary social discourse, which used to take place in various traditional or moral terms, is increasingly couched in legal terms. But law as a cultural symbol and mode of cultural discourse has a life of its own quite apart from (though interact-

---

[21] Oliver Wendell Holmes made a similar point when challenging Austin's 'command' theory of law as inadequate because it failed to recognize that private law rules create options rather than lay down commands (see Grey 1989: 831).

ing with) what the state legal apparatus actually does. The advantage of interpretive-oriented approaches to law is their capacity to account for this meaning based dimension; that does not, however, imply discarding the behaviour-oriented approaches, which insist that we must keep an eye on the material effects of law.

Whether the centrality of law thesis is correct is an empirical question that cannot be determined by the analytical map alone. The map only suggests that we have compelling reasons to be skeptical of the most sweeping version of the thesis, and it reveals that the notion of the legalization of society encompasses several qualitatively distinct processes, which can be benign, beneficial, or threatening depending upon their nature and how they operate.

The Nature of the Concept of Law

Donald Black was correct when he concluded that science can know only phenomena not essences. Yet he went on to make an essentialist claim about law when he declared that, 'law *is* governmental social control.' His concept was artificially constricting in two directions: it removed from the field of inquiry all those other functions law provides, and it conceptually eliminated the possibility that the government has other mechanisms of social control besides law. Black should have just said 'governmental social control' is an important phenomenon which must be studied.

The same is true of 'institutionalized norm enforcement', 'institutionalized social control', 'institutionalized dispute processing', 'living law', 'concrete patterns of social ordering', and all of the other many variations of scientific concepts of law. Each such concept created a legitimate and useful framework—an analytical tool—that allowed scientists to compare and study various phenomena in relation to the functions or criteria identified.

The error in each case was to take the additional step and assert that a given concept *is* law. This move limited our ability to observe and analyse law to the parameters proscribed by the social scientific framework. When, for example, law is defined as the institutional enforcement of social norms, the question, 'do legal institutions in fact enforce social norms?', is analytically precluded, for an affirmative answer to this question is a presupposition of what it means to be a legal institution. Likewise, from their respective functionalist perspectives, the following questions are incoherent: 'Do legal institutions resolve disputes?'

'Does law effect social control?' These are not just academic questions. Analysts have observed that the presence of law sometimes *produces* disputes (Schur 1968: 84). The analytical map and sociological studies suggest that law is not the most important mechanism of social control, and that social control may not be the most important function law fulfills. Yet the belief that law fundamentally involves social control persists in the scientific as well as legal literature, sturdily resisting all evidence to the contrary. By their nature, all functionalist concepts inhibit an inquiry into whether law fulfills the stated function, for law has been defined in terms of that function.

What law is and what law does cannot be captured in any single scientific concept. The project to devise a scientific concept of law was based upon the misguided belief that law comprises a fundamental category. To the contrary, law is thoroughly a cultural construct, lacking any universal essential nature.[22] Law *is* whatever we attach the label *law* to. It is a term conventionally applied to a variety of multifaceted, multifunctional phenomena: natural law, international law, primitive law, religious law, customary law, state law, folk law, people's law, and indigenous law on the general level, and an almost infinite variety on the specific level, from the state law of Massachusetts to the law of the Barotse, from the law of Nazi Germany to the Nuremberg trials. If there is a shared trait to the various phenomena which carry the tag 'law', it's that they all lay claim to legitimate authority, to rightful power. This quality more than anything else is what makes law—in all of its many incarnations—so potentially dangerous.

A realistic socio-legal studies examines each of these phenomena, individually, to ask what they are, what they do, and what we do with them. In the following Chapter, I will outline the elements of one of these phenomena—state law—in terms of a 'social' theory of law which focuses equally on behaviour and meaning.

---

[22] This assertion does not deny that the ideal of law in a given community may indeed have an essential nature that can be analytically identified. Lon Fuller's *The Morality of Law* (1964) is an attempt at specifying the essential elements of law. However, this is the nature of the ideal of law as it exists within the Western liberal rule of law tradition. If in the distant future this tradition prevails around the world, there will be one (world) cultural version of law, and its essential nature will be much as Fuller describes.

5 A Social Theory of Law by Comparison to Legal Positivism

The primary theoretical strategy driving the previous Chapter can be described as decentreing. This decentreing consisted of prying apart the close association law and social order have in our minds, then challenging the dominance of both. This effort involved denying the belief that law plays *the* central role in the maintenance of social order, and disputing the assumption that *the* core activity of law is social control. Both beliefs continue to exert a grip on thinking in the field.

At the conclusion of a recent review of the sociology of law which emphasized the many changes in the field corresponding to the new realities of 'postliberal society', legal sociologist Frank Munger (1993: 119) urged that, '[t]he key to theory is understanding . . . the problems of social order that we deem to be important; for this task, theory must be ambitious.' But no theory centred on social order can be ambitious. The 'social order problematic' is a time-worn view about law and society we inherited from 17th Century Enlightenment concerns about legitimating the application of state power. Not only has this problematic pervasively shaped our view of law; it has also been a core obsession of both anthropology and sociology throughout their existence. When law and social science came together in socio-legal studies, each reinforced the assumption of the other that social order was the central concern. Thus it is understandable that a recent review by John Conley and William O'Barr (1993: 41) chronicling the history of legal anthropology and its current homeward turn, concluded, like Munger, that, '[t]he ultimate challenge, as it has always been for anthropology as a whole, is to prescind from studies of individual communities in pursuit of a theory of social control in America.'

If we know that law is 'one of many mechanisms that facilitate social control,' as Conley and O'Barr (p. 63) observed, and recognize that 'law itself is a form of authority in decline . . . [and] we understand its limits as a force shaping the social order,' as Munger (1993: 119–20) observed, why should we construct socio-legal theory around social control and social order? As long as social order provides the framework for the study of law we will be trapped into exploring the dilemma that defines liberalism: the reconciliation of order with liberty. This liberal antinomy insures that we will be stuck exploring a narrow dialectic between the state (with its interest in order) and the individual (desiring freedom from oppression by the state or by other individuals through the state). I am not suggesting that this is insignificant or unimportant, by any means, only that we should discard the framework as too limiting, especially in an age in which the relative power of the state appears to be diminishing.

The secondary theoretical strategy driving the foregoing Chapter can be described as stripping. I tried to strip away several core beliefs about law, including the two beliefs already mentioned—that law is the central force in the maintenance of social order and social control is the central activity of law. I also tried to strip away the taken for granted assumptions that legal norms represent or reflect or restate social norms—that legal norms are derived from lived social norms or help generate lived social norms. The underlying belief I was trying to get at, which gives rise to all of the above beliefs, is that law involves consensual social order. My argument is that all of these are *normative* beliefs about law, yet they have masqueraded as *descriptions* of law, even within social scientific studies which have prided themselves on being purely descriptive. Again I do not deny that law sometimes satisfies these descriptions, only that they should be viewed as questions rather than assumptions.

After this decentreing and stripping, what remains for socio-legal studies to focus on are the many phenomena cited at the conclusion of the last Chapter which go by the name of law. These phenomena can and should be studied through the application of any social scientific technique or paradigm in existence or imaginable, without restriction. Although I lack the capacity to elaborate on the myriad possibilities in any great detail, in this Chapter I will outline one particular approach to *state law*, based upon interpretive theory, especially pragmatism-inspired symbolic interactionism. In descriptive terms, state law involves a loosely co-ordinated complex of activities comprising one aspect of the state apparatus—that aspect identified as the 'legal' system. What the people involved in this complex of activities (the legal actors) claim to do, and in fact do or don't do, and what other people (non-legal actors) do with this complex and its products, are the questions. I call this a 'social' theory of state law.

I will begin by comparing legal positivism, which is the dominant view of law held by members of the legal community, to the behaviour-based social scientific views of law set out in the previous Chapter. This comparison will demonstrate that a rigourous legal positivism would actually be grounded in the social theory of law I present. The point of conjunction of these two approaches lies in the claim of both to be grounded in social practices, in meaningful social behaviour.

The Normative Nature of Hart's Legal Positivism

One of the interesting implications of the behaviour-oriented social scientific approaches to the concept of law described in the previous Chapter is that they appear to dispute the fundamental claim of legal positivism—that it identifies what law *is* (not what law *ought* to be) (see Hart 1957–8). According to the social scientific approaches, positive law norms are *oughts*; the law *is* only what people routinely do (first category) or what legal actors do (second category), regardless of whether what they do is consistent with the positive law norms. Examining the relation between these apparently conflicting ways of looking at law 'descriptively' proves illuminating, and will help locate the social theory of law I set out.

Neil MacCormick (1981: 158–9) summarized the legal positivist position as follows:

In Austin's words, 'The existence of law is one thing; its merit or demerit another.' Hence jurists ought to distinguish carefully two tasks: the task of elucidating what are the prerequisites of any law's existence, coupled with a description of the laws which do actually exist; and the task of reviewing the moral merits and demerits of existing laws, coupled with proposals for reform of the unmeritorious ones.

Legal positivism takes a realistic (though not Legal Realist) approach to law. What is law is a question of fact, whether or not we approve of the laws. Legal positivists were contesting the notion that only laws consistent with natural law dictates have the status of 'law'. Thus legal positivists focused on distinguishing what is law from *moral oughts*, whereas the social scientists focused on distinguishing what law is/does from *legal oughts* (from the norms cited as law but not lived or not enforced). At this level these approaches do not necessarily conflict—they can coexist in the pursuit of distinct objectives—but there is a point at which their claims come into conflict.

H. L. A. Hart took Austin's approach a step further by locating the criteria for the existence of law in social facts. Again, MacCormick states (p. 159):

[Hart's] theory of legal rules as social rules is presented as a preferable alternative to Austinian or other like accounts of laws as commands of sovereigns. What he does hold is that legal rules as social rules have social sources, being rooted in the actual practices (doings, sayings and thinkings) of persons in society. Legal rules neither are, nor include, nor derive from objectively pre-existing and valid natural standards of human conduct. They derive exclusively from social practices.

According to this account, the fact of law is entirely dependent upon what people do and the attitude they take toward these activities. This grounding in actual social practices is what led Hart (1961: v) to claim that his theory was an exercise in 'descriptive sociology'. Against Austin's theory that law involves the commands of the sovereign habitually obeyed by the populace, Hart (p. 56) argued that law also consists of an internal normative ('critical reflective') attitude of acceptance towards the laws, at least among the legal officials.

The social practices referred to by Hart (pp. 78–96) consist of his classic distinction between primary rules of obligation (the rules of behaviour governing social interaction) and the secondary rules of recognition, adjudication, and change (the rules legal actors use to identify and apply the primary rules). For Hart (p. 113) these two rules form the essence of a legal system:

> There are therefore two minimum conditions necessary and sufficient for the existence of a legal system. On the one hand those rules of behavior which are valid according to the system's ultimate criteria of validity must be generally obeyed, and, on the other hand, its rules of recognition specifying the criteria of validity and its rules of change and adjudication must be effectively accepted as common public standards of official behavior by its officials.

The secondary rules, in particular, were the key for Hart. Although the citizens must generally obey the primary rules, strictly speaking they do not have to like them or feel a normative obligation to abide by them (though Hart added that this would be the sign of a healthy legal system). However, according to Hart, the legal officials did have to feel a normative commitment to the secondary rules.

The potential for conflict derives from the fact that, identical to Hart, the behaviour-based social scientific approaches to law also claimed to be 'descriptive', to identify what law is, and to focus on social behaviour (on what people are doing, on their actual practices), yet their versions of law differ from Hart's. The difference can be demonstrated in Hart's (p. 100) discussion of the distinction between validity and efficacy:

We can indeed simply say that the statement that a particular rule is valid means that it satisfies all the criteria provided by the rule of recognition . . . Some of the puzzles connected with the idea of legal validity are said to concern the relation between the validity and the 'efficacy' of law. If by 'efficacy' is meant that the fact that a rule of law which requires certain behavior is obeyed more often than not, it is plain that there is no necessary connexion between the validity of any particular rule and its efficacy . . .

A rule that satisfies the rule of recognition is a valid law even if people in the social community do not generally obey the rule, and even if the legal system takes no action to enforce it. According to the behaviour-based social scientific approaches, however, this would not qualify as a law under either the first or second category, respectively. Ehrlich gave the label 'rules for decision' to valid positive law rules which can lie in slumber for a century but be resurrected at any time to serve as a justification for a judicial decision.

The presence of legally valid but totally ineffective (not followed and not enforced) laws might seem to be so rare that it is not worth discussing, but that was the case with the anti-sodomy law in *Bowers*, with many longstanding laws on the books which have fallen into disuse, with certain provisions of the Austrian Civil Code studied by Ehrlich, with many transplanted laws and codes in developing countries which are validly enacted yet lie unobserved and dormant, and with laws of exclusively symbolic import, like the provisions in a number of constitutions around the world which affirmatively recognize, for example, social rights such as a right to good health or employment. Indeed, I would venture to assert that in every state legal system that exists there are more than a few valid legal rules which are neither observed by the populace nor affirmatively implemented by legal officials.

The above argument, Hart might have responded, shows only that his approach would differ from the social scientific approaches with regard to the existence of individual laws on the books, but not on the question of the existence of a *legal system*, at least in relation to the second category of the concept of law (several versions of which were actually constructed upon Hart's analysis). This response is correct. As I will show, however, the consequences of this match are profoundly unpalatable for Hart: it eliminates the acceptance requirement, defeating his attempt to avoid Austin's command theory of law, and it eliminates the necessity for the first condition Hart cited for the existence of a legal system, that laws are generally obeyed. This argument will reveal the ways in which Hart's approach is in fact normative rather than descriptive.

Hart's concept of law and the second category of the social scientific concept of law converge on the assertion that a legal system will exist where there is a complex of legal actors who co-ordinate their actions to enforce norms. The very fact of co-ordination requires some degree of agreement in their social behaviour, which would be satisfied through shared adherence to the secondary rules. If, for example, legislators promulgate laws and judges agree about which laws are validly enacted, and take action to apply them, a legal system will exist. *This is true without any mention of the legal officials' attitudes toward the secondary or primary rules, or without regard to whether the primary rules are generally obeyed.* And remember that the analytical map challenged the assumption built into the second category of the concept of law that the rules enforced by legal institutions are necessarily derived from or reflect lived social rules—that was the underlying point of the tension between the two categories.

Primary rules of obligation take on a completely different character when viewed in this light. It appears that they may indeed be draconian commands of the sovereign, or the gunman writ large. Michael Payne (1982: 503) has recognized that Hart's account leads to the conclusion that *no one*, neither the populace nor the officials, need accept the primary rules:

[Hart's] two minimum conditions require *obedience* by citizens of the primary rules and *acceptance* by officials of the secondary rules. Consequently, the two minimum conditions imply that a legal system may exist in which neither officials nor citizens accept the primary rules . . . Therefore . . . such a system may be reduced to a system based on power alone.

Payne's point is that people must obey the primary rules because an institutionalized power apparatus forces it, regardless of acceptance.[1] But Payne did not go far enough. Despite what Hart asserted, it is also not necessary that the legal officials 'accept' the *secondary rules* (in Hart's sense of being normatively committed to them),[2] as long as they adhere

---
[1] Roger Shiner (1992: 59–84) accepts the thrust of Payne's critique, but attempts to rehabilitate Hart's account by recharacterizing 'acceptance' as merely acceptance in the long run through acquiescence (or not revolting).

[2] Shiner (1992: 64) recognized that it would 'be excessive to require that the offical's acceptance had to be a full-blooded commitment to the moral worth of the secondary rules.' Thus Shiner (p. 65) asserts that the acceptance requirement must be interpreted 'as thinly and minimally as possible'. The officials will wield power if they co-ordinate their activities, so they do. However, if the only degree of acceptance necessary is following out of pure self interest, this is so minimal an interpretation that there is nothing left in the content of Hart's original view of acceptance.

to them. It is easy to conceive of the existence of a corrupt legal system manned by officials who take a cynical view toward the entire body of rules they administer, primary and secondary (cf. Edgeworth 1986: 132). Acceptance is thus not a necessary aspect of either primary or secondary rules.

Contrary to his avowedly descriptive stance, Hart's assertion that law consists of rules which enjoy a degree of acceptance is a normative view of law. That is the way members of the legal community in Western countries, like the United States and United Kingdom, typically view the law. Hart saw law as legitimate and built this legitimacy—through the notion of acceptance—into his formulation of what is needed for the existence of a legal system. However, the *only* condition that is needed for the existence of a legal system is the presence of a co-ordinated complex of actors adhering to a shared set of secondary rules who do things *in the name of law*. Because I am developing a social theory of state law, in this context I would add the further requirement that these actors enforce, and apply norms in the name of *state* law. A legal positivism which takes seriously the assertion that it identifies what law is (regardless of whether the legal system is one we would approve of), would be led to this minimalist description, which provides the starting point for the social theory of law I set out in a later Section.

Viewing law in these terms leads to a further step: rejecting Hart's first requirement for the existence of a legal system—that people generally obey the primary rules (even if they don't accept them). As I indicated above, the fact that legal officials co-ordinate their activities (through shared secondary rules) to enforce primary rules does not of itself imply that the primary rules are generally obeyed by the populace. It depends upon the power wielded by the legal system and the degree of resistance by the populace.

Fulfillment of the first condition does not follow from Hart's description in the same sense that the existence of actually followed secondary rules is a necessary requirement for the existence of a legal system. Rather, Hart (p. 100) appeared to believe that the first requirement was a matter of practical reality:

From the inefficacy of a particular rule . . . we must distinguish a general disregard of the rules of the system. This may be so complete in character and so protracted that we should say, in the case of a new system, that it had never established itself as the legal system of a given group, or in the case of a once-established system, that it had ceased to be the legal system of the group . . . In such cases it would be generally *pointless* either to assess the rights and duties of particular persons by reference to the primary rules of a system or to assess the validity of any of its rules by reference to its rules of recognition (emphasis in original).

Hart would seem to be obviously correct that it is pointless to say there is a legal system when the rules are generally disregarded, but he is demonstrably wrong, and wrong in legal positivist terms.

Ehrlich showed that in the region of Austria he studied substantial aspects of the Austrian Civil Code dealing with social behaviour were generally disregarded. Ehrlich did not contend, and surely Hart would not, that the Austrian legal system did not exist, or even that it did not exist in that part of the country. Hart might assert that some people did obey certain portions of the Code, at least in certain locations (the cities), but the point remains that there can be general disobeyance without leading to the conclusion that there is no legal system. A legal system exists, even in legal positivist terms, because there are legal actors engaged in producing and reproducing a legal system through shared secondary rules, regardless of their efficacy in generating widespread conformity to the primary rules.

Another example can be found in my study of law in Yap, Micronesia (Tamanaha 1993a). Yap had a legal system, with a legislature, a handful of judges and attorneys, a small police department, and a complete legal code based in its entirety on laws transplanted from the United States. But vast portions of the Code have never been applied, few lay people have any knowledge of the content of the laws or of the nature of the legal system, a large proportion of social problems are dealt with through traditional means without participation of the legal system, and indeed on most of the islands there is no legal presence at all. Their day-to-day behaviour is not governed by state law, but by their own system of cultural norms. Social order is maintained by sources other than the law. They do not identify with the legal system in any way. For most Yapese, when confronted with the law, it is like being confronted with the command of the sovereign (an alien sovereign). While they do not routinely act in conflict with law, it could not be said that they are 'obeying' or complying with the primary rules in Hart's terms. Hart (1961: 54–60) defined obedience to include a minimum element of knowing (though not necessarily willing), passive compliance. '[O]ne might be said to *follow* or be guided by a rule when and only when someone performs an act *because* the rule indicates that it be performed' (Schauer 1991: 113, emphasis in original).

Although almost the entire populace live in general disregard of the overwhelming majority of the rules of the legal system, it is wrong to say their legal system does not exist. I worked there as a busy assistant attorney-general for almost two years. They have a full-fledged legal system, mostly occupied with the affairs of running a government or with commercial activities (i.e., mostly non-social control activities). The existence of state law in Yap is a social fact, based upon the activities of legal officials. Conceivably, Hart might assert that there are also other (non-state) 'legal' systems operative in Yap—which do satisfy his two minimal conditions—but that would not refute the fact that the state law system does exist despite the failure to meet his first condition.

To save his assertion that general obedience of primary rules is a necessary element for the existence of a legal system, Hart can respond that the counter-examples I have identified are relatively rare products of unusual circumstances. Perhaps, at least to Western eyes where law looms so large, but the situation in Yap is repeated in varying ways and degrees in situations of transplanted law around the world. Hart's analysis purported to be analytical and descriptive. The more exceptions we tack on the less it can claim to be either. It would appear that state legal systems can exist without fulfilling either of Hart's two minimum conditions—obedience by citizens of the primary rules and acceptance by officials of secondary rules—as long as there are officials coordinating their activities in the name of state law. Hart mistakenly believed that his account was an account of law as such, rather than an abstracted account of the Western incarnation of state law, because he assumed the existence of a close association between legal norms (primary rules) and social norms. If you assume a close association, then general obeyance automatically follows.

This almost universally assumed article of faith is extremely difficult to disloge. Here is one final attempt to sever the assumed link.

Positive Law Norms and Social Norms

My aim is to present positive law rules in a manner that allows their open and complex relations with lived social rules to be better observed. The best way to accomplish this is to examine how they operate in an unusual context. Therefore, I have reprinted *Rex* v. *Palamba s/o Fundikila*, 14 E.A.C.A. 96 (Tanganyika 1947), judgment delivered by Sir G. Graham Paul, CJ:

138   *Realistic Socio-legal Theory*

The two appellants, jointly charged in the High Court of Tanganyika at Kigoma, were found guilty of the murder of a woman Wamlunda d/o Kulyungumba and sentenced to death. From their convictions they appeal to this court . . .

The statement by the first appellant is quite short and may be quoted verbatim. It is as follows:

Q. Do you wish to make a statement?

A. Yes, I wish to say that I personally saw my eleven children dead. After that, through sorrow, I made my two wives, my mother and my daughter take Mwavi to see that they had not killed my children, and as a result my wife and my mother were dead.

Q. What is Mwavi?

A. Mwavi is a medicine (dawa) used by witchcraft. If a person takes this medicine and he has done wrong he dies, whereas if a person takes this medicine and he or she has not done wrong, he (or she) does not die but only vomits. I have nothing more to say, but I agree to this charge of killing people.

The woman Wamlunda d/o/ Kulyungumba in respect of whose death the appellants were convicted of murder was the senior wife of the first appellant.

Apart from the succinct voluntary statement of the first appellant there was evidence in some detail of what was undoubtedly a trial by ordeal organized and directed by the first appellant. The gist of that evidence was that the two appellants went to a particular medicine man—a six hours' journey—to get certain 'medicine' called by the witness 'Mwavi'. The medicine man has since died. Four women of the family were compelled to take this 'medicine' and to swallow large quantities of water—a certain amount of formality being observed, with the first appellant presiding with a gun and intimating that anyone refusing to take the 'medicine' would be shot. Of the four women who took the medicine two vomited and survived; the two older women did not vomit and they died. All four women were in good health before the administration of the Mwavi. The whole business was admittedly a trial by ordeal to discover who had by witchcraft caused the death of eleven children.

The body of Wamlunda to whom the murder charge relates was apparently burnt after her death so no post-mortem examination could be made to ascertain scientifically whether she had died as a result of taking Mwavi or not . . .

Even if there had been proper proof that the woman Wamlunda did die as the result of the dose of Mwavi given to her there would still remain the very difficult question of malice aforethought on the part of the first appellant. Even on the hearsay evidence of the local lore Mwavi of itself is not a fatal poison. It requires, in order to be fatal, an additional element, namely the guilt of the person taking it, that is to say guilt of witchcraft. This court cannot possibly proceed on any other basis than that Wamlunda was innocent of witchcraft, which so far as this court is concerned does not exist. On the basis that Wamlunda was innocent of witchcraft where is the malice aforethought in the first appellant who, ex hypothesi, believed that the administration of Mwavi to a person innocent of witchcraft would not cause death? To bring him within the Penal Code as a murderer there must be under section 200 of the Penal Code (omitting those parts of the section inapplicable to this case) one or more of the following circumstances:

> (a) an intention to cause the death of, or to do grievous harm to any person, whether such person is actually killed or not;
>
> (b) knowledge that the act or omission causing death will probably cause the death of or grievous harm to some person, whether such person is the person actually killed or not, although such knowledge is accompanied by indifference whether death or grievous bodily harm is caused or not, or by a wish that it may not be caused.

On the necessary hypothesis that Wamlunda was innocent of witchcraft none of these essential circumstances was present in the case as regards the first appellant.

Taking that view of the case we have no alternative but to allow the appeals and quash the convictions and sentences.

With its juxtaposition of contrasting norms, this case provides an excellent vehicle through which to demonstrate the variable relationship between legal and social norms, but first a couple of preliminary observations.

Section 200 of the Penal Code is part of a standard murder statute, in all likelihood modelled upon a similar provision in the United Kingdom. Observe that the statute is not phrased in normative terms; it consists of a series of definitions or elements which must be satisfied. This is the typical form of the vast majority of state law provisions— they construct categories to which legal consequences are attached when fulfilled. Perhaps to belabour the obvious, at least with regard to state law, the impression that legal norms literally restate social norms should be dismissed. Concepts of law which centre upon the enforcement of social norms—'a social norm is legal if'—tend to generate this misimpression.

Obviously the judge is not a native. Only two legal rules play a prominent role in the case. The primary legal rule is section 200 of the Penal Code. The second legal rule is the one which implicitly informed the judge's understanding of his judicial obligation: his duty was to interpret and apply the plain meaning of section 200 to the facts of the case, regardless of whether the outcome was one with which he agreed.

Several indigenous social norms are discernable from the opinion, relating to: the appropriate response to mass death in the family; what is a legitimate method of identifying wrongdoers; the nature of the relationship between a man and his mother, wife, and daughters in situations where wrongdoing is suspected.

The first point this case illustrates is that the answer to the question, 'What norms are enforced by this case?' depends upon who you ask. If you asked the defendants, and perhaps the villagers, the answer would probably be that the court (rightly) recognized the validity of the indigenous social norms set out in the preceding paragraph (though the deceased wife's friends or relatives might well take an altogether different view). If you asked the same question of the judges or of a group of lawyers, the answer would undoubtedly be that the decision enforced the penal code requirement that murder requires intent to kill, and perhaps also the legal norm that judges are bound to follow the law.

A second point is the obvious one that these legal norms were not derived from lived social rules, yet the outcome in effect upheld these rules, at least from the perspective of the defendants.

A third point is that the local social rules were vindicated despite the fact that the judge apparently was not interested in upholding these rules (note his reluctance: 'we have no alternative . . .'). The immediate focus of the judge was on whether the events which occurred fit within the categories defined by the applicable legal rules. His reasoning indicates that he was immersed in the ideosyncratic logic which judges engage in when confronted with legal cases, a logic determined by the internal demands, traditions, customs, and habits of thought which thickly encrust a given practice of judging.

The above three points suggest that if law does enforce social norms, it does so because the legal decision is perceived that way by the various individuals who receive it, more so than because the legal rules correspond to the social norms; and it does so as a contingent matter, not necessarily because the persons in the legal arena or the available body of legal rules are oriented to vindicating social norms. Judge Paul was entirely focused on applying the legal rules, which is a common disposition of judges in 'rule of law' systems where the legal rules are considered binding.

Moreover, what matters about the decision from the standpoint of the social community is the outcome, not the content of the decision, which few members of social communities have access to, or have the desire or capacity to read and fully understand. The bottom line for members of the social community, at least for those who are at all interested, is who won or lost, and usually that bare fact alone is what people interpret when forming their opinions about which norms were enforced. In addition, it must not be forgotten that different people in the community may interpret the same outcome in vastly different ways. The sharply divergent response to the O. J. Simpson acquittal is striking confirmation of this, and also demonstrates that the same phenomenon exists in our own system as well.

Although this case arises out of unusual circumstances, the basic points it illustrates about the uncertain relationship between legal norms and social norms are sound. There is another point of relevance to Hart's analysis. Hart's primary rules of obligation referred to social rules which members of the community are bound to follow. However, contemplate the following: 1) the distinction between legal norms and social norms, and judges' emphasis in rule of law systems on following *legal* norms; 2) the fact that people regularly behave without much thought about or concrete knowledge of the law (often consulting the law only after what's done is done); and 3) the fact that people usually interpret only the outcomes of cases rather than the content of legal decisions. The combined impact of these points would indicate that the primary rules are, above all, articulated rules which serve as directions to and resources for legal actors, lawyers, and judges. Taking into account their tedious volume and detail, their incomprehensible (except to the initiated) legalese, and their general obscurity outside of members of the legal community, a truly descriptive legal sociology would be forced to conclude that primary rules—indeed all legal rules—are tools in the trade of legal discourse.

That is not to say that Hart was wrong. Primary rules have a dual existence: they are rules which articulate standards of behaviour (keeping in mind that many legal rules are not about behaviour), but they are also the basic materials with which legal actors work. The problem is the former view is so dominant that it tends to obscure the latter— and the latter view is a critically important reminder that the former view cannot always be taken at face value. When addressing the broader social community legal actors may refer to the vindication of social norms as a systemic justification for their activities, but this self-understanding serves as a means of legitimating the legal enterprise, and should not be mistaken for a description of the legal process.

A Social Theory of State Law

When asking the question, *what is law?*, legal theorists as well as social scientists have striven to identify law *as such*, to locate a concept or definition of law that could be universally applied as an analytical category (whether the outcome was that law exists everywhere or that some places did not have law). This quest, I argued in the previous Chapter, has produced many insights (and the paradigms formulated have comparative uses), but insures eternal quibbling because law has no essential nature. I also argued that most of the definitions of law—the second category—were in fact abstractions from the state law model, and these abstractions had the effect of isolating upon one aspect of state law, leaving out much of what law involves.

A social theory of law draws upon these lessons to identify as the starting point for a study of law the very real presence of state law. Attempts to locate *the* concept of law were popular in an age when the state legal apparatus was a fledgling by comparison to its massive form and the range of activities it undertakes today, at least in the West. Although we cannot talk about law as such, we can talk about state law, which is a reality of modern society, though a reality that exists in an extraordinary variety of manifestations throughout the world. Compare, for the example, the (presently) all but defunct state legal system of Somalia with the solidly entrenched presence of the legal system of Massachusetts.

Across this variety there is a common element, which is necessary for the purposes of identification. This element takes as its point of reference the state; if there is no state, there is no state law. Within the state governmental apparatus, law involves those activities having to do with articulating, effectuating and applying the law of that state system. The prototypical (though not exclusive) forms of this are the legislative, judicial, administrative, policing, sanctioning, and prosecutorial apparatuses within the government, which include all persons allowed to participate, from court clerks, to prison guards, to private attorneys. Questions will arise at the margins with regard to any particular system over whether a certain activity is part of the state legal system. But the criteria of inclusion should be applied liberally, including as an aspect of state law whatever can be informatively seen in this way for a given study. Since this approach has no essentialist pretensions, nothing is at stake in identifying as law in one situation what might not be treated as law in another, as long as there are good reasons for seeing the phenomena in such a manner.

This is a 'social theory' of law in the sense that it builds around these elements in a way which focuses on the social presence of law. This is the same view I applied earlier in the discussion of philosophical pragmatism to argue that, while there is nothing distinct about scientific reasoning, science is distinct in the sense that it consists of various communities of persons trained in the various scientific traditions, engaged in various scientific practices, talking about the same subjects drawing upon shared bodies of knowledge, and supported by various institutions, and the products of science course through social life. That is the social presence of science; likewise with the social presence of law.

I will now identify the core ideas underlying this approach, building upon the insights of interpretive social science, especially symbolic interactionism. These insights are consistent with Alfred Schutz's analysis of meaning presented in Chapter Three.

Symbolic interactionism is a school of thought developed by George Herbert Mead out of pragmatism. Mead also made major contributions to philosophical pragmatism in relation to the intersubjective aspects of thought, though he is better known as a sociologist. Like philosophical pragmatism, symbolic interactionism, as the name suggests, constructs a sociological approach around the ways in which we act in the world. Among existing sociological approaches, it stays the closest to the facts and contains a minimum of abstractions.

The core idea behind symbolic interactionism is that all social interaction 'is characterized' by an immediately reciprocal orientation' (Joas 1993: 16; see also Schutz 1962: 11). We assume that in a given context of action the 'other' more or less sees and understands things the same way as 'self'. The symbolic codes (including speech, gestures, clothes, posture, etc.) drawn upon in the course of interaction are interpreted consistent with social typifications (interpretive schemes or constructs) shared by most everyone in the group or culture at large, especially contained within and transmitted through language. In Mead's (1934: 268) formulation, '[a] person who has in himself the universal response of the community toward that which he does, has in that sense the mind of the community . . . this community includes anyone who can understand what is said.' Our individuality is thus, in a direct sense, a social product, though each of us is nonetheless unique because we are socialized into different groups and different combinations of groups, we have unique life experiences, and we have innate differences in character and capacity.[3]

Shared intersubjective ideas and beliefs are what allow collective action to proceed, based upon mutual behaviour expections. Symbolic interactionists describe social interaction in terms of a reflexive monitoring process. In a given context of action, we begin with a set of objectives or possible alternatives, which are then adjusted in accordance with the manner in which the situation plays out, all the while interpreting the 'other's' behaviour as well as our own (by seeing it as if through the eyes of a third party), and making instrumental calculations in relation to achievement of our goals.

Of particular interest to law is the interpretivist view of rules. Rather than characterize rules as determinants of action, interpretivists see rules more as possibilities which are fully realized only in actual use:

> Rules are not abstract, fixed, and unchanging. They are open to continual reinterpretation, depending on the actor's goals, the setting in which the action takes place, and who else is involved in the encounter. Rules, then, do not exist independently of their use. Their precise meaning (their real meaning) is defined in use, as the action unfolds and the situation becomes more clearly defined ... the rules are not treated as determinants of action, as forces impinging on the actor from the outside. The rule-governedness of the interaction is something the actor helps bring about in concert with other actors (Wilson 1983: 113).

Moreover, symbolic interactionists see roles 'not as positions people must fill in order to be social but as a set of expectations or understandings which they can invoke, ignore, manage or change' (p. 131). The general picture of social interaction presented is one grounded in norms, rules, and roles which are nonetheless flexible and open to negotiation within the constraints provided by social convention, by the views and actions taken by others in the same context of action, and by surrounding material conditions.

From this basic set of ideas about social interaction and communication, Mead and his followers were able to construct an action-based sociological approach which accounts for the basic forms of social interaction. Institutions are co-ordinated complexes of human interaction, usually supported by a material base (office buildings, factories, etc.).

---

[3] Alfred Schutz (1962) has developed many of these same ideas through mundane phenomenology, and in certain respects with greater detail than Mead. For a detailed elaboration of Schutz's ideas on these issues, see Tamanaha (1993a: 79–94).

Herbert Blumer (1969: 58), a leading successor to Mead, elaborated this view of institutions:

It sees [large societal organizations] as arrangements of people who are interlinked in their respective actions. The organization and interdependency is between such actions of people stationed at different points. At any one point the participants are confronted by the organized activities of other people into which they have to fit their own acts . . . Instead of accounting for the activity of the organization and its parts in terms of organizational principles or system principles, it seeks explanation in the way in which the participants define, interpret, and meet the situations at their respective points. The linking together of this knowledge of the concatenated actions yields a picture of the organized complex.

According to this view, the institution is characterized more as a process than a static structure; structures are produced and reproduced on an ongoing basis through these interactive processes.

The overarching dynamic contained within interpretivism is the tension between freedom and constraint, or (in social science terminology) between agency and structure. A rough generalization is that positivists have tended to emphasize the constraint side while interpretivists the freedom side. This problematic—to what extent are we constrained and to what extent free?—underlies the most difficult questions in social theory, as well as, not coincidentally, legal theory. There appears to be a growing recognition, reflected in the work of social theorists like Anthony Giddens (see Cohen 1987), that we are free, within constraints, and that agency gives rise to structure and is in turn partially determined by structure.

Building upon this interpretive view of social interaction, institutions, and rules, I will now set out a series of analytical distinctions to help organize the study of the legal-social field. Fortuitously, Mead (1934: 261) used law as an example in his discussion of the nature of institutions:

The institution represents a common response on the part of all members of the community to a particular situation. This common response is one which, of course varies with the character of the individual. In the case of theft the response of the sheriff is different from that of the attorney-general, from that of the judge and the jurors, and so forth; and yet they all are responses which maintain property, which involve the recognition of the property rights in others. There is a common response in varied forms. And these variations, as illustrated in the different officials, have an organization which gives unity to the variety of the responses. One appeals to the policeman for assistance, one expects the state's attorney to act, expects the court and its various functionaries to carry out the process of the trial of the criminal . . . such organized sets of responses are related to each other; if one calls out one such set of responses, he is implicitly calling out others as well.

Observe how closely this description matches the everyday lawyers' view of how law works. Flushing out the details of Mead's description will help identify the basic elements involved.

First consider the common response—the overall story which co-ordinates the actions of 'all members of the community to a particular situation'. In broad terms, the common response is the basic cluster of beliefs about law adhered to by most people in the community as well as people who make up legal institutions. The police are the street level enforcement muscle of the law, to be called upon for assistance by community members in distress; the state's attorney is the enforcer at the next stage, after the police have delivered the suspected wrongdoer; the judge/jury are there to apply the law, vindicating community norms (like property). Among the central participants in the process, only the law-makers, the legislators (including judge as law-maker), were left out of Mead's description, though they were implicitly present in the presupposed legal prohibition against theft. Other contributors were also left out, like support staff, the clerk's office and the prison service. In addition, it must not be forgotten that Mead's example entirely left out the vast realms of civil law and administrative law, though for immediate purposes I will remain with Mead's focus.

Although we regularly refer to state law as a hierarchically structured *institution*, when broken down into its constituent elements it becomes apparent that state law is more closely described as a collection of institutions, each with their own characteristic activities, and each with their own internal hierarchy of authority, often located in separate buildings with their own material and financial resources, often with conflicting interests and concerns, loosely connected to one another at certain points of intersection or co-ordination. Each institution itself consists of distinct, co-ordinated complexes of activities. To see how the whole comes together—or fails to come together, or works at cross purposes—two different angles must be examined: the inner functioning of each constituent institution and the specific points of linkage (where, how, under what circumstances participants from each interact with others).[4]

---

[4] An example of this kind of analysis can be found in R. M. Emerson and B. Paley (1992).

We tend, for example, to see police under the authority of state's attorneys, and that often is how the official chain of command is constructed, but the actual everyday relation is one in the which the latter is substantially reliant upon the former for co-operation and assistance in providing the material necessary to successfully make a case. Each has power in different aspects of the relationship.[5]

Recognition of the variegated components involved corrects a tendency in socio-legal studies to see law as a whole, which licenses blanket observations like law serves the interests of the elite class. While it is correct to say that the activities of these institutions, taken as a whole, constitutes the *state legal system*, in actual operation the 'wholeness' of law is more a projection than a reality. To provide an example, law is often defined in monolithic terms as governmental social control. But many police will say *they* are the ones doing the social control dirty work, whereas the courts and state's attorney regularly hamper these efforts by quickly releasing crooks to the streets or letting them off lightly or by setting unrealistic restraints on police activities. After all, social control would be vastly more effective if we simply incarcerated everyone captured by the police. A more discriminating look might suggest that the police are involved in social control, whereas judges, prosecutors, and defenders are representing other interests like preserving society's notion of fairness, protecting the innocent, or serving as bulwarks against the excessive application of police power.

Following the pragmatic emphasis on action, the best analytical point of entry to each constituent institution is to hone in on its core activities—that is where the notion of a *practice* comes in. Each of these separate institutions are characterized by particular practices or activities: police do policing, judges do judging, state's attorneys do prosecuting, legislators do legislating (defence lawyers defend, social workers monitor and counsel, the court clerks administer, and so forth). Their individual supporting institutional structures are built around facilitating and perpetuating these activities. And each practice is an integral part of the overall complex of action that makes up the legal institution or legal system.

The notion of a practice, which will be elaborated on in depth in the next Chapter, contains integrated aspects of both meaning and doing. Clifford Geertz (1983: 155) captured a part of the meaning aspect: 'the various disciplines (or disciplinary matrices), humanistic, natural

[5] This observation is based upon my experience as a former Assistant Attorney General, and also as a former Assistant Federal Public Defender.

scientific, social scientific alike, that make up the scattered discourse of modern scholarship are more than intellectual coigns of vantage but are ways of being in the world . . . In the same way that Papuans or Amazonians inhabit the world they imagine, so do high energy physicists or historians of the Mediterranean in the age of Philip II . . . Those roles we think to occupy turn out to be minds we find ourselves to have.' And the same is true of police, judges, prosecutors, defense lawyers, legislators, corporate lawyers, legal aid attorneys, and so forth.

For analytical purposes, two inseverable aspects to this meaning dimension must be distinguished. Geertz's description alludes to the phenomenological dimension, to the way in which thinking within the activity is experienced and conducted. This first aspect involves the framework of thought connected with the activity. Alfred Schutz (1962: 341) argued that engaging in activities involve thinking within 'finite provinces of meaning' which are characterized by distinct 'cognitive styles'. For example, when pressing a legal argument before a judge, lawyers (thinking in the *internal legal attitude*) take a predominantly instrumental attitude towards legal rules, selectively bending, stretching and shaping them to fit their cause, and it doesn't really matter on which side of the case they happen to fall. But a judge engaging in judging (thinking in the *internal judicial attitude*) takes a very different view of the same rules, feeling rather more of their binding character and striving to cut through the lawyer's rhetoric to get at the meaning of the rules involved. This comparison shows how their respective frameworks of thought differ in ways connected to the practices in which they are engaged.

The second aspect has to do with the shared bodies of meaning that set apart and define groups or communities as distinct, what Mead referred to as the mind of the community, and Stanley Fish has introduced into legal theory as the notion of an 'interpretive community'. Interpretive communities consist of groups of people bound together by shared knowledge, language or terminology, and often a basic corpus of ideas, beliefs, and attitudes. One becomes a member of an interpretive community by undergoing indoctrination—by learning and internalizing the shared 'meaning system' of the interpretive community. While interpretive communities are often linked to practices, they often rise above both practices and institutions.

All persons who complete the rigours of legal education are members of the *intersubjective legal community* (the interpretive community of persons trained in law in a given legal tradition). They draw upon and think within the *legal meaning system* of that community whenever doing law, regardless of whether they are lawyers, judges, or law professors. They understand the legal language and communicate with one another about legal rules in ways outsiders cannot fully comprehend, even though they are connected to different institutions and participate in different practices. Of course, individual lawyers do not possess all the knowledge contained within the legal meaning system. As a function of the practice in which they engage, certain lawyers know more about corporate finance and antitrust law, and others about public housing regulations or divorce law. However, all members of the intersubjective legal community of a given legal tradition possess knowledge of a core set of linking aspects of the overall legal meaning system, primarily that inculcated in the course of legal education, including basic knowledge about property, contract, tort law, procedural law, how to find an answer to a legal question, and basic ideas about how legal institutions operate.

The analytical notions, legal meaning system and intersubjective legal community, entail one another, referring to different aspects of the same phenomenon, two ways of looking at what Fish merged into the single notion of the interpretive community. The meaning system consists of shared meaning strains and the legal community is the group that shares it.

Stated summarily, this is how the above elements relate: the legal meaning system refers to a discrete cluster of shared meaning strains; intersubjective legal community refers to the group informed by this shared legal meaning system; there are individual state legal institutions (i.e. legislature, judiciary, prosecutor's office), which are co-ordinated complexes of activities with a material base, usually organized around a practice or set of practices; a practice involves integrated aspects of engaging in (doing) a distinct activity; the internal attitude is the (phenomenological) cognitive style or framework of thought which characterizes thinking while engaging in a given practice; the state legal system consists of the state legal institutions and their constituent practices, considered as a whole. Each of these elements can also be broken up into lesser inclusive sub-units, where appropriate, as I will illustrate in the discussion of practices in the next Chapter.

All of the above elements, taken in combination, can be placed under the umbrella notion of a *legal tradition*. Legal tradition encompasses all aspects of a particular embodiment of state law, including legal education, the various practices of law, the actual historical individuals who have had a prominent influence on the nature and shape that law takes, the prevailing beliefs that inform and define the tradition, and more, everything about law in a given incarnation. Legal traditions can be viewed as wholes at any level of examination (i.e. state, federal, or local). There is only one of each tradition. Legal traditions have a history, often with ancestors, offspring and relatives (through transplantation or borrowing).

The final major component to draw out of Mead's account is the social community, the community of non-legal actors, who I have mentioned thus far mostly in passing. Mead described the community in homogeneous terms when he suggested that there is 'a common response on the part of all members of a community'. In pluralistic societies we must distinguish those members of the community, or members of sub-communities, who neither share in the common response, nor look at the law in terms of the picture presented by the rule of law story. Immigrant communities in the chinatowns or hispanic sectors in major cities in the United States, for example, whose inhabitants often do not speak English, and who tend to fear government officials, especially the police, do not see law the way Mead described; nor do gang members in South-Central Los Angeles. So the common response often is not in fact common to the entire community or society. In situations like those in Yap, very few people in the social community share in the common response; indeed for most purposes the common response in that context is all but limited to the legal actors alone.

Focusing on the social community involves a flip in perspective—which is grounded in a status distinction between those who are legal actors and those who are non-legal actors (including legal actors in their non-legal capacity). Non-legal actors face the law in the posture of potential consumers or users or subjects or victims, voluntary or involuntary. They can be examined in relation to a variety of factors, including knowledge about law, attitudes towards the legal system, resort to (or avoidance of) the law, uses of the law, and so forth. The social order problematic, and the view of law as social control, have a built-in bias which views law from a total societal standpoint. This leads to an overemphasis on the criminal law aspects of a legal system. If we instead examine non-legal actors and their relations to law and the legal apparatus—a focus on the social presence of law—social order and criminal law become less predominant. Law can instead be seen as a complex of institutional structures constituted by people (legal actors and supporting actors), operating within a material base, serving as a resource used by people for innumerable purposes, though usually still only at the margins of social interaction.

The civil law system, for example, is a resource drawn upon by members of the community for a multitude of reasons in the pursuit of their interests, including providing security when engaging in transactions, formalizing a transaction for the purposes of organization or record-keeping, seeking recourse after some harm has occurred, or seeking revenge upon or harassment of some opponent for personal satisfaction or gain. Even the government, itself made up of individuals acting in the pursuit of state-related projects, is a consumer of the legal system (as when enforcing contracts or defending against tort suits)—a major consumer—and as such is just one more player in the social community no different in status from other community members (which includes businesses and corporations as well as ordinary people). Indeed the government itself, unlike some forms of social association like the family or friendships, is internally constructed upon specified legal rules—law thus provides the background framework for its existence, as it does, to varying degrees, for other forms of institutions and associations (including corporations). The situation and nuances of non-legal actors in their posture as active or passive users of law is so complex and varied that nothing more of a general nature can be said about it.

These are middle-range concepts, abstract only to the extent necessary to identify the elements at play, designed to facilitate careful and close observation and description. A number of the above ideas have already made their way into legal theory—albeit not in precisely the same terms—under the label, 'Conventionalism'. Stanley Fish (1989), Owen Fiss (1985; 1982), and Stephen Burton (1985), among others, have articulated (differing) accounts of law and legal interpretation which include references to the shared meaning of the legal community, to the significance of practice in determining the meaning for rules, and to the overarching influence of the legal tradition in shaping legal activities. Although the direct inspiration for much of this work has been Wittgenstein, especially as it relates to the pre-eminence of practice,[6] it is also consistent with the interpretive insights articulated above.

Applying their own terminology, socio-legal scholars who identify themselves as interactionists or naturalists have also begun to build a baseline of knowledge consistent with this approach (see e.g. Manning

---

[6] Dennis Patterson (1990a; 1990b) has written several informative articles which develop Wittgenstein's views of a practice, and their relevance for law.

and Hawkins 1990). Moreover, many socio-legal studies already explore one or another of the above elements or their interrelations, albeit not in the specific terms or categories I have set out. Much of this work can be directly mapped onto the approach I have constructed, to contribute to the preparation of a comprehensive picture of the social presence of the state legal system.

In many respects this approach corresponds to the way lawyers and legal theorists look at law, which should facilitate a translation between the work of socio-legal studies and that of legal theorists, as I will demonstrate in the next three Chapters of this book. Indeed, as I argued in the first Section of this Chapter, a legal positivism based on actual social practices should itself be grounded in the social theory of law I set out. Law is what the legal actors say law is, as determined by their shared meaning system; and the question of whether legal officials or the populace generally obey or accept the primary or secondary rules are empirical questions that must be answered in relation to the particular system at hand.

The greatest strength of this approach is that it is inclusive: everyone, scientist and lawyer alike, can do it without specialized terminology or any particular skill beyond an ability for acute observation. Shorn of its technical social science talk, symbolic interactionism is not really a specific method. Rather, it is a sophisticated exhortation (which leads by example) to keep an eye on how people interact and communicate, and to follow closely how these interactions connect within broader complexes of action, all in the course of striving to understand what is going on.

The approach I have set out serves more as an organizing framework than as dictates about what must be done. The ultimate test for this approach is whether it contributes to the central task of a realistic socio-legal theory: producing informative descriptions that get to the facts of the matter about law. To demonstrate its value, in the following three Chapters I will elaborate on various aspects of the social theory of law through application to issues in legal theory, beginning with the nature of practices and the internal/external distinction.

6 The Internal/External Distinction and the Notion of a 'Practice'

The internal/external is gradually assuming a central position in legal theory and in socio-legal studies. H. L. A. Hart (1961: 55) introduced this distinction to legal theory when he argued that 'a social rule has an *internal* aspect' which distinguishes it from mere habit and must be taken into account as an essential characteristic of legal rules. The distinction arose again in a dispute between Hart and Ronald Dworkin over the propriety of descriptive jurisprudence. Dworkin's 'central objection seems to be that legal theory must take account of an *internal* perspective on the law which is the viewpoint of an insider or participant in a legal system, and no adequate account of this *internal* perspective can be provided by a descriptive theory whose viewpoint is not that of a participant but that of an *external* observer' (Hart 1994: 242). *Law's Empire* (1986), Dworkin's latest elaboration of his theory, is essentially constructed upon this very point: 'This book takes up the *internal*, participants' point of view' (p. 14). Moreover, Dworkin argues that the internal view 'must be judged *internally* by its own standards' (Moore 1989: 953), and cannot be judged by standards external to the practice.

The internal/external distinction has also been invoked as the essential element which distinguishes the scholarship of Critical Legal Studies (CLS) from mainstream doctrinal analysis. According to David Trubek (1984: 589), 'CLS follows this tradition: Analyzing the law from the *outside*, . . .' And the distinction has been identified as the core characteristic which unifies legal sociology, as well as distinguishes it from traditional legal studies. Legal sociologist Roger Cotterrell (1983: 242) described it thus: '[t]he numerous approaches to legal analysis which can be characterized as sociological in the broadest sense are unified only by their deliberate self-distancing from the professional viewpoint of the lawyer. It is implicit in the aim of empirical legal theory that law is always viewed "from the *outside*," from the perspective of an observer of legal institutions, doctrine and behavior, rather than that of a participant.'

Thus the internal/external distinction has arisen in a variety of seemingly unrelated contexts—involving the nature and study of rules, the status of jurisprudence, the propriety of rendering evaluative judgements on the practice of law, the relation of CLS work to mainstream scholarship, and the thread which unifies as well as distinguishes legal sociology. Despite its appearance in these wide-ranging issues, the internal/external distinction itself remains obscure and largely unanalysed.

This Chapter will explicate the nature and implications of the internal/external distinction by going back to its source of origin in the philosophy of social science. I will describe the development of the distinction in two different contexts: 1) in a dispute over the nature of social action and the methodology required to study it; and 2) in relation to what is called the 'strong programme' of the sociology of science. I will reveal the many complex implications which follow from the distinction, which range from questions of methodology to epistemology.

Then I will articulate the notion of a practice, briefly introduced in the previous Chapter. This notion provides an analytical tool for understanding many references to the internal/external distinction. Using detailed legal examples, I will elaborate on the notion of a practice, and indicate the differences and interconnections between practices and two other closely related contexts to which the distinction has been applied—institutions and interpretive communities. Finally, with this background information in hand, I will return to analyse each of the legal contexts mentioned at the outset.

The underlying purpose of this Chapter is to flesh out selected elements of the social theory of law presented in the preceding Chapter by bringing them to bear in concrete contexts, and to further elaborate the methodological and epistemological underpinnings of the realistic approach I urge. An important aspect of this discussion will be to indicate how the issue of indeterminacy—central to legal theory—arises in the philosophy of social sciences. This will set the stage for the final two Chapters, in which the realistic approach is applied to explore the nature of the practice of judging.

Science and the Study of Social Life[1]

For well over a century there has been a philosophical debate over the nature of science and its knowledge claims. A central part of this debate focused on the similarities and differences between the natural sciences

---

[1] This account is drawn from many sources, but the following have been especially helpful, Bohman (1991); Rosenberg (1988); Giddens and Turner (1987).

and the social sciences. As I have indicated, until the relatively recent 'interpretive turn',[2] the positivistic view of science was dominant. According to this view the natural sciences (especially physics and chemistry)—which have proven their mettle through the extraordinary technological advances that have made the modern age—were paradigmatic of science. On this model, science entailed the causal *explanation* of phenomenon by subsuming them under universally valid covering laws which allowed for reliable prediction. The prevailing view was that the natural sciences were gradually progressing through the cumulative gathering of knowledge, leading to an ever more accurate and comprehensive map of and direct correspondence with objective reality.

The widespread view that the natural sciences were the epitome of science, combined with the ideal of the unity of science, had dire consequences for the social sciences. The social sciences have never lived up to the standards set by the natural sciences. As philosopher of science, Mary Hesse, (1980: 193) appraised it, '[o]n the actual present situation one can only observe what underlies complaints about the backwardness, theoretical triviality, and empirical rule-of-thumb character of most social science, in spite of limited success in establishing low-level laws in isolated areas.' The historical development of the social sciences has been marked by internecine battles over competing paradigms and explanations with scant agreement over what counts as valid knowledge.

One reaction to this state of affairs was to deny that the social sciences were in fact 'sciences'. But the reaction of many social scientists was a determined effort to emulate the natural sciences to the extent possible. The predominant factor that kept the social sciences from meeting the requirements of positivism was the presence of human beings—seen by science as fallible, sometimes arbitrary, often irrational or deluded—in the social equation. In particular, the subjectivity of human actors was considered to be inherently inaccessible to science, especially in light of the 'other minds' problem generated by the Cartesian world view.

The solution to this problem was obvious: social science must eliminate any reference to subjectivity and focus only on externally observable social action, which is physicalist in the same way as are the objects studied by the natural sciences. Durkheim embraced this view:

---

[2] Hiley, Bohman, and Shusterman (1991) contains an informative collection of articles on the influence of interpretivism in various fields.

I consider it extremely fruitful this idea that social life should be explained, not by the notions of those who participate in it, but by more profound causes which are unperceived by consciousness, and I think also that these causes are to be sought mainly in the manner according to which the associated individuals are grouped. Only in this way, it seems, can history become a science, and sociology itself exist (quoted in Winch 1958: 23–4).

Social actions are 'caused' by social factors, in particular by the functional needs of the social group, regardless of the self-understandings or motivations of the individual actors involved.

B. F. Skinner's behaviourism, which claimed that stimulus-response conditioning is the 'cause' of behaviour, provided another example of the elimination of the thinking subject. 'The fundamental insight of behaviourism was strategic: instead of trying to analyse consciousness and states of the mind, scholars could make more progress in psychology by looking at the actions of men and women and at the observable states of people and of their environment to which the actions could be lawfully related' (Homans 1987: 58). Although his behaviourism differs from that of Skinner's,[3] legal sociologist Donald Black, extensively discussed in Chapter Three, took the methodological aspects of behaviourist ideas to an extreme in his proclaimed 'assassination of the person'. A third example was structuralism, which sought to identify invariant structures (in linguistics, personality, and cultural symbol systems) that contain an intrinsic logic or intelligibility. 'As Levi-Strauss puts it, one must avoid the "shop-girl's web of subjectivity" or the "swamps of experience" to arrive at structure and science . . . Structuralism seals its formalized language off from discourse, and therefore from the human world' (Rabinow and Sullivan 1979: 10–11).

These examples highlight two characteristics of the leading versions of positivist social science: they discounted or eliminated consideration of the meaningfully-oriented human subject, and they did so for the purpose of meeting the strictures of naturalistic science. These two characteristics are internally connected. The faith that science held the key to knowledge justified the priority accorded to the scientific method, which in turn led to and legitimated disregard for the understandings of lay social actors. 'There is an idea common to a number of different social sciences that the participants in a social practice are benighted and that the accounts they offer of their own attitudes and actions are

---

[3] The basic difference is that Skinner argues that behaviour is the result of operate conditioning, whereas Black argues that it is caused by a series of social 'laws'.

poor and should be discounted and replaced with other, richer, more enlighted or profitable [scientific] lines of explanation' (Root 1993: 74).

Max Weber was one positivist social scientist of note who took exception to this general trend. Weber recognized that social reality is largely comprised of the meaningful ideas and beliefs of social actors. Without attention to these ideas and beliefs, the actions of individuals and the complexes of social action they jointly produce cannot be fully understood. Although he agreed that social science must generate law-like causal explanations of social action, Weber (1964: 88) insisted that the 'specific task of sociology must be the interpretation of action in terms of its subjective meaning'. 'Only if a sociologist can see the world from the perspective of *their* values, and appreciate what these values mean to *them*, can he explain how the behavior of his subjects is influenced by the values they hold and construct an empirical causal explanation of the sort he seeks to provide' (Kronman 1983: 16–17).

An entirely different reaction to the debate was to reject the unity of science thesis and hold instead that the natural sciences and the social sciences are fundamentally distinct and should remain so. Peter Winch's *The Idea of a Social Science and its Relation to Philosophy* (1958) contained a widely influential argument to this effect, and is especially instructive for our purposes because it was the source cited by Hart in his touting of the internal view.

Although Winch endorsed Weber's argument that sociology should focus on interpretive understanding, he criticized Weber for his residual positivist desire to explain action by reference to causal laws. The problem with formulating laws is that society is constructed by internally connected systems of ideas and theories which are constantly developing and changing (Winch 1958: 133).[4] Thus Winch went beyond Weber to argue that positivist methods are inappropriate to the social sciences—in this domain *understanding* should be the objective. ' "Understanding" . . . is grasping the *point* or *meaning* of what is being said or done. This notion is far removed from the world of statistics and causal laws: it is closer to the realm of discourse and to the internal relations that link the parts of a realm of discourse' (p. 115, emphasis in original).

[4] Other analysts have pressed different arguments for the separation of the natural and social sciences. An often cited argument can be found in Taylor (1979). Taylor's argument is that unlike the objects studied by the natural sciences, the subjects studied by the social sciences are thinking, acting, reflecting beings who can read and react upon the scientific accounts to change their behaviour, all of which precludes the formulation of invariant causal laws. See also Dreyfus (1986).

According to Winch, understanding social action involves grasping the 'form of life' in which it takes place. Access to this form of life requires uncovering the operative social rules which make it intelligible for the participants involved as well as for the scientific observer. Winch (p. 52) made the strong claim that 'all behavior which is meaningful (therefore all specifically human behavior) is *ipso facto* rule governed.' '[I]t is only by reference to common rules that anyone can grasp what others are doing. Thus the concept of following a rule implies the anticipations, reactions, and expectation of other people in the social, intersubjective context of action in a "form of life" ' (Bohman 1991: 61).

Winch's conception of the internal view is not limited to the subjective attitudes or motivations of the actors, but rather more broadly encompasses the (rule based) webs of meaning in which the social action takes place. This is what Schutz referred to as meaning between social actors, and Geertz as public meaning. This socially generated and shared context of meaning is what renders the action intelligible to those involved. Hence it is not necessary for the actors themselves to be able to articulate, or even be conscious of, the operative social rules identified by the scientific observer, although they should be able to recognize these rules once they have been articulated.

Two particular responses to Winch's account are relevant to the legal context. The first response was to dispute Winch's overly rule-saturated, rule-bound view of social action. Social theorist James Bohman (1991: 64–5) recounted the objections:

The fact that some social actions follow rules does not require a distinctive or autonomous explanatory approach, nor do the rules themselves even ultimately explain most cases of rule following. As Robert Edgerton points out, there are many different types of rules, rules with exceptions, rules enforced without exceptions, rules about the exceptions to rules. Winch's view belongs to the older conformist models of rule following. As Edgerton describes this conformist 'normative theory,' 'people everywhere not only followed the rules of their societies—but also made these rules a part of themselves and became, almost literally, inseparable from them.' But theories challenged this view based upon the indeterminacy of rules—that is, the fact that people often do not follow them, do not incorporate them and frequently use them strategically to further their own interests. Under the new perspective of strategic interactionism, embodied in the works of theorists like Erving Goffman, rules are treated as flexible, negotiable and subject to exceptions.[5]

---

[5] Bohman cites to R. Edgerton's *Rules, Exceptions and the Social Order* (1985).

Given these objections, a methodology which over-emphasizes rule following is simply inadequate.

The second response to Winch focused on the relativistic implications of his analysis. In a famous debate with anthropologist E. E. Evans-Pritchard and philosopher Alasdair MacIntyre, both of whom argued that it was permissible (or even inevitable) to pass judgements on the beliefs and rationality of primitive societies, Winch (1964) argued that the forms or modes of life studied are '*non*-logical', by which he meant that the criteria of logic are inapplicable to them. For Winch (1958: 100), 'the criteria of logic are not a direct gift of God, but arise out of, and are only intelligible in the context of, ways of living or modes of social life. It follows that one cannot apply criteria of logic to modes of social life as such.' Moreover, because all modes of social life—including science, religion, or a primitive society—have their own internal criteria of intelligibility, the logic internal to one mode of life cannot be applied to evaluate the logic internal to another.

Winch carefully qualified his position. He agreed that a scientist could, taking the internal view, describe a belief without personally adopting or endorsing or ageeing with it: 'I do not mean, of course, that it is impossible to take as a datum that a certain person, or group of people, holds a certain belief—say that the earth is flat—without subscribing to it oneself' (p. 110). His point was rather that what this belief *means* and its logic can only be assessed within the context of its form of life. Furthermore, all societies have persons who hold beliefs that would be considered irrational or wrong when evaluated against the standards of judgement derived from within their own form of life (1964: 309), and a correct understanding of the situation would be to see that it is irrational within that context.

Winch's argument spawned a debate on the nature of rationality which has yet to be resolved (see Hollis and Lukes 1982). The nuances of the debate need not be reproduced here—just two basic aspects will suffice, both of which were briefly mentioned in the discussion of pragmatic philosophy. The first aspect is that careful analyses of the *natural* sciences have led to wide-ranging doubts about *their* claim to rationality, as summarized by philosopher Joseph Margolis (1986: 234):

Quite sensibly, Hempel (and with him, Davidson) took the hypothetico-deductive model of explanation in science to provide the most promising model . . . of rationality: a rational agent, on that view, is one who behaves (implicitly or explicitly) in accord with the most powerful cognitive model we possess. The generally admitted fact of scientific progress draws us in this direction. The trouble is that that model is in the deepest of trouble itself, because the logical status of scientific laws is in doubt, because the deductive model of explanation is in doubt, and because the conceptual connection between explanatory models and the living, historical practice of scientific inquiry is unclear. This, of course, is precisely what is associated with the difficulties unearthed by such investigators as Kuhn, Lakatos, and Feyerabend. We simply do not have a suitable model of the rationality of science, though we do have some clues.

The second aspect relates to the implications of the 'holist' view of epistemology and the thesis of the underdetermination of theory, advanced by Willard Quine and Mary Hesse, among others. 'Holism' involves 'the claim that theoretical sentences (within either natural language or more formal theories) have their meaning and their evidence only as parts of a theory' (Roth 1987: 7).[6] One implication of holism is that theoretical statements cannot be sharply distinguished from observational statements. Theories consist of mutually supporting and inseparable networks of theoretical and observational statements. '[T]here is no theoretical fact or lawlike relation whose truth or falsity can be determined in isolation from the rest of the network' (Hesse 1980: 86). 'Any statement can be held true come what may, if we make drastic enough adjustments elsewhere in the system . . . Conversely, by the same token, no statement is immune to revision' (Quine 1953: 43). Truth is therefore relative to the theory (Roth 1987: 46).

The thesis of the underdetermination of theories holds that 'there are in principle always an indefinite number of theories that fit the observed facts more or less adequately' (Hesse 1980: viii). Therefore, given an actual situation where two theories are equally adequate to the facts, resort to the facts cannot determine the correctness of one theory over another (especially since what will count as facts are partially determined within each theory). In combination, underdetermination and holism can be read to support Winch's views about the nature of rationality (cf. Roth 1987: Chapter 9). Indeed, in a manner reminiscent of Winch's (1964: 318) claim that rationality is relative to forms of life as developed in actual use, Quine argued that the norms of science change as the practice of science changes, and that there are no extra-scientific constraints on scientific methodology—the practice of science itself is the final determinant (though Quine differs from Winch in concluding that natural science is the final determinant of truth in empirical matters and can be applied to evaluate other beliefs) (see Roth 1987: 32).

[6] Roth's (1987) book provides an excellent introduction to the implications of Quine's work for the philosophy of the social sciences.

Holism (in one variation or another) and the thesis of the underdetermination of theories are adhered to by many of the leading philosophers of today.[7] These ideas have led to what I earlier called 'antifoundationalist' philososophy—the view that there is no way to get outside of theories as such (no unmediated access to the world), no Archimedan standpoint from which to evaluate theories, and no way to ground knowledge in any foundation more solid than the theory which gave rise to it. Much of the discussion in the philosophy of social sciences today revolves around a struggle to deal with the relativistic implications of this position.

One reaction was to declare the 'epistemological unity of humankind', the thesis that (for various reasons, usually related to human nature and the capacity to survive and function in a hostile world) primitives and moderns share the same basic notion of rationality and perceive the world in more or less the same way, so there is no problem with rendering judgements (see Roth 1987: 130–51). An often cited postion is Donald Davidson's 'Charity Principle', which leads to basically the same outcome, though in less strong terms. Davidson argued that if beliefs and actions are to be intelligible (for the participants as well as the scientific observer), they must be largely correct (by the participants' standards as well as the observer's)—'interpretation is possible at all only on the background of shared and largely true beliefs' (Roth 1987: 134). 'Charity is forced on us; whether we like it or not, if we want to understand others, we must count them right in most matters' (Davidson 1984: 197). Consequently, the more error the scientist finds in the participant's actions and beliefs, the more likely it is that the scientist's understanding is incorrect (Root 1993: 175–6). Davidson's Charity Principle in effect softens the gulf between alternative forms of life, or at least suggests that there is always some common ground to be found between forms of life upon which evaluative judgement can be based (see Davidson 1984: 183–98).

There is, of course, *much* more to the philosophical issues so expediently related above, including conditions, qualifications, refinements, and competing views of the matter. But that is sufficient background for our purposes. In the preceding discussion two different implications

---

[7] For a list of holists see Bohman (1991: 251 n. 30, 31). Among other luminaries, Bohman lists Richard Rorty, Charles Taylor, Hans Georg Gadamer, Jacques Derrida, Hubert Dreyfus, Stanley Fish, John Searle, Donald Davidson, Jurgen Habermas, Clifford Geertz and Alasdair MacIntyre, though he points out that there are different versions of holism ('strong' and 'weak'), and that these theorists draw different conclusions from holism.

where drawn from the internal/external distinction, the first *methodological* and the second *epistemological*. The methodological component relates to the contrasting strategies applied by positivists and interpretivists to the study of social life, the latter taking the position that the internal understanding of participants must be taken into account, and the former focusing on external patterns of action. Epistemological issues arise when the scientist moves beyond description to evaluate the beliefs or knowledge by standards external to that form of life.

Finally, I will identify the moral overtones to the internal/external distinction with regard to both methodological and epistemological aspects. As is familiar to all anthropologists, the epistemological aspect has moral implications for the reason that it insists upon respect for the integrity of different ways of being and thinking. The methodological aspect has moral implications because it insists that social science must not abolish the thinking subject. Positivistic social sciences regularly characterize human subjects as deluded or 'judgmental dopes' (see Bohman 1991: 76–7), or as mere pattern carriers whose very existence and actions are in the service of perpetuating the social system. Besides the spectre of determinism raised by these characterizations, people become mere things, and things (especially deluded things) lack moral standing. Taking seriously the internal view restores this moral standing.

Some theorists would assert, as Richard Rorty (1983: 169–70; see also 1979: 349) has, that this moral component is *the* central reason for considering the internal view: the 'need to look for *internal* explanations of people or cultures or texts takes civility as a methodological strategy. But civility is not a method, it is simply a virtue . . . [the contrast] seems to me a contrast between fellow feeling and moralizing condescension—between treating men as moral equals and as moral inferiors' (emphasis in original).

The 'Strong Programme' of the Sociology of Science

The sociology of knowledge involves the assertion that knowledge and modes of thought cannot be understood without taking into account their social origin. In a classic example of this kind of analysis, Marx argued that the ideational superstructure of society masks or distorts reality, leading to false consciousness among the economically oppressed for the benefit of the elite. 'Particular ideologies, then, are held to be not only distortions of reality, but *socially induced* distortions, arising from the class interest of the proponents and victims of the ideological beliefs' (Hesse 1980: 30, emphasis in original). Karl Mannheim, the 'father' of the sociology of knowledge, extended Marx's partial theory of ideology to a total theory of ideology: 'all beliefs about man and society are induced by social context, and have social functions' (p. 30).

But this extension to all beliefs was problematic:

For if *all* beliefs distort, how can there be *true* beliefs about the real, and in particular how do we know there is a 'real' to be distinguished from the distortion? This reflexive argument certainly hits Mannheim's own theory, for this is quite clearly a social theory of the same kind as it refers to, and must therefore itself be socially induced according to its own principles (p. 31).

To avoid this self-refutation, Mannheim suggested that 'the intelligensia is a disinterested class whose beliefs are minimally distorted' (p. 31). Moreover, Mannheim specifically exempted mathematics and the natural sciences from his vision of total ideology. In these areas true knowledge could be distinguished from false belief because the natural world and its characteristics are unchanging and universal. 'Valid knowledge about such objective phenomena, he maintains, can be obtained only by detached, impartial observation, by reliance on sense data and by accurate measurement' (Mulkay 1979: 11).

The 'strong programme' of the sociology of science is a school of thought which extends the sociology of knowledge to the areas previously excluded by Mannheim.[8] According to the strong programme, all knowledge, including that produced by math and the natural sciences, has underlying social causes. Strong programmers distinguish internal *reasons* from external social *causes*, and assign determinative efficacy to the latter. 'Internal reasons' are the rational-teleological explanations given by scientists themselves for their discoveries and beliefs, reasons that focus on logical analysis, testing, fitting the evidence, coherence, simplicity, and other commonly cited norms for science; 'external causes' are social factors like class interests or professional interests. The strong programme postulates that external (social) factors are the causes of true as well as false beliefs in science; whereas the standard view of the matter is that scientific rationality is the source of true beliefs.

Proponents present the strong programme in strongly positivist

---

[8] The leading works in the strong programme are Barnes (1974); Bloor (1976). A collection of articles written by followers and critics of the strong programme can be found in Brown (1984).

terms, insisting that they provide explanations of beliefs through causal laws (Bloor 1976: 4–5; Bohman 1991: 40). Similar to most positivist accounts which attempt to formulate causal laws for human behaviour, the strong programme discounts the explanations given by the scientists for their own actions, substituting external causes for these internal reasons. The key to their argument is the way in which strong programmers—citing Kuhn, Feyerabend, and Wittgenstein—justify discounting the participants' explanations: by arguing from indeterminacy. Holism implies one kind of indeterminacy—which suggests that the question of when contrary evidence will disconfirm a theory—as opposed to result in an internal adjustment of theoretical statements—is not determined by the theory or the facts; underdetermination of theories implies another kind of indeterminacy—that objective reality cannot be used to select between empirically equivalent competing theories. Thus, the strong programme concludes, social interests must be the decisive factor.

Opponents have argued that neither kind of indeterminacy gets the strong programme very far. Holism is a philosophical doctrine that specifies the nature of theories as such, at the highest level of generality, but it does not specify how in a given instance the choice between making an adjustment in the theory or discarding the theory is determined. Kuhn's study of normal science and paradigm revolution suggests that the ultimate pressure for an overthrow of accepted theory comes from internal considerations.[9] '[A]lthough [Kuhn] eschews the project of attempting to specify just when a given paradigm is going to be overwhelmed by anomalies, he nonetheless perceives the motivation for change as arising within the context of the testing of a theory against experience and in the face of competitors' (Roth 1987: 178).

Similarly, the underdetermination of theory argument is an *in principle* argument, that is, in principle there are an indefinite number of theories that could fit the facts just as adequately. While there may have been historical instances where the available competing theories fit the facts equally well,[10] that does not of itself indicate that social influences (as opposed to adherence to internal norms like a preference for sim-

[9] As Kuhn (1977: 119) put it: 'The problems on which such specialists work are no longer presented by the external society but by an internal challenge to increase the scope and precision of the fit between existing theory and nature . . . In short, compared with other professional and creative pursuits, the practitioners of a mature science are effectively insulated from the cultural milieu in which they live their extraprofessional lives.'

[10] Quine (1975) has indicated that it is an open question whether there have been actual instances of two logically incompatible but empirically equivalent theories.

plicity) were the determinative factor in a given instance of theory choice (see Laudan 1984: 68–70); and anyway in most cases competing theories do not fit the facts equally well, especially with regard to the more mature sciences.

The strong programme has one more version of indeterminacy to fall back on—the indeterminacy of the scientific norms themselves. Strong programmers cite Wittgenstein to argue that adherence to norms (or rules) cannot explain behaviour. Wittgenstein (1958: 81) held: 'no course of action could be determined by a rule, because every course of action can be made out to accord with the rule.' 'For this reason, every rule and every explanation is, in the end, grounded in routine, habit and custom' (Bloor 1984: 305). What people *do* determines what the norm means, which implies that the norms are unavoidably open to change brought on by a new course of action that (in effect) alters the meaning of the rule. David Bloor, a leading strong programmer, uses this action-based theory of meaning ('meaning is created by use, not by meaning' (p. 309)) to argue that internal factors *are* external (p. 303). According to this analysis, the content of scientific norms, including theoretical coherence, logical consistency and satisfying the evidence, are themselves determined by social convention, and are therefore social.

However, since *all meaning* is conventionally determined in the sense conveyed by Wittengenstein, to claim that scientific norms are social in this sense is true but trivial; strong programmers are claiming much more—that specific social interests, like those of the elite or the scientific profession, are served by and determine the nature of scientific knowledge. To establish this thesis, adherents of the strong programme must show that the (social) conventions of science are in turn themselves determined by external (non-scientific) social interests.

The above objections to the strong programme emphasize the point that one cannot argue from a demonstration of indeterminacy alone to the conclusion that social influences are the causal factors. First, the causal mechanism must be specified to show how the social influences are translated into the specific theories selected or generated (Bohman 1991: 43). Strong programmers have acknowledged that establishing causal links are essential to their case, and that this has been problematic: '[t]here is simply not, at the present time, any explicit, objective set of rules or procedures by which the influence of concealed social interest upon thought and belief can be established' (Barnes 1977: 34–5). Furthermore, because they argue from indeterminacy, and indeterminacy is ubiquitous, strong programmers cannot evade the sting of their own argument. They 'are unable to determine, on their own principles [holism and underdetermination], if the coincidences noted are a function of the interests of those under study or of those doing the study' (Roth 1987: 208).

Some theorists have tried to defuse the entire debate by denying that the internal/external distinction can be drawn intelligibly. According to Ian Jarvie (1984: 170–1), the institution of science includes:

> science lessons in school, people in white coats in laboratories, shelves of books and journals in libraries, conferences like the AAAS, historical traditions of endeavor, the invisible college, university departments and degrees, Nobel prizewinners, expert witnesses in court, medical researchers, and so on . . . To even conceive of this highly abstract social institution as having an inside and outside strikes me as ludicrous.

Jarvie's position, shared by many, is that scientific knowledge is developed through the influence of both scientific norms and social interests. Hesse (1980: 52) offered a weak interpretation of the strong programme: 'The strong thesis as I have explicated it requires only that all aspects of social structure, including its cultural manifestations in ideas, beliefs, religions, art forms and knowledge, constitute interlocking systems of causation.' Sometimes social interests are the primary causal factor; sometimes it is the influence of local rational rules. 'Every historical case has to be examined on its individual merits' (p. 52). And Hesse also identified a characteristic special to the natural sciences which explains it progress over time: 'the pragmatic criterion of predictive success' (p. 190). The natural sciences are based upon the gathering of instrumental knowledge which makes correct prediction a necessity. As these predictions accumulate, the pragmatic criterion effectively filters out value judgements.

To conclude this discussion I will show how the strong programmer's use of the internal/external distinction relates to the usage urged by Winch. In short, although they rely upon the same basic internal(actor's understandings)/external(disregard actor's understandings) distinction, and they both draw upon holism and Wittgenstein's views about rule following and meaning, the strong programme directly violates the spirit of Winch's approach.

Winch's advocacy of taking into account the internal dimension of social action led to the epistemological point of respect for the internal coherence of forms of life. Davidson's Charity Principle suggests that for such forms of life to be intelligible, the knowledge and beliefs of participants must be largely correct, and the greater the proportion of error the scientist attributes to actors the more likely it is that the scientist's understanding is wrong. In contrast, the strong programme accepts the internal/external distinction for the purposes of identifying the internal beliefs, but then procedes to discount almost entirely these beliefs. The strong programme thus transgresses the Charity Principle. Or as social theorist Stephen Turner (1981: 141) put it, their 'interpretations [of the internal view] are remarkably uncharitable'.

Despite their lack of charity, nothing prohibits the argument of the strong programmers; whether or not they are correct is an empirical question. The epistemological issues raised earlier regarding the propriety of rendering judgements on alternative forms of life do not even arise in this context. Strong programmers are avowedly scientists applying the scientific method to science itself. Thus at all times they are pressing a critique of science through the application of norms internal to science.

The Notion of a Practice

Although the internal/external distinction has been extensively elaborated upon in social science, and increasingly so in law, neither discussion has sufficiently focused on what, specifically, the distinction hinges upon. For Winch it hinged upon a form of life. Jarvie assumed it hinged upon institutions. It may also hinge upon interpretive communities. Or it may hinge upon any given social situation, like a trial, or social event, like the Convention at which the US Constitution was drafted. All that is required to invoke the distinction is the presence of meaningfully oriented social actors who can be understood and analysed in terms of some discrete group or whole.

Herein I will develop the distinction in relation to the notion of a practice, which will help make sense of many references to the internal/external distinction in legal discussions. There are several variations of the notion of a practice. I will build upon and reformulate the versions articulated by Alasdair MacIntyre and Stanley Fish, then provide a detailed development of the notion through application to two examples: the practice of judging and the practice of legal theory in the US legal tradition.

A. Practices, Institutions, and Interpretive Communities

Alasdair MacIntyre (1984: 187–8) defined a practice as follows:

By a 'practice' I am going to mean any coherent and complex form of socially established cooperative human activity through which goods internal to that form of activity are realized in the course of trying to achieve those standards of excellence which are appropriate to, and partially definitive of, that form of activity, with the result that human powers to achieve excellence, and human conceptions of the ends and goods involved, are systematically extended. Tic-tac-toe is not an example of a practice in this sense, nor is throwing a football with skill; but the game of football is, and so is chess. Bricklaying is not a practice; architecture is. Planting turnips is not a practice; farming is. So are the enquiries of physics, chemistry and biology, and so is the work of the historian, and so are painting and music . . . Thus the range of practices is wide: arts, sciences, games, politics in the Aristotelian sense, the making and sustaining of families, all fall under the concept.

MacIntyre's definition shows the variable nature of practices, large and small, general and specific, trivial and momentous, and it shows that practices can be nested within other practices and can overlap with other practices. It also shows the difficulty of pinning down precisely what a practice is beyond the broad statement that it involves a coherent form of socially established co-operative activity which has its own standards of excellence. What that actually means can best be filled in by examples; nor need we agree with his examples. Considering the care, skill, and knowledge which bricklayers bring to their task, it is not obvious why bricklaying is not a practice. Furthermore, MacIntyre's examples and his references to excellence should not give the impression that practices are limited to positively oriented social endeavors, at least not in my construction of the notion. Professional drug-dealing or terrorism (both of which involve complex and coherent forms of socially established co-operative activities) involve practices, each with their own internal standards of excellence and goods, perverse as these might seem from a societal standpoint.

MacIntyre (p. 194) further clarifies that, '[p]ractices must not be confused with institutions. Chess, physics and medicine are practices; chess clubs, laboratories, universities and hospitals are institutions.' He is quick to add, however, that practices cannot survive for long without institutions—'institutions and practices characteristically form a single causal order . . .' (p. 194). MacIntyre thus counters Jarvie's dismissal of the internal/external distinction. Jarvie's view was premised upon characterizing the distinction as connected to science as an 'institution'. Institutions, however, are distinct from practices. Judging is a practice; the court is an institution. Doing legal theory is a practice; the philosophy department or law school is an institution. Practising law is a practice; the legal system is a collection of institutions. Institutions often provide the support structure within which practices take place, but the two are nonetheless distinct.

MacIntyre (p. 190) also describes the process by which a person is initiated into a practice:

A practice involves standards of excellence and obedience to rules as well as the achievement of goods. To enter into a practice is to accept the authority of those standards and the inadequacy of my own performance as judged by them. It is to subject my own attitudes, choices, preferences and tastes to the standards which currently and partially define the practice. Practices of course . . . have a history: games, sciences and arts all have histories. Thus the standards are not themselves immune from criticism, but nonetheless we cannot be initiated into a practice without accepting the authority of the best standards realized so far.

MacIntyre's description evokes the image that to become a participant in a practice involves giving oneself over to that practice. Interpretive theorist Stanley Fish (1989) used even stronger terms in relation to practices generally, and specifically in relation to law:

. . . you will always be guided by the rules or rules of thumb that are the content of any settled practice, by the assumed definitions, distinctions, criteria of evidence, measures of adequacy, and such, which not only define the practice but structure the understanding of the agent who thinks of himself as a 'competent member.' The agent cannot distance himself from these rules, because it is only within them that he can think about alternative courses of action or, indeed, think at all (p. 323).

. . . to think within a practice is to have one's very perception and sense of possible and appropriate action issue 'naturally'—without further reflection—from one's position as a deeply situated agent (pp. 386–7).

. . . the initiated student who has thoroughly internalized the distinctions, categories, and notions of relevance and irrelevance that comprise 'thinking like a lawyer,' cannot see anything *but* the practice (nor can he remember what it was like to not see it) and along with it, because it is inseparable from the practice, he sees the set of principles of whose unfolding the practice is the story (pp. 364).

By Fish's description a participant in a practice virtually becomes a living embodiment of that practice.

But MacIntyre's and Fish's descriptions raise a serious question that neither adequately answers. Both theorists see practices in overly monolithic terms, as if they were internally homogeneous, unified, and coherent in pursuit of the common enterprise of which the practice consists. To be a participant in that practice one must conform to the norms of that practice (MacIntyre), or even have the norms of that practice colonize your mind (Fish). The question is this: how do practices change? Since both theorists emphasize that practices have histories, they must change.

In an essay dedicated to the question of change in relation to practices and interpretive communities—concepts which he fails to distinguish sharply—Fish (pp. 152–3) faces it head on:

. . . there would not seem to be enough room . . . to make change a possibility. In the preceding pages this impasse has been negotiated by a demonstration that neither interpretive communities nor the minds of community members are stable and fixed, but are, rather, moving projects—engines of change—whose work is at the same time assimilative and self-transforming. The conclusion, therefore, is that change is not a problem; . . .

The answer to the question 'what can cause change?' is 'anything'[.]

Fish's answer, in the final analysis, appears to be that it is in the nature of practices to change, so they do. While there is truth in this answer, there is more to say.

The fuller answer has to do with the non-uniform nature of practices and their participants, and the relation of practices to their environment. While practices are based upon a shared set of organizing rules and standards, nonetheless they are internally heterogeneous. Some practices are more internally coherent than others, but all practices contain norms that potentially conflict or lean in differing directions. Participants in the practice of chess or football, for example, will share many of the norms internal to the practice yet differ on such matters as to whether conservativeness or risk-taking (alternative norms available within the practice) is the best way to succeed. More complex and general practices, like the practice of judging, are even more internally heterogeneous. The practice of judging contains norms oriented toward the application of rules but also norms oriented toward doing justice, demands which sometimes clash. Beyond the minimum necessary to constitute a practice as such, there is no reason to postulate or assume that the entire body of norms contained within that practice are internally consistent. To believe in such unity and coherence is an analytical imposition upon an otherwise unruly reality, in much the same way anthropologists in the past projected tightly knit, unchanging sameness onto primitive societies.

The other source of change is the heterogeneity of the participants themselves. At least in highly differentiated societies, every individual participates in more than one practice and is a member of more than one interpretive community. People do not enter practices *tabula rasa*. The influence of other practices and interpretive communities shape the manner in which participants take up aspects of the practice at hand, leading them to adopt certain interpretations of norms over others (within the range allowed by the indeterminacy of rules). That is why two lawyers engaged in the practice of law can sincerely understand the selfsame legal norm differently.

In short, practices can change because no practice is perfectly homogeneous or internally consistent, either in its body of norms (and their range of interpretations) or in the pool of participants. Added to these internal factors are the influences exerted on a practice by its environment, especially its relationship to the institution that supports the practice and to other closely connected or interacting practices. Given this more nuanced picture of the nature of practices, which softens the overly unified and conformist characterizations of MacIntyre and Fish, change is no longer a mystery.

The final aspect to be clarified is the relationship between interpretive communities and practices. These two notions are distinct and must be understood as such. Interpretive communities are groups of people bound together by socially generated and shared clusters of *meaning*—complexes of ideas, beliefs, knowledge, symbols—what I have called intersubjective meaning systems. In law, this is the *legal meaning system* that all persons trained in law (lawyers, judges, legal academics) partake in when thinking about or doing law. A practice as such is not limited to the realm of meaning—it involves an *activity*, it involves doing, which contains aspects of both meaning and behaviour. Similar to the close relationship between practices and institutions, practices are accompanied, supported, indeed constituted by the meaning system of an interpretive community. Like practices, interpretive communities are internally heterogenous and members pick up and internalize different internal clusters of meaning, though all members share a baseline of knowledge and beliefs and basic facility with the language or terminology which characterizes a given interpretive community. Finally, a cautionary note: while it is possible to analytically separate the dimension of activity from that of meaning, in reality the two are inseverable, since the meaning is what informs the activity, and the activity can be understood only by attending to the meaning.

B. The Practices of Judging and Legal Theory

Many of the above points can best be understood through legal examples. The practice of judging is separate from a legal institution. However, one cannot participate in judging unless one holds the position of judge within a legal institution. Thus the nature of a given practice of judging is strongly influenced by the legal institution to which it is connected, because the nature of judging is shaped by the mix of people who actually participate in that practice; the legal system determines (according to its own criteria) who gets to participate, and it specifies their institutional roles.

Doing legal theory is a practice separate from judging—the former is usually connected with academic institutions and the latter with legal institutions—and their internal norms are quite distinct, but the two are often closely related and exert reciprocal influence. That is because many influential participants in one practice have been participants in the other (like Benjamin Cardozo and Oliver Wendell Holmes), and because the Anglo-American practice of legal theory takes judging to be a central concern. This close interaction is made possible by the fact that, although judging and doing legal theory involve separate practices, both of these practices are informed by the broader interpretive community that consists of all those trained in law. They substantially share the same baseline of ideas, beliefs, and general knowledge about law, much of which was inculcated in the course of legal education and through their participation in their various types of practices.

While there has been an essential continuity to the historical practice of judging in the US legal tradition, it is widely recognized that the nature of this practice has gone through several fundamental changes over the last two hundred years, in response to surrounding social pressures and in response to changing theories about law and the judicial role—which in turn were influenced by changes in the practice of judging itself—thus forming a circle of mutually influencing factors. In general terms, the practice of judging has gone from the grand style to the classical formalist style, to an uncertain mix of rule and policy considerations.[11] Because all practices change in piecemeal fashion—altering

---

[11] For an essay on the different styles of judging see Mensch (1990).

only one part, holding the rest more or less constant—with different aspects changed or held constant over time—the original form of a practice may well be quite unlike the selfsame continuous practice two hundred years later. It is, nonetheless, the same historical practice.

Continuing with the example of legal theory helps illustrate two further aspects of practices: practices can be nested within other practices at higher levels of generality; and the best way to distinguish among practices and to locate the levels at which they exist is to identify the set of shared norms that constitute the practice.

Reflecting the close relations between the practice of judging and the practice of legal theory, the Legal Realists had a major influence on the aforementioned shift in the practice of judging from the formalist style to the current mix of rule and policy consideration by demonstrating the indeterminacy of legal categories, rules, and principles, which in turn exposed the reality that judges were constantly faced with choices in the interpretation of law (see Singer 1988). From our standpoint today, it is obvious that the Legal Realists were involved in the practice of legal theory; but the same point can be established by attending to the then prevailing norms about what it meant to be doing legal theory, including, *inter alia*, thematizing law itself, conducting doctrinal analysis, exhibiting rigourous reasoning, publishing in legal journals according to the highest standards of the day, and engaging in polemical discussions with their theory-oriented opponents. To a significant extent the Realists altered the theoretical discussion by using arguments which did not previously exist and were not previously recognized as valid or relevant, but this change was effectuated only by adhering to most of the norms that defined the practice while challenging certain others. Otherwise their work would never have been recognized as a part of the same theoretical conversation about law, and would not have succeeded to the extent that it did.

Nested within the practice of legal theory, the Realists formed their own sub-practice—as defined by the loosely associated cluster of norms, beliefs, attitudes, and strategies that allow us (as well as the Realists themselves) to see Legal Realism as a discrete complex of common endeavor. This example demonstrates that more inclusive practices—practices at higher levels of generality—require less in the way of shared norms defining that practice, and thus are more internally heterogenous than lower level practices. Theoretical practices in particular are often highly heterogeneous, because they are held together by the very general normative requirements that they be 'theoretical' and concern the same subject matter (broadly defined, and always changing), neither of which imposes any restrictions about conformity to any particular view about the subject itself. Indeed just the opposite is true—theoretical practices thrive upon disagreement about the subject. Moreover, because theoretical practices in particular have a well developed capacity to be reflexive—to thematize themselves—they have a built in openness to change.

Now I will briefly apply the above distinctions to the situation today. The current practice of legal theory is one and the same historical practice described above. Within this general practice, a number of discrete sub-practices exist, including the critical practice, the liberal practice, the economic practice, the feminist practice, the critical race practice, the natural law practice, and the socio-legal practice.[12] Although each of these sub-practices are internally heterogenous, they are nonetheless defined by the shared norms, attitudes, and strategies that make them what they are, and set them apart from the other sub-practices. The fact that these sub-practices exist on the same level of generality (all nested within the practice of legal theory) can be demonstrated through a comparative analysis—along with adhering to the general requirements of being 'theoretical' in relation to the subject 'law', each of them offers prescriptive as well as descriptive claims about law, about the relationship between law and society, and about legal theory. Regardless of the very different look each of these sub-practices presents, they are all participating in the same practice: legal theory.

For some time the basic tool used to analyse law has been the institution. Now there are additional concepts—practices, and interpretive communities and their shared meaning systems—which help open up new dimensions and draw different lines. Practices add an *activity* related dimension that cuts across the institution at many different levels. Operating within legal institutions are many practices: judging, policing, legislating, lawyering, and nested sub-practices, like prosecuting, defending, tax practice, insurance practice, corporate practice, legal aid practice, appellate judging, trial judging, and so forth. Each has its own complex of norms and standards that define a given practice, although nested sub-practices also share a substantial body of norms and standards with parallel level sub-practices and the higher level practice which encompasses them. There are also practices uncon-

---

[12] I should emphasize that one can participate in more than one sub-practice, and one can participate in the practice of legal theory without being a participant in any particular sub-practice.

nected to legal institutions—like doing legal theory and teaching law (usually connected to academic institutions)—that influence the practices attached to legal institutions.

Interpretive communities and their shared meaning systems add a *meaning* related dimension that rises above institutions as well as practices. Judges, lawyers, legal theorists, law professors, retired legal practitioners, law students near graduation, all those who have undergone the scholastic indoctrination necessary to obtain a grasp of legal language and basic knowledge and beliefs about law—and thereby gain access to legal discourse—are members of the interpetive community of a given legal tradition (or the 'intersubjective legal community'), regardless of what practice they participate in or whether or not they are connected to a legal institution. And while practices require a shared meaning system to function, institutions do not. People occupying different positions in an institution or complex of institutions need not be members of the same interpretive community, as evidenced by the fact that police have an important role in the overall complex of the legal system but most are not members of the intersubjective legal community.

Despite their close and overlapping connections, institutions, practices and interpretive communities are distinct and must be understood as such for analytical purposes.

The Structure of the Internal/External Distinction

The structure of the internal/external distinction consists of two fundamental elements: *observed* and *observer*. While social action can be studied by social scientists in a variety of ways and from many angles, when an investigator specifically intends to examine the internal view of an activity, the methodological starting point is to identify the practice that activity embodies—that practice becomes the observed. Taking an internal view of the practice means viewing that activity in consideration of the understandings of the participants involved (interpretivism); taking an external view means ignoring these understandings and instead focusing on the patterns of behaviour reflected in the activity (positivism).

In contrast to the observed element, in the scientific discussion of the internal/external distinction there is virtually no mention of the status of the *observer*. The observer is presumed to be a scientist, because the subject of the discussion is how social science should be conducted, and the unstated assumption is that science necessarily entails a scientist in the position of observer. One must, after all, have substantial training and specialized knowledge to qualify as a truly scientific observer. Furthermore, one of the most cherished norms of science—impartiality—has the effect of automatically disqualifying participants. Scientists assume that a participant in a practice cannot be impartial—to participate is to be biased. Although scientists have begun to emphasize participant observation, rather than recognizing true participants as observers, 'participant observation' invariably means that the *scientific* observers should see things 'as if' they were participants, a kind of pseudo-participation. This denial of observer status to actual participants helps preserve the authority of scientists vis-à-vis participants.

There are indications that this failure of science to accord true observer status to actual participants will change (see Root 1993: 239–49). Increasing attention to the understandings of participants, combined with recognition of the value-laden nature of the social sciences and growing skepticism about their knowledge claims, generate pressure in this direction. Law, however, is already there. Many of the most influential observers about law have been participants. To accommodate the legal context, the observer element must be further subdivided into *participant observer* and *non-participant observer*. The line which separates the two is solely based upon experience. A participant observer has at some time participated in the practice observed; a non-participant observer has not participated in the practice observed.

The core of what actual participation means is obvious—either the observer has done it, or not. But the distinction is not always clear cut. To use a familiar legal example, Justice Cardozo's book *The Nature of the Judical Process* (1921) is the product of a participant observer. He was a judge who reflected upon and wrote about the nature of judging. Ronald Dworkin's *Law's Empire* (1986) and Duncan Kennedy's 'Freedom and Constraint in Adjudication: A Critical Phenomenology' (1986), to the extent that they offer observations about judging, are the products of non-participant observers. Dworkin and Kennedy have never been judges. Their experience as judicial law clerks gave them intimate access to judging, and allowed them to experience aspects of it, but they have not been true participants.

Other difficult questions arise. The questions, how much participation is enough? (when the person feels 'comfortable' in the practice, is able to engage in it 'without thinking'), and does participation long ago still qualify one as a participant? (yes, if the practice has not substantially changed), and similar questions at the borders, must be determined in each context. But the general distinction is evident.

Distinguishing participant observers from non-participant observers has the effect of creating a second internal/external distinction, one regularly made in the legal discussion but mostly ignored in the scientific discussion. Recall that the focus of the scientific discussion involved taking an internal or external view of the *observed*. This second distinction specifies whether the *observer* is someone internal or external to the practice observed. By this analysis, there is an inseverable tie between observer and observed. In each case it is necessary to identify what is being observed *before* the status of the observer can be specified.

In summary, the two basic elements at issue—observer and observed—each have their own variation of the internal/external divide. For the observed element, one can take an internal view of the practice or an external view of the practice; for the observer element, there are participant observers (internal) and non-participant observers (external). Legal and socio-legal scholars have mixed and matched these various senses of the internal and external without recognition that different analytical categories are involved.

There are four possible combinations, as follows, filled in with examples related to the practice of judging:

Practice of Judging

	Observer	
Observed	*Participant Observer* (Internal)	*Non-Participant Observer* (External)
As Meaningful Subject (Internal)	Internal/Internal Cardozo's *Judicial Process*	External/Internal Dworkin's *Law's Empire*
As Object— Patterns Only (External)	Internal/External	External/External Donald Black's *The Behavior of Law*

I have already mentioned the examples in the top row. For an example of the External/External category, I have listed Donald Black's *The Behavior of Law*. Therein he strictly applies the behaviouristic view to the legal system (the above reference is limited to those aspects of the book that refer to judging); that is, he focuses solely on the patterns of activities of legal actors and postulates causal laws based upon these patterns. No examples are provided for the Internal/External box because it is unusual—not impossible—for participants in an activity to observe that activity externally, though Judge Richard Posner's (1990a) inconsistently behaviouristic view of judging arguably qualifies.

The final point which must be emphasized is that the above box relates exclusively to *observing*, and has nothing to do with actually *doing* or *participating* in a practice. That is because the internal/external distinction arose in the context of a scientific discussion over how to study social practices, not about actually participating. The distinction between observing and participating tends to get lost in the legal discussion because many legal observers have been participants, and because of the close relationship between the cluster of practices that make up law, especially judging and theorizing about law. For example, when writing *The Nature of the Judicial Process*, Cardozo was making observations about judging (not engaging in judging) and he was doing legal theory (the practice engaged in). In relation to reflexive practices like theorizing, it is possible for a work to make observations about a practice while at the same time participating in that practice, but as a general matter observing and doing are distinct orientations with different intentional objects, though the transition between the two is easily accomplished—each time a person pauses to reflect upon their own activities.

The Internal/External Distinction in the Legal Context

A. Hart's Internal View of Social Rules

Hart's introduction to law of the internal view of social rules has, almost in the same breath, been praised as a major contribution to jurisprudence, and criticized as confused and inadequate. To set up the distinction, Hart (1961: 86–7) wrote:

The following contrast again in terms of the 'internal' and 'external' aspect of rules may serve to mark what gives this distinction its great importance for the understanding not only of law but of the structure of any society. When a social group has certain rules of conduct, this fact affords an opportunity for many closely related yet different kinds of assertions; *for it is possible to be concerned with the rules, either merely as an observer who does not himself accept them, or as a member of the group which accepts and uses them as guides to conduct.* We may call these respectively, the 'external' and the 'internal' points of view. Statements made from the external point of view may themselves be of different kinds. For the observer may, without accepting the rules himself, assert that the group accepts the rules, and thus may from outside refer to the way in which they are concerned with them from the internal point of view. But whatever the rules are, whether they are those of games, like chess or cricket, or moral or legal rules, we can if we choose occupy the position of an observer who does not even refer in this way to the internal point of view of the group. Such an observer is content merely to record the regularities of observable behavior in which conformity with the rules partly consists and those further regularities, in the form of the hostile reaction, reproofs, or punishments, with which deviations from the rules are met . . .

Hart's two crucial (and flawed) observations came in the italicized sentences: first, in identifying external with non-acceptance, and internal with acceptance; and secondly, in associating external with observer, and internal with participant. Hart ended up with the external view representing that of non-participant observers who do not accept, and the internal view representing that of participants who do accept.

Hart then went on to distinguish two different external stances: 1) that of observers who do not themselves accept the rules, but recognize and take into account that the participants themselves do; and 2) that of an observer who completely ignores the internal views of the participants, like behaviouristically-oriented scientists, and just records their patterns of action. This latter perspective was Hart's intended target, which he equated with Austin's argument that the existence of rules could be determined through habits of obedience to commands. As I indicated in the preceding Chapter, Hart felt that a focus on habit alone obscured the normative aspect of rules, which could only be recognized through the internal view.

Hart recognized that there was a problem with his identification of the internal view with acceptance. As he admits on the following page (p. 88), there are participants in a practice who can function quite well without entirely 'accepting' the norms of that practice. Instead of taking this possibility as a cue to disassociate internal from acceptance and external from non-acceptance, Hart makes matters worse by declaring that this non-accepting internal view 'very nearly reproduces' the external view.

Hart's analysis led Joseph Raz (1979: 154) to conclude that, '[i]nternal statments are thus full-blooded normative statements. Making internal statements is thus a sign of endorsement of the rules concerned.'

Raz (p. 155) argues that Hart's internal/external distinction tends 'to obscure from sight the existence of a *third category* of statements'. This third category, according to Raz (p. 156), consists of participants (like lawyers and legal scholars) who 'can use normative language without thereby endorsing the law's moral authority'. Neil MacCormick (1981: 39) also argued that there are '*three* distinct points of view, not a simple internal/external dichotomy' (emphasis in original). But MacCormick's third view was not the same as the third view suggested by Raz. MacCormick labelled his third view the 'hermeneutic' perspective. According to MacCormick, the hermeneutic perspective is that of the external observer who recognizes that the participants themselves accept the rules, without the observer himself or herself accepting or endorsing the rules.

Raz and MacCormick thus both argue that there is a third perspective to add to Hart's internal/external distinction, though each identifies a *different* third perspective: Raz focused on uncommited participants, whereas MacCormick focused on uncommited observers. As indicated above, Hart actually mentions both possibilities. Thus it is not surprising that Hart (1983: 14) later concurred with both critiques, though he (implicitly) merged the two into a single third perspective:

In terms of Raz's distinction, already mentioned, such statements of legal obligation or duties are 'detached,' whereas the same statements made by those who accept the relevant rule are 'committed.' Of course those who make such 'detached' statements must understand the point of view of one who accepts the rule, and so their point of view might well be called 'hermeneutic.' Such detached statements constitute a third kind of statement to add to the two (internal and external statements) which I distinguish. To have made all this clear I should have emphasized that as well as the distinction between mere regularities of behavior and rule-governed behavior we need a distinction between the acceptance of rules and the recognition of acceptance by others.

And that is the state of matters today. We have an internal category and an external category, in some uncertain relation to a third category representing committed versus detached. Besides being confusing, the inadequacy of this solution can be demonstrated by raising yet another possibility. An observer may describe the internal norm oriented action of participants and 1) withhold any judgement about the norms themselves (detached); 2) endorse or accept these norms (committed); or 3) criticize these norms (critical). The flaw in their respective analyses is they failed to keep separate the two different, observer-observed senses of internal/external, and they mixed up observing with doing.

The Internal/External Distinction 181

I will now entirely reconstruct the distinction, drawing upon the earlier discussion of Winch (who was the original source cited by Hart). Assume that the practice at issue is judging, and that the observer is a legal sociologist, or a legal theorist like Hart. Neither the sociologist nor Hart is a judge, so their position is that of non-participant observers—persons outside the practice making observations about the practice. As a *methodological* matter, they each have two perfectly legitimate alternatives. They can apply the *internal* view to take into account the understandings of judges and the complex of rules and meaning that constitutes the practice of judging; or they can instead just observe the patterns of actions judges engage in—for example, matching statistics on sentencing to the social background of the judge or the race of the defendants—and draw conclusions about these patterns, thereby taking an *external* view. This, in a nutshell, is the internal/external distinction in the sense developed in the social sciences.

Note that I have said absolutely nothing about the alternative possibilities of the observer being committed, detached, or critical of the judge's understanding. These alternatives have nothing to do with the methodological aspects of the internal/external distinction. Rather they are *evaluative* questions which arise after the internal view has been *described*. These are the questions which led to the epistemological debate I mentioned earlier. Winch argued that we need not and should not render any evaluative judgement, that we should remain detached. And that is the stance Hart (1961: v) assumes when he describes his work as 'descriptive sociology'. But this is a matter for the observer to decide, as a function of the interests and concerns of the observer, entirely separate from the methodological decision.

Everything I have just said also applies to a participant observer, like Judge Cardozo. Although he articulated an internal view of judging in *The Nature of the Judicial Process*, Cardozo could have viewed judging in an external way. Moreover, Cardozo could have stopped after the description of the internal view and not rendered any judgement on the practice of judging. Or he could have gone on to endorse it, be critical of it, provide prescriptions for it, or do a mix of all three, as he did.

That is all there is to the internal/external distinction. However, a final issue must be addressed. A great deal of confusion in the discussion was caused by the fact that Hart, Raz, and MacCormick kept mixing in observations about what the participants were *doing*, not just about how to *observe* the participants doing what they were doing. They were sent on this wrong track by Hart's initial assertion that an internal statement is from one who accepts the rule. Yes, many participants accept the rules that infuse their practices, but the range of possible attitudes of participants toward a rule or complex of rules runs from detached, to committed, critical, contemplative, instrumental, manipulative, playful, distant, to being so deeply in the rule that it is not even thought about but routinely done, and more. Which attitude is held depends upon the social action at issue—a particular instance of judging or context of social behaviour—and the particular complex of norms involved. By defining the internal perspective in terms of acceptance, Hart in effect stipulated the answer to what can only be determined through case-by-case inquiry. When borrowing from Winch, Hart carried over the overly rule-bound view of social action for which Winch has been soundly criticized.

To function as a judge, the judge certainly must internalize (and therefore accept, though not necessarily consciously) a great deal of the norms applicable to the practice of judging. Many of these norms are trivial (like referring to oneself in the third person object form—'the Court finds that . . .'), though most are not (like norms related to fairness, the proper judicial temperament, following the law, the style of writing judicial decisions, judicial ethics, and so forth). A judge can be cynical about some of these norms—and flout them or follow them while laughing on the inside—and a judge can have no opinion about them, or even embrace them, or have any one of many possible attitudes toward them, but most often judges don't even think about them, they just do them. A judge can thematize some of these norms and question them, but to be recognizably functioning as a judge—to engage in the practice of judging (to be doing)—the judge will have to adhere to most of these norms, and will do so naturally without thinking about it. That is what participating in a practice means. None of this, however, specifies the attitude a judge must have toward any subset of these norms at any given time. Nor does it rule out the possibility of an entirely corrupt or disheartened judiciary which functions quite effectively even though the majority of judges take a detached or critical view towards the rules they apply.

All of these observations apply full force to primary and secondary rules, which on this level are just a subset of norms contributing to shaping the practice of judging, though prominent ones to be sure. The interpretive view opens up a whole realm of norms operative in the practice of judging that Hart left out. Many of the norms which define the practice of judging are not secondary rules (rules about primary rules), nor primary rules (rules about social behaviour), but are rules relating to how judges behave when judging. Moreover, aspects of the practice of judging go beyond norms or rules (or at least are not easily characterized as such), like attitudes or dispositions or the situational logic involved in decision-making.

The practice of judging forms the behaviour-based, norm-laden meaning context within which judges do judging. Attending to that in its entirety is what taking the internal view means. The notion of a practice, because it consists of both specifically legal norms (primary and secondary rules) as well as of social norms and psychological factors that influence the interpretation and application of legal norms, is an analytical construct within which the interests of legal theory and socio-legal studies converge.

B. Dworkin's Internal/External View of Legal Theory

In his recent Postscript to *The Concept of Law*, completed just prior to his death, Hart (1994: 239–44) took pains to defend his approach against what he saw as Dworkin's 'imperialistic' view of legal theory. In *Law's Empire* (1986) and elsewhere, 'Dworkin appears to rule out general and descriptive legal theory as misguided or at best useless' (Hart 1994: 242). Significantly, both theorists assert that legal theory must take account of the internal view. Hart says it is essential to describe the internal view, but insists he need not go further. Dworkin argues that legal theory is an evaluative interpretive project which cannot stop at description. Moreover, when Dworkin says 'evaluative', what he actually means is positive rationalization—legal theory should make law the best that it can be.

As Hart (ibid.) notes, it is 'hard to follow Dworkin's precise reasons for rejecting descriptive legal theory . . .' His reasoning, set out in the introductory Chapter to *Law's Empire*, appears to be as follows: 1) the practice of law is a normative activity based upon sense (meaning); 2) this practice can be studied externally or internally; 3) external legal theories have not been useful for the participants; 4) so legal theory must be internal; and 5) taking the internal view means making the law the best it can be (see Dworkin 1986: 13–14;1987: 9–20).

The earlier elaboration of the notion of a practice established that legal theory is a practice at a high level of generality with a great deal of internal heterogeneity. Within the practice of legal theory today there are many different varieties (sub-practices), including the critical approach, the economic approach, the socio-legal approach, and Dworkin's liberal approach, among others.

Dworkin's point, therefore, cannot be that these competitors are not a part of legal theory. His argument must be the more limited one that these other legal theories are not helpful to the practice of judging, and legal theory should provide that service. Dworkin's view represents what is called a 'perfectionist' approach to theory, which takes an openly value-committed stance toward the subject at hand. But perfectionist approaches can be critical or rationalizing (or a combination of both) in relation to the practice at issue. Which stance one adopts depends upon one's values and the nature of the legal system involved. Without this freedom, legal theory would be beholden to the legal system even if it were evil. Many critical scholars, for example, are sincerely trying to make law better, and believe that doing so requires total critique. Practices develop positively in relation to criticism as well as rationalization. There is no way to declare in advance that rationalization is the most useful or best for the practice, because only the passage of time, only the historical development of the practice of judging, can determine what shape the practice takes and what has been the most influential factor in leading to that state.

Perhaps Dworkin was led to his 'imperialism' by his belief that *law is a practice*. He (1986: 90) asserts that 'no firm line divides jurisprudence from adjudication or any other aspect of legal practice.' According to the analysis herein, there is a clear dividing line between jurisprudence (legal theory) and adjudication (judging)—they are different practices attached to different institutions with different internal norms and standards of excellence.[13] The more fundamental point is that there is no such practice as 'legal practice as a whole' (Dworkin 1986: 90) within which adjudication and legal theory are situated.

The practice of law as I have used the term is what lawyers (practitioners) do, their activites, and the norms and standards they follow in pursuit thereof (norms and standards regarding good and bad lawyering which are to be found in the actual practice of law, not in the provisions of the Codes of Professional Responsibility). Judges, lawyers, and legal theorists in a given legal tradition are all members of the same overar-

---

[13] It might be said that every time a judge decides a difficult case that judge is theorizing about law, and thus in a sense doing legal theory. That would misapprehend what is involved in the practice of legal theory, which is a specific practice that goes beyond just thinking about law in a theoretical way. The practices of judging and legal theory I have elaborated herein do not have a monopoly on 'judging' and 'theorizing about law', which occur in a multitude of contexts across a wide variety of practices.

ching intersubjective legal community with its shared legal meaning system (which enables them to communicate and see law in more or less the same way), but they nevertheless participate in different practices. These practices can be viewed as a cluster, and can be added together with other practices like policing and legislating (whose participants need not be members of the intersubjective legal community) to be viewed as the cluster of practices associated with a given society's legal system. But these practices added together do not amount to an overarching practice called 'legal practice' for the reason that there is no single practice—defined as a socially established coherent activity with its own standards of excellence—which encompasses all these divergent practices.

Unlike science as a whole, which arguably consists of a coherent set of broadly stated standards, like the pursuit of knowledge and attention to the facts, the many practices that cluster around law cannot be joined under any single set of defining norms or standards of excellence. The most plausible candidate in law is the dated theoretical view that law involves subjecting society to the governance of rules. That defines law from a societal standpoint, and perhaps describes a norm common to the practices of judging, legislating, prosecuting, and policing, but it is not a norm or standard which characterizes either legal practice generally (lawyering involves a strategically-oriented instrumental view of rules) or the practice of legal theory (which takes a multitude of views toward rules and the legal system).

Dworkin has made another extraordinary assertion based upon the internal/external distinction. Legal theorist Michael Moore (1989: 953) summarized it as follows:

Thus Dworkin tells us that each interpretive practice must be judged internally by its own standards of validity, objectivity, independence from convention, and even truth, meaning and reality. For Dworkin, it is impossible to judge the propositions central to any interpretive practice by the (external) standards of science. Rather, we should 'proceed more empirically' by ascertaining what counts as a good reason within each such enterprise and judge the objectivity of the practice accordingly.

Dworkin in effect claims that law as a practice is unto itself, insulated from the application of externally generated standards. Setting aside the objection that this is an extremely dangerous position (as Moore argues), and ignoring my objection that there is no overarching 'law practice' as such, I will limit the response to demonstrating that Dworkin's claim is not supported by the philosophical doctrines surrounding the internal/external distinction.

Winch argued that the standards taken from one *form of life* should not be drawn upon to evaluate another form of life, and the examples he used were that the knowledge produced by our science should not be used to judge the beliefs of primitive societies, historical societies, or religion. Two characteristics should be noted about these examples. First, they refer to all encompassing cultures or cosmologies, not to individual practices within these cosmologies. Secondly, these cosmologies were at a great distance from modern science, so great that there were few apparent commonalities upon which evaluative judgement could be based.

Even if we grant the first point that law comprises a total cosmology in the same way that science or religion or the culture of a primitive society does (which seems highly contestible), the second point is patently inapplicable. Science and law in modern society are very close, with many shared beliefs, knowledge, and standards of rationality. Both science and law understand and apply inductive, deductive, and analogical reasoning in much the same way, as well as attention to the evidence, the attitude of impartiality, what truth means, and much more. Law has many of its own tradition-based peculiarities (like legal fictions), as does science. But they have so much in common—because both are grounded in our culture, *our form of life*—that there is absolutely no problem with rendering evaluative judgements on the law from the perspective of science—the standards are substantially the same. Dworkin is correct that to truly understand law one should examine the activities of legal actors from the internal view (methodology), but he is wrong to raise any epistemological barriers to a critical evaluation of this view.

Finally, I will question Dworkin's (1986: 14) central methodological assertion:

This book takes up the internal, participants' point of view; it tries to grasp the argumentative character of our legal practice by joining the practice and struggling with the issues of soundness and truth participants face. We will study formal legal argument from the judge's viewpoint, not because only judges are important or because we understand everything about them by noticing what they say, but because judicial argument about claims of law is a useful paradigm for exploring the central, propositional aspect of legal practice.

That is how Dworkin characterized his exercise at the beginning of the book.

Consistent with the internal approach set out in this book, what one would expect to follow is a detailed anthropological or sociological account of the practice of judging in the eyes of judges, or at least references to such accounts. What instead follows are a series of theoretical arguments against his polemical opponents, then equally abstract arguments that 'integrity' should be the overarching guide for adjudication. Only after this is there any discussion about the practice of judging, but this discussion is mostly in relation to an imaginary superhuman judge (Hercules) who proceeds to reason using the abstractly derived suggestions Dworkin produced about how judging *should* be practised. And on the penultimate page of the book that is precisely how Dworkin (p. 412) characterizes what he has accomplished: 'I described the nested interpretive questions a judge should put to himself and also the answers I now believe he should give to the more abstract and basic of these.'

There is nothing wrong with Dworkin's project of offering suggestions to judges about how they should engage in judging. But that is not what is meant by taking the internal view, at least not as developed in the social sciences. Dworkin passed over the investigation and description of the practice, which forms the core of the internal view, and went straight to prescription.[14] Calling his Herculean account of judging the internal view of actual participants is therefore misleading.[15] The actual practice of judging is much more complicated and mundane than Dworkin's suggestion that judges make the law 'the best that it can be'. It involves a mix, among other factors, of trying to be fair, do the right thing, follow the law, satisfy the parties before them, look good among colleagues, act judicially, move the cases along, and not make any serious or obvious mistakes, all in the context of the case at hand. A legal theory built upon this reality would be interesting indeed.

Dworkin laid claim to the internal view mostly to legitimate his account. This claim allowed him to assume the mantle of spokesman for the practice of judging without first demonstrating what that practice actually entails. The normative complex that shapes the practice of judging cannot be derived by any idealizing technique. It must be shown through a detailed interpretive and behavioural investigation of the practice itself, as I will undertake in the final two Chapters.

[14] Dworkin may respond that I am raising the old 'is' versus 'ought' distinction, which cannot be maintained in the face of holism. He is correct as a philosophical matter, but this does not blunt the fact that there is a real difference in our common usage and understanding between saying what judges do, and saying what they should do.
[15] Perhaps this also explains why Judge Harry Edwards (1992: 47), who complained that most legal theory is divorced from reality, declared that 'Dworkinian scholarship . . . has little direct utility for practitioners, judges, administrators, or legislators.'

C. CLS as Interpretivists On the Outside

CLS scholars have made a great deal of the internal/external distinction, though in a highly questionable way. They are vehemently against scientific positivism; and have endorsed the basic tenets of interpretivism, especially the view that social reality is socially constructed through ideas and beliefs, and therefore these ideas and beliefs—the internal view—must be taken seriously (see Trubek 1984; Gordon 1990). At the same time, critical scholars have constructed their identity on the claim that they study law from the 'outside'.

This claim is not offered lightly. David Trubeck (1984: 615) explicitly associated the CLS outside view with that of empirical legal science: 'Both groups look at law from the outside, as it were, questioning its own self-understanding.' He wrote (p. 589):

> While Critical legal scholars take doctrine seriously, they also think they are examining the social role of law. The Critical scholars clearly believe that when they conduct a critique of legal thought, they are not doing doctrinal research, but rather are looking at law from the outside and tracing relationships between law and social action.

The difficulty critical scholars face in making this claim of looking 'from the outside' and 'not doing doctrinal research' is that, as Trubek (p. 588) admits, 'much of the writing produced by CLS focuses on the ideas in legal doctrine or legal scholarship.'

Beyond their repeated insistence that it is so, it is difficult to find a clear articulation of precisely why or how it is that CLS is on the 'outside'. Again Trubek (pp. 588–9):

> Unlike the judges and scholars whose work they study, those who *critique* legal thought do not try to determine, for example, the appropriate rules for wildcat strikes or whether it is necessary to prove discriminatory intent as a condition of liability under antidiscrimination laws. Rather, the Critical scholars seek to expose the assumptions that underlie judicial and scholarly resolution of such issues, to question the presuppositions about law and society of those whose intellectual product is being analyzed, and to examine the subtle effects these products have in shaping legal and social consciousness (emphasis in original).

The bulk of law review articles are aimed at assisting practitioners and judges to understand and deal with particular social problems or legal regimes, concerns which do not occupy critical scholars. Many of these practice-oriented articles include a dose of critical analysis and end with constructive suggestions. Critique, at least to some extent, is an expected aspect of legal scholarship. Moreover, other schools of legal theory, including law and economics, as Richard Posner's (1990a) highly sceptical jurisprudence text reflects, are as critical of the law and legal understandings as CLS. Thus the fact of criticism itself does not set CLS apart in any way. The most that can be said is that CLS articles are different in precisely the same way that all theory-oriented articles differ from practice-oriented articles.

In the end the basis for the distinction appears to be in the last sentence in the above quote, regarding their focus on legal consciousness: they are on the outside because, 'CLS reads doctrine as ideology, thus distancing itself from mainstream scholarship' (p. 619). CLS adherents assert that their almost exclusively doctrinal analysis is 'non-doctrinal' because their objective is to get beneath the doctrine itself, to reveal its ideological source in external social interests. As Robert Gordon (1990: 419) put it, '[t]he [legal meaning] systems, of course, have been built by elites who have thought that they had some stake in rationalizing their dominant power positions, so they have tended to define rights in such a way as to reinforce existing hierarchies of wealth and privilege' (see also Trubek 1984: 606). This claim is similar to that made by the strong programme of the sociology of science; indeed, in many respects the strong programme stands in relation to science as CLS does to law, despite the fact that the former are avowed positivists and the latter avowed interpretivists. The difference is that the strong programmers were social scientists who focused on producing case studies to demonstrate the existence of the connections between scientific knowledge and the social interests which purportedly shaped them, and they have explicitly acknowledged that this complex connection is exceedingly difficult to uncover and has yet to be conclusively established. In contrast, CLS has produced few such studies,[16] which cannot be conducted through exclusively doctrinal analysis. Doctrinal analysis can

---

[16] One outstanding exception to this is the work of Morton Horwitz. His detailed historical analysis is combined with doctrinal analysis in an integrated and powerful way, although like the strong programmers the most he has been able to establish are interesting parallels. More important, the progression of his work suggests that CLS may have given up its strong association of legal rules with ideology. His first major work, *Transformation of American Law 1780-1860* (1977) is a straight Marxist analysis that links the development of the content of law to class interests in society. In contrast, his recently published second volume (1992) is a much more nuanced account, which speculates on the influence of all sorts of factors, from social to psychological, and draws fewer links between the content of the law and external interests. While this second account is much more persuasive than the first, the cost of this persuasiveness is, it seems, giving up the claim that law is ideology.

demonstrate indeterminacy and contradiction, but only by going outside the texts can they demonstrate causation.

What CLS scholars are doing is legal theory from a left to radical-left critical standpoint, just one of many sub-practices currently nested within the general practice of legal theory. Neither their critical stance nor the objectives and beliefs which motivate this stance places them on the 'outside' in any way. The claim to being on the outside is a rhetorical feint, a stylized way of declaring an oppositional stance which situates them apart and above, while placing everyone else inside. The imagery of 'outside' is powerful: you can hold the observed, see the whole of it inside and out, get behind it, subject it to your penetrating gaze. False consciousness arguments often work from the claim to being on the 'outside', because that move licenses a wholesale dismissal of the knowledge and beliefs of those being examined.

This conclusion raises doubts about another assertion made by CLS scholars, that they are interpretivists who take the internal view seriously. By their own account, 'Critical studies research seeks to discover the false but legitimating world views hidden in complex bodies of rules and doctrines and in legal consciousness in general' (Trubek 1984: 579). Again, the close parallel between CLS and the strong programme is evident. Like the strong programme, CLS claims to take the internal view seriously, but mostly for the purpose of asserting that much of it represents false consciousness. Not only does this violate the spirit of the interpretive approach—which is to strive to *understand* the internal view—it runs afoul of the Charity Principle. This does not necessarily imply that CLS is wrong, only that we have reason to be suspicious of *their* understanding. Perhaps CLS is wrong about the facts of the matter, or perhaps the internal view is much more realistic than they portray. Ironically, despite their hostility to positivism and declared allegience to interpretivism, CLS scholars discount a body of shared beliefs held by a group in precisely the morally condescending way positivists (like the strong programmers) have traditionally done in the past. This does not mean the internal view cannot be criticized; only that there must first be a sincere effort at understanding.

Critical scholars simultaneously assert an odd combination of positions: they hold to the interpretive view that ideas and beliefs construct social reality, yet insist that entire swaths of prevailing ideas and beliefs about law are false, which means that at least *these* ideas and beliefs are not in fact constructing social reality. Interpretive tenets do not easily co-exist with claims about wholesale false consciousness (which imply positivist notions of truth). The CLS joinder of these two indicates that a deeply problematic internal tension exists in the theoretical underpinnings of CLS. This tension is the same one I revealed in Chapters Two and Three in relation to their belief that deep down, beneath ideas and beliefs, there is some bedrock truth to which critical scholars have access.

D. Legal Sociology on the Outside; Not Socio-Legal Theory

Roger Cotterrell (1983: 242) described the sociological position:

The numerous approaches to legal analysis which can be categorized sociological in the broadest sense are unified only by their deliberate self-distancing from the professional viewpoint of the lawyer. It is implicit in the aim of *empirical legal theory* that law is always viewed 'from the outside,' from the perspective of an observer of legal institutions, doctrine and behavior, rather than that of a participant, although participants' perspectives may be taken into account as data for the observer. Indeed from a phenomenological standpoint the interpretation of participants' perceptions may be of primary importance. Yet that interpretation becomes possible only through a scientific distancing as determined and thoroughgoing as the empathy which the observer (or better, encounterer) may seek with the observed (or encountered). Sociological analysis of law has as its sole unifying objective the attempt to remedy the assumed inadequacy of lawyers' doctrinal analysis of law (emphasis in original).

Cotterrell's description is presented in classic interpretive science form, up until the last sentence. His final sentence openly defines the legal scientific community in terms of an empirical and political precommitment: to demonstrate and remedy the assumed inadequacy of lawyer's doctrinal analysis of law.

Cotterrell means 'inadequacy' in two senses. The first sense is the uncontroversial assertion that there is much more to know about law and its relation to society than can be found in legal doctrine alone; the second sense is that legal doctrine itself is not what it purports to be and that legal actors are deluded or have a mistaken understanding of the nature of their own activities. This second sense is close to the stance assumed by critical scholars,[17] though as I indicated earlier it is also a relatively common attitude taken by social scientists generally toward

---

[17] Among a number of examples, the work of critical socio-legal theorist Alan Hunt epitomizes this close connection. Hunt (1987) writes, 'Internal theories exhibit a predisposition to adopt the self-description of judges or lawyers as primary empirical material; their stated views on what they do and why they do it are treated as direct evidence about the nature of legal practices. There is thus a naive acceptance of leal ideology as reality.'

their object (or subjects) of study. Once again, this is not in the spirit of the internal approach or the Charity Principle. Identical to CLS, it appears that legal sociologists often claim to take the internal view mostly for the purpose of discounting it.

However, closer examination renders questionable whether most social scientists who study law are even capable of taking the internal view. Anthropologists would scoff at the suggestion that a scientist could take the internal view of a culture without first learning the language of that culture; but few legal anthropologists and sociologists have made the effort to learn legal language or how that language is used to construct law. CLS scholars can take the internal view because they have access to this internal understanding and indeed participate in shaping it through their involvement in legal discourse, which is also why they are not outsiders. Most legal sociologists and anthropologists are non-participant observers looking at law from within their own scientific practice, truly 'outside' law in the way CLS is not. But also for this reason, in the absence of attempts to learn the legal language and how it works, the claim of taking the inside view rings hollow, as if it were a perfunctory nod to current scientific views about the proper methodology which is then all but ignored. Perhaps that explains why there are few sociological or anthropological accounts of how judges and lawyers understand their own activities.

Cotterrell's formulation is instructive in another way. Contained within it is the implication that participants themselves cannot be observers, at least not scientific ones. That is the thrust of his twice repeated reference to the necessity for 'scientific distancing', language which in a single swoop discounts the view of participants (not objective because not enough distance) and boosts the authority of the scientific observer (more objective because distant). Distance is especially important when you believe the subjects you study are suffering from delusion, for that is the only way to escape the delusion (see Hunt 1987).

As I illustrated with the table on the practice of judging, a fully complemented set of observers would include participant observers, non-participant observers taking the internal view (interpretive scientist), and non-participant observers taking the external view (positivist scientist). For a long time science allowed only the last alternative; the middle alternative has recently gained popularity; if interpretivism takes itself seriously, there will be greater recognition of the value of the first alternative. An understanding of the nature of social life requires attention to all three. Social scientists have yet to come to grips with one of the more threatening implications of interpretivism: there is 'no a priori ground for the superiority of a sociological over a 'lay' interpretation' (Bauman 1989: 51).

The final revealing aspect of Cotterrell's description is that, while it is a correct characterization of the external nature of most work in legal sociology, *what he says does not apply to himself*, nor to most of the body of works that fall under the label socio-legal theory. Unlike most legal sociologists who actually engage in empirical studies, Cotterrell is trained in law and his work is largely theoretical.[18] He takes the information produced by sociologists and anthropologists and applies that within the theoretical discussion of law. Cotterrell—along with many other legally trained academics (often teaching in law schools) who identify themselves as socio-legal scholars—does socio-legal theory, and this is a practice nested within legal theory generally.

It's not just that socio-legal theory satisfies all the norms for participating in the practice of legal theory—publishing in the same journals, talking about the same subjects, engaging in polemical debates with other legal theorists. The practice of legal theory itself has changed to now include discussions of and resort to sociological material; consider, for example, the work of Hart, Dworkin, and CLS. This change in the practice of legal theory is partly due to the success of the Realists. And it is also a credit to the last twenty or so years of CLS and socio-legal studies. But the broader reason is that theory itself, as a general practice in many fields, has become increasingly 'sociological' due to the pervasive influence of interpretivism and anti-foundationalism, as reflected in the fact that academic 'Philosophy' appears to be gradually metamorphosing into 'Social Theory'. There are still works in legal theory that do not include resort to sociological insights, but they are diminishing, and this is only a reflection of the internal heterogeneity of the practice of legal theory anyway.

Cotterrell is standing on the cusp of a sea-change in the nature of the practice of legal theory, claiming to be outside when that practice has already expanded to encompass him. Cotterrell is thus very much an 'insider' despite his claim to 'outsider' status. That makes him a

---

[18] There are socio-legal scholars who do both sociological studies and write about the application of these studies to legal theory. That is just a reflection of the fact that people can and often do participate in more than one practice. But that does not erase the distinction. The practice of the empirical study of legal phenomenon consists of a quite different set of norms than the practice of applying these studies to legal theory.

highly qualified participant observer who resorts to sociological arguments to lend insight into legal arguments, but he is in no way an externally situated scientist observing legal theory from a distance (though he is an outsider to the practice of law, and to the practice of judging),[19] as he repeatedly claims, and the same holds true for socio-legal scholars generally.

The broader point is that theoretical practices in particular, because of their self-reflective capacity, have a relentless ability to absorb whatever begins as external to the practice when first introduced. Nothing can confine a practice to its original borders; which explains the futility of attempts to begin theoretical discussions by parsing and distinguishing among, for example, legal philosophy, legal theory, and jurisprudence, as if these practices stood still. Consistent with the trend in other theoretical disciplines, a large part of legal theory today consists of socio-legal theory.

The objective of this Chapter goes beyond just providing criteria by which to evaluate internal/external claims. Increasing references to the internal/external distinction are part of a broader change in the way we see and talk about social reality. Interpretive analysis and the logic of holism inexorably lead to the internal/external distinction because they link all meaning and knowledge to social groups. Being inside or outside a group used to be seen mostly as a matter of one's identity; now it is the very grounds from which one generates and assesses knowledge.

Keeping up with this change will require a new set of orienting concepts. Seeing activities in terms of discrete practices allows us to draw an analytical border around them in a way that helps us study them internally as well as observe their interrelations with their environment. The notion of a practice is an essential concept for a realistic approach because it joins behaviour (activity) with interpretation (the meaning which informs that activity). Practices are, to be sure, just another abstraction, heuristic device, and way of organizing the subject for the purposes of analysis and observation. There are limits to the application of this notion and it contains a number of weaknesses, but it nevertheless is a useful analytical tool, as I will show. In the next Chapter

---

[19] It might be argued in Cotterrell's defence that he has claimed only to be outside legal practice, not outside legal theory. However, in his text, *The Politics of Jurisprudence* (1989), Cotterrell explicitly claims that he is on the outside, applying sociology to legal theory itself. The problem with this claim is that his thought-provoking book is indistinguishable from most works in legal theory today.

I will elaborate on what behaviourist and interpretive studies, and judges have said about the nature of judicial decision-making. In the final Chapter I will draw upon this information to present an account of the practice of judging, then address issues in legal theory that relate to judging.

7 Studies of Judicial Decision-Making

Rule Following Behaviour and the Indeterminacy of Rules

The indeterminacy of rules, a subject which has arisen in several different contexts in this book, is a puzzling phenomenon within legal theory as well as within the social sciences. Although norms or rules are thought to determine and serve as guides for action, studies have shown that often they are sources of rationalization for action, regularly adhered to yet also subject to manipulation and departed from when necessary or convenient. Thus rules which were to serve as the explanation of behaviour appear so indeterminate that an explanation of the rules is called for, regarding their nature, how it is we determine what they mean, and why and under what circumstances they are followed or not followed. Through the influence of the behaviour-oriented views of the pragmatists as well as Wittgenstein, lately there has been a return to behaviour to explain the rules themselves.

Wittgenstein (1958) put it thus:

> 198. 'But how can a rule shew me what I have to do at this point? Whatever I do is, on some interpretation, in accord with the rule.'—That is not what we ought to say, but rather: any interpretation still hangs in the air along with what it interprets, and cannot give it any support. Interpretations by themselves do not determine meaning.
>
> 'Then can whatever I do be brought into accord with the rule?'—Let me ask this: what has the expression of a rule—say a sign-post—got to do with my actions? What sort of connection is there here?—Well, perhaps this one: I have been trained to react to this sign in a particular way, and now I do so react to it.
>
> But that is only to give a causal connexion; to tell how it has come about that we now go by the sign-post; not what this going-by-the sign really consists in. On the contrary; I have further indicated that a person goes by a sign-post only in so far as there exists a regular use of sign-posts, a custom (p. 80).
>
> 201. This was our paradox: no course of action could be determined by a rule, because every course of action can be made out to accord with the rule. The answer was: if everything can be made out to accord with the rule, then it can also be made out to conflict with it. And so there would be neither accord nor conflict here.
>
> It can be seen that there is a misunderstanding here from the mere fact that in the course of our agreement we give one interpretation after another; as if

each one contented us at least for a moment, until we thought of yet another standing behind it. What this shews is that there is a way of grasping a rule which is *not* an *interpretation*, but which is exhibited in what we call 'obeying a rule' and 'going against it' in actual cases.

Hence there is an inclination to say: every action according to the rule is an interpretation. But we ought to restrict the term 'interpretation' to the substitution of one expression of the rule for another (p. 81).

202. And hence also 'obeying a rule' is a practice. And to *think* one is obeying a rule is not to obey a rule (p. 81).

217. 'How am I able to obey a rule?'—if this is not a question about causes, it is about the justification for my following the rule in the way I do.

· If I have exhausted the justifications I have reached bedrock, and my spade is turned. Then I am inclined to say: This is simply what I do' (p. 85).

219. . . . When I obey a rule, I do not choose.
I obey the rule *blindly* (p. 85).

Following a rule, according to Wittgenstein, is basically a matter of unthinking doing. The distinction he draws between this doing and interpretation opens up a space between two things we sometimes conflate: following the rule, and formulating the rule (or interpreting the rule, which is the same as coming up with a formulation). One is a matter of doing, the other a form of talking—this is the behaviour/talk axis.[1] By talk I mean more than just what people say or write; I mean conscious articulation, regardless of the form (or whether it is made express). This axis has been articulated in various ways in preceding Chapters. What people do is one thing, what they or others say or think they are doing (their meaning or the rules they are supposedly following) is another.

Let us return to the question: why do people do what they do when engaged in following rules? The answer—now in unthinking behavioural terms—is routine, usage, habit or custom, primarily inculcated through language learning and socialization. Rule following occurs through regularized behaviour when the rules are often unarticulated or at least not a matter of conscious contemplation by the actors. Articulation or conscious contemplation—the formulation of norm talk—implies a space between behaviour and rules. With articulation comes an entirely different activity—the activity of the formulation of

---

[1] Talk is also a form of behaviour. Here the contrast between behaviour and talk is one which refers to the substantive component of the talk, to its content, to what the talk refers to or means.

and talk about rules (as in legal discourse, or everyday discourse in which we resort to norms to justify our actions). In the context of norm talk, rules are subject to whatever degree of manipulation is conventionally (through habit and custom) allowed within that particular realm of norm talk. This is the space in which the indeterminacy of rules is exploited. The indeterminacy of rules, in other words, is a function of norm talk.

But surely, it must be said, not all rule following is unthinking, even if the vast bulk of it is. We can pause to contemplate an action, and decide upon a course of conduct based upon the normative import of a rule, either because we agree with the content of the rule, or because the fact that it is a rule provides us with an independent reason to comply (regardless of whether we like the course of action dictated) (see Schauer 1991: 112–62). Wittgenstein's observations are not inconsistent with the presence of this reflective moment of choice. The point is, rather, the decision aside, what it means to be 'following the rule' is still a matter of doing (that is, of satisfying the conventional course of action involved in 'following the rule' being contemplated).

Both the question *whether* to follow the rule, and the prior question, *what is the rule?*, involve norm talk, not doing; the separation between these two inquires—'should I follow the rule?' and 'what is the rule?'—is indistinct and dialectical, and often cannot be specified in a given instance of behaviour. Norm talk—the formulation of and contemplation of the norm at issue—can result in behaviour, and indeed in patterns of behaviour. Accounting for this type of rule following requires a reinjection of the thinking subject, a subject who does various kinds of operations within the grey border between deciding whether to follow a rule and articulating what that rule is. This is also where rational choice theory or strategic interactionism come into play. The considered social scientific view of the nature of this choice involves a bounded means-end calculus, with the ends particular to the (socially defined) individual, and the means identified through a rational calculation (limited by time, resources, and information constraints) of the best available way to achieve the end desired.

A bifurcated picture of rule-following is thus presented. Routinely followed rules, of language as well as behaviour, are generally the product of inarticulate habit or custom, behaviour just being carried on. Articulated or consciously thematized rules, however, are subject to explicit consideration and capable of manipulation. In the latter context social patterns of behaviour may arise as a result of the normative import of the rule (assuming others also abide by it), and/or as a by-product of the means-ends calculation. Social patterns of behaviour emerge from individual purposeful decisions because norms are shared and ends are often shared (since they are socially informed), and people often act under shared constraining conditions, which when combined lead to similar decision outcomes and hence similar behaviour.

Though the focus on indeterminacy in legal theory differs from that in social science, the same elements are involved. The Realists, who brought attention to bear on the indeterminacy in law, were concerned with law as an articulated body of rules—thus focusing on the second aspect related above, norm talk—and their primary concern was to refute a specific belief that prevailed about this body of rules: that they could mechanistically, without the interposition of choice, lead to definite outcomes. Once the indeterminacy of rules was demonstrated, it became clear that judges must often make choices when they interpret and apply the law. And the burning issue which threatened the legitimacy of the law itself was: what informs these judicial choices? If the answer is the personal values of the judges, then the claim that we are ruled by law, not by the person who happens to be the judge, is false.

So effective were the Realists that few legal theorists, judges or lawyers in the United States today deny that choice arises in the interpretation and application of law or that this choice is to some extent influenced by the values of the judge. Now the question is whether the amount of choice made available by the indeterminacy of law is so great, and whether the influence of personal values so strong, that what judges do is not distinct from politics in any meaningful sense.

CLS theorist Mark Tushnet (1991: 1538) described the current views on indeterminacy among legal theorists:

The point may be made by imagining that we have developed a measure of the determinacy of a set of legal rules, the 'determinile.' A completely determinate legal system would measure 100 determiniles, while a completely indeterminate one would measure zero. Cls adherents at present defend the position that the proper measure of legal systems is probably between five and fifteen; that is, no system is completely indeterminate, but the level of determinacy is relatively low. Mainstream legal theorists at present defend the position that the proper measure of a well-functioning legal system like that of the United States is somewhere between forty and sixty; that is, such systems have a substantial amount of indeterminacy, but not nearly as much as the cls position claims. The positions differ, as is suggested by the existence of a gap between the 'most deteminate' version of the cls position and the 'least determinate' one of the mainstream position. In addition, among cls adherents there is disagreement about the primary reason for the degree of determinacy that there is: power relations associated with gender differences, race differences, and class differences are all candidates of some. Yet at this point we are simply arguing over a mere detail, the question of degree.

Although one may quibble with the representativeness of Tushnet's estimates, most legal theorists do believe there is substantial indeterminacy.

Tushnet is also correct in the general tenor of his observation, to the effect that we have reached an impasse on this issue with no obvious means to discern whether the critical view or the mainstream view is correct. Mainstream legal scholars point to H. L. A. Hart's (1961: 12) observation that many legal rules 'have a central core of undisputed meaning, and in some cases it may be difficult to imagine a dispute as to the meaning of a rule breaking out'. Similarly, scholars like Ken Kress (1989) point to the pervasiveness of easy cases and the high degree of predictability about how cases will be decided. Other scholars, like Owen Fiss (1982), point to the presence of shared 'disciplining rules' which limit the range of plausible and appropriate interpretations. Still others follow Stanley Fish (1989: 138) in arguing that the conventions of the interpretive community of law and of the nature of the practice of judging yield determinate results and therefore fear of indeterminacy is unfounded 'because the necessary constraints are always already in place'. Fish's response refers to the first half of the bifucated view in social science described above, to the mostly unarticulated rules and ways of doing that underlie patterns of behaviour: 'To be . . . "deeply inside" a context [like adjudication] is to be already and always thinking (and perceiving) with and within the norms, standards, definitions, routines, and understood goals that both define and are defined by that context' (p. 127). This is the strong conventionalist view, and Fish's position is in accord with Wittgenstein's on rule-following: judges largely do so through customs and usages, through unthinking doing learned in the course of legal training and practice.

But these responses are not entirely convincing. Hart (1961: 12) made his observation about a core of settled meaning in the context of pointing out that '[i]n most important cases there is always a choice.' Moreover, Hart observed that clarity of the rules is only part of the equation: '[p]articular fact-situations do not await us already marked off from each other, and labeled as instances of a general rule, the application of which is in question; nor can the rule itself step forward to claim its own instances' (p. 123). The prevalence of easy cases and the predictability pointed out by Kress can be explained by extralegal factors, like the fact that the overwhelming majority of judges have been middle aged white males whose elite attitudes and values are what render indeterminate legal rules determinate. Fiss's solution founders on the recognition that even disciplining rules require interpretation and thus are also subject to indeterminacy, which in turn threatens an infinite regress. And Fish's answer is unconvincing because it denies by analytical fiat concerns which are based upon observation and experience. Lawyers know that there is a substantial degree of flexibility in the rules, reflected in the fact that skilled advocates can almost always work up a legal argument, no matter which side of a case they fall on.

Legal theorists, then, are divided among critical scholars, many of whom believe there is rampant indeterminacy in law[2] (say about 90 per cent on the determinile scale), and mainstream scholars, many of whom believe there is substantial but not overwhelming indeterminacy (say 50 per cent or less), and a number who think indeterminacy is not even a concern.

What do judges think? Here are the opinions of several judges on the issue, expressed by Judge Alvin Rubin of the Fifth Circuit US Court of Appeals. I quote extensively to convey the full flavour of Judge Rubin's (1987: 310–12) beliefs:

Fifty-four percent of our decisions are rendered without oral argument.

Every one of the cases we decide without oral argument is, I think, of the kind Justice Cardozo called cases that should not have been appealed, for perhaps 90% of all appealed cases, he said, were destined to be decided one way. Realists and criticalists disregard or discount these cases for the same reason. That is, they are not 'interesting' cases . . .

Such cases are all doctrine-controlled, even if the doctrine involved is only deference to the findings of fact made in the trial court . . .

Let's turn to the forty-five percent of the cases in which we think the outcome is at least debatable. After the case is argued, it is assigned to a judge for an opinion. Every judge has had the experience of attempting to write an opinion in accordance with the tentative vote, and then finding that he could not accept the result. In the craft, we say the 'opinion would not write' . . . We all know what is meant by the phrase. It means that a good lawyer, a good judge,

---

[2] There is disagreement among critical scholars about the degree of nature of the indeterminacy involved, though all agree that it is substantial. For a discussion of the indeterminacy thesis by a critical scholar, see Singer (1984). For a critique of the critical view of indeterminacy, see Solum (1987).

a good law professor—that is to say a craftsman in the law—would on reading the opinion know, as the author has come to realize, that it does not adopt accepted methods of analysis and does not follow accepted rules, but is arbitrary in result or superficial in reasoning. So we reach a result that differs from our initial opinion and personal predelictions because something that we recognize as 'law' (together with its careful exposition) demands it . . .

Let me approach in a somewhat different way the question whether decision-making is pure result-selection followed by rationalization. Judge Harry Edwards was appointed to the District of Columbia Circuit Court after many years as a law teacher. He and I have each thought that, given the varying political backgrounds and philosophies of the judges on his court and those on mine, the number of dissents would indicate whether opinions are but 'stylized rationalizations.' If they are, then judges should differ fairly frequently on either result or rationalization or both.

Judge Edwards found that, despite the widely reported differences in political background and personal philosophy of the judges on his court, ninety-four percent of its cases in the one year he reviewed were decided without a dissent. He looked also at what he called 'mixed' panels consisting of a mixture of judges who would be labeled 'liberal' and those who would be labeled 'conservative.' In less than ten percent of these cases did the judge who was in the political minority file a dissent. Judge Edwards writes that, even in the cases he considered 'very hard' to decide, cases in which each judges's political, social, and moral beliefs inevitably influence the view he takes, most judges feel bound to resolve the case in what he called a 'principled fashion,' that is, with result determined by rule.[3]

Judge Rubin made several points. First, over half of the cases are so clearly controlled by the law that there is no need for a hearing. These are the easy cases that are *positively* determined by legal rules. Secondly, for the remaining cases, although personal predelictions may influence the initial decision, the law (including the requirement that decisions be plausibly justified for a legal audience) at least provides a *negative* check that disallows certain outcomes. Thirdly, over ninety-percent of the appellate cases, including those with panels comprised of judges holding contrasting political views, are unanimous, and the source of this high degree of consensus is agreement over the import of the applicable legal rules. Fourthly, he described the process in terms of being a 'craftsman', which, as I indicated earlier, the pragmatists characterized as intelligently conducted doing (doing within a practice). Finally, neither Judge Rubin nor Judge Edwards denied that the values of the judge had an influence on the decision-making process, though both felt

[3] Rubin cited to Cardozo (1924: 60), and Edwards (1985: 629).

that the law still ultimately controlled. Judge Rubin's views, which appear to be representative of the general view of judges, need not be accepted as correct. As critical scholars and social scientists are given to assert, he may well be deluded about the nature of his own activities, or he may be prevaricating in the interest of preserving the prestige of the judiciary. Judge Rubin is a participant whose views are necessarily suspect from the standpoint of the critical and social scientific communities.

The confounding aspect of this problem is that it is not obvious how to go about proving which view—CLS, mainstream, or judges—is correct. The very exercise of constructing a scale of determinacy and then pegging the level of a given legal system reeks of indefensible conjecture. Discussing indeterminacy in the abstract, in the manner articulated by Tushnet, is surely mistaken. Deconstructionists have demonstrated that any text, including legal rules, no matter how apparently certain, can be rendered indeterminate by challenging the interpretive assumptions we subconsciously apply to that text to stabilize its meaning. The lesson of desconstruction, and of the behaviour-oriented views of meaning and rule-following articulated by the pragmatists and Wittgenstein, must be that the key to understanding indeterminacy is to focus not on the rules themselves but on behaviour in relation to the rules, and on the circumstances under which persons dealing with the rules desire to or have an interest in exploiting the latent indeterminacy contained within rules (and language).

There is an indirect way to determine the extent of indeterminacy in law, one which focuses on the run of cases rather than on the application of rules in an individual case, a way which should help us evaluate whether the CLS view of affairs, or the mainstream and typical judge's view, is more correct. That involves consulting social scientific studies of judicial decision-making.

Social Scientific Studies on Judicial Decision-Making

The bulk of social scientific studies on judicial decision-making have been conducted in behaviourist terms; that is, by identifying patterns of judicial decisions (dependent variables) and trying to locate the sources that led to these decisions (independent variables). 'For instance, social scientists have put a lot of work into discovering the influence that judges' political party affiliation and other personal background characteristics have on decisions' (Glick 1983: 242). A strongly held predisposition dominates the field: 'much social science research assumes that . . . judges are "politicians in black robes" ' (p. 243) (see also Brace and Hall 1993: 916).

Twenty five years ago C. Herman Pritchett (1969: 31), one of the pioneers in the behaviourist study of law, formulated the social scientific view—called 'political jurisprudence'—by way of contrast to the legal view, in the following terms:

> Political jurisprudence, then, asserts that judges are inevitably particiants in the process of public policy formulation; that they do in fact 'make law'; that in making law they are necessarily guided in part by their personal conceptions of justice and public policy; that written law requires interpretation which involves the making of choices; that the rule of *stare decisis* is vulnerable because precedents are typically available to support either side in a controversy.

It is rather ironic that social scientists claim this view to be their own, since Pritchett acknowledged that this view originated in Legal Realism (p. 28–9); and, perhaps with the exception of the word 'typically' in the final clause, it nicely characterizes what is the dominant *legal view* today, and has been for some time.

Judge Rubin made many of the same observations, as have influential legal theorists like H. L. A. Hart, and echoes of it trace back as far as the writings of Oliver Wendell Holmes and Benjamin Cardozo. Here is a more recent assertion, in the straightforward words of Judge Dallin Oaks (1985: 147): '[j]udges also make law. They do so inevitably as they interpret statutes passed by the legislature, since interpretations can never be free from choices illuminated by the creative instinct and motivated by personal preference.' Or consider the observations of Judge Ruggero Aldisert (1985: 259–60):

> Modern jurisprudence, however, recognizes that the judge can, and indeed must, make law as well as apply it . . . Yet there are limits. In 1917 Holmes counseled: 'I recognize without hesitation that judges do and must legislate, but they can do so only interstitially; they are confined from molar to molecular motions.'
>
> Although the precise limits of judicial lawmaking have not been staked out, the power undoubtedly is a broad one. Holmes and his followers propounded the 'interstices' doctrine, but judicial lawmaking has often exceeded interstices. In practice it might appear that the only limitations are those which are 'functional'—such as the inadequacy of facilities for extensive fact gathering, confinement to the facts of record, and the like. Ultimately the test of judge-made law, as with any law, is its effect on social welfare and its acceptance by society.

Although it is not correct to assert that all judges would agree with these statements in their entirety, many more such observations by judges can be presented. As political scientist Joel Grossman (1966: 1551) recognized three decades ago, '[l]egal scholars and social scientists [have] long since disabused themselves of the aesthetically pleasing but inaccurate view of the appellate judge's task as primarily mechanical and syllogistic.'

But there is still an important difference in views between social scientists and judges reflected in the above quotes. Judges continue to assert that there are limits to lawmaking and that the law does control; whereas social scientists who see judges as politicians in black robes believe that politics control even within the limits. Significantly, of late social scientists have begun to move more toward the legal view, as I will relate.

The following exposition will highlight social scientific findings about the influence of judges' values on their decisions in three separate areas: US Supreme Court decision-making, appellate court decision-making (including state supreme courts), and district or trial court decision-making.

A. *Studies of Supreme Court Decision-Making*

Owing to its prominence, an inordinate number of social scientific studies have been conducted on decision-making in the US Supreme Court. In the view of many political scientists, 'the literature has demonstrated conclusively that judicial policy preferences, which are organized so as to constitute well-defined ideologies, are a primary determinant of choices in the Supreme Court' (Brace and Hall 1995: 11). These studies usually identify a collection of background characteristics (conceived of as indicia of attitudes) to group or scale justices in relation to three basic categories: liberal, moderate, and conservative. Their votes in cases are then compared against the ascribed background.

Perhaps the most powerful study was conducted by C. Neal Tate (1981). Tate used four basic categories of background characteristics: 1) upbringing—including region of birth, religion, urban or rural background, and prestige of educational institution attended; 2) career prior to court—including prior judicial experience, work as a prosecutor, elective office, federal government employment; 3) age at employment and length of tenure on the court; and 4) partisanship—including the justice's party affiliation and the judical selection partisanship of the appointing President. He then examined all split decisions between

1946 and 1978 in two categories (totalling 2,327 cases): civil rights and liberties cases (1,452) and economic cases (875). A 'liberal' vote in civil rights and liberties cases was a vote in favour of granting the claimed right, a 'conservative' vote was against. In economic cases, a 'liberal' supported unions over management, government regulation of business, worker claims against employers and small business claims against large corporations; a 'conservative' did the opposite.

The results of this study are striking. There is a significant correlation between votes in these two types of cases, indicating that judges liberal in civil liberties cases also tend to be liberal in economic cases, and likewise for conservatives. Justice Douglas, for example, voted liberal in 94.3 per cent of the civil liberties cases and 82.1 per cent of the economic cases; Justice Rehnquist voted liberal in 4.5 per cent of the civil rights cases and 15.6 per cent liberal in economic cases (p. 357). More important, Tate was able to use the background characteristics of the justices (their degree of liberalness or conservativeness suggested by their backgrounds) to 'explain' 87 per cent of the variance in civil liberties cases and 72 per cent of the variance in economic cases. Consequently, knowing the background of the individual justice tells us that justice's vote (over the run of non-unanimous cases) with a high degree of reliability.

A later study by Jeffery Segal and Albert Cover (1989), which directly tested for the effects of the attitudes of the Justices on their decisions in civil liberties cases from 1953 through 1987,[4] had similar results—overall there was an 80 per cent correlation between the Justices' attitudes and their votes (p. 62).

Before addressing other studies conducted on the Supreme Court, it is worthwhile to consider how these studies match up with the legal view of Supreme Court decision-making. Many a professor of constitutional law will read this with at least a hint of smugness. The political

---

[4] Background studies have been criticized on the grounds that the background variables are too crude. (see Goldman and Sarat 1978: 374). They assume that people with similar socializing experiences will have similar attitudes or values. Attitude studies responded to this objection by using articles about the Jusitices to rank them along an ideological scale.

A different critique of both background and attitudes studies has been pressed by J. Woodford Howard (1968). He has argued that misleading inferences are drawn from counting the raw vote of the justice, because it conceals all kinds of intervening variables (like different reasons for the votes) or intensity of position (see also Brenner and Dorff 1992). Howard highlighted the 'small group dynamics' that led to the decisions, including the pressure of heavy schedules, the influence of law clerks, the presence of negotiation and vote trading, etc.

nature of the Supreme Court is hardly news. Eighty years ago Felix Frankfurter (1916: 683) wrote, '[c]alled upon late in life to teach constitutional law, a great teacher of property law, after a brief trial, gave it up in despair on the ground that constitutional law "was not law at all, but politics." ' More recently, Justice Thurgood Marshall delivered a speech in which he opposed the 'Missouri plan' proposing a value-free, merit-based method of the selection of judges. According to Marshall (1977: 179), endorsing an observation by Supreme Court Justice Charles Clark: 'judging is more than just an exercise in technique or craft; it calls for value judgments.' The influence of personal values on Supreme Court decision-making is no secret to legal academics or judges.

Nonetheless, these studies are important. They have been conducted through a rigourous focus on behaviour over a large number of cases, and the high degree of correlation they establish between attitudes and decisions is powerful evidence. With regard to the Supreme Court, at least in relation to civil rights cases and economic cases, law appears to be politics. On this score CLS has been vindicated by positivist social science.

There is more to consider before a conclusive judgement can be rendered, however, for other studies of the Supreme Court have produced additional findings which intimate a more nuanced picture than the one presented thus far. Sidney Ulmer (1986) conducted a study to test whether Tate's results were 'time-bound'. He sought to discover whether social background factors are equally useful at 'explaining' judicial decisions over a longer period of time than the recent 30-year period selected by Tate. Ulmer used a different set of independent variables: 1) whether the Justice's father was a state or federal officer; 2) whether the Justice was the first-born child; and 3) the political affiliation of the judge. Earlier studies have shown that each of these factors, especially the third, had some correlation with judical decisions. For the dependent variable, Ulmer examined the votes of Justices in cases in which the government was pitted against 'underdogs' in two different periods: 1903–1935 and 1936–1968. His prediction was that Republican Justices who were first-born sons, with fathers who had worked for the government, would tend to support the government in cases against underdogs.

Ulmer found that the background factors 'explained' 72 per cent of the variance in the later period, but only 18.4 per cent of the variance in the earlier period, thus demonstrating that background studies are indeed time bound.[5] A minor and a major point can be taken from Ulmer's study. The minor point is that statistical correlations must be interpreted with caution; the fact that a Justice's birth order is shown to have a statistical relation with his or her decisions does not establish any causal relationship. Correlation may just be coincidence. The major point—one of significance for the purposes of legal theory—is that, as Ulmer suggests, background factors may not always have had a dominant influence, or the same kind of influence, on the Justices' decisions, at least not to the extent they apparently have now. Although Ulmer's study was not sufficient to establish anything of a positive nature, it does hint at the possibility that after the Realists made their impact, and more specifically after the patently political about-face of the Supreme Court under pressure from President Roosevelt's 'Court-packing plan', Justices were *more political* in their rendering of decisions—they felt freer to allow their attitudes to influence how they interpreted the law.

A study was published by Jeffrey Segal in 1984 which raises puzzling questions about the robust findings of the attitude model. Segal (1984) explicitly set out to test the validity of the legal model in search and seizure cases. He identified four independent variables from the case law as the essential factors in determining whether a challenged search and seizure would be upheld as valid: 1) the prior justification for the search—including whether it was conducted pursuant to a warrant and whether the lower courts found the existence of probable cause; 2) the nature of the intrusion—whether it occurred at home, in the car, or on the person in a public place; 3) the extent of the search—a full search or a more limited one like a frisk and questioning; and 4) whether the lower court found that the search was incident to a lawful arrest or not, and whether or not any exceptions were applicable.

Segal then examined all such cases decided between 1962 and 1981. His model correctly predicted (or retrodicted) 76 per cent of the Court's decisions. In this instance, the legal model 'explained' three-fourths of the cases, which is about as much as the earlier described attitude models 'explained'. Recall that Segal also produced the 1989 study cited earlier which demonstrated that attitudes correlated to votes in 80 per

[5] In a response to Ulmer, Tate conducted another study over a period of time longer than his original study. His results showed a sharp reduction in the percentage of variance 'explained', from 87% and 72% in the first study to 47% and 51% in the second study (see Tate and Handberg 1991). Although Tate claimed his second study showed 'a very worthwhile outcome', in fact it supported Ulmer's basic point that background has not always had the same amount of influence.

cent of civil liberties cases (which includes search and seizure). Thus the very same scholar has produced two different studies, one showing that legal factors explain the outcome and the other showing that extralegal factors explain the outcome, to about the same degree, in the same kind of cases, involving the same Justices, during basically the same period of time.

So which is it: does the law or the attitudes of the Justices determine the decisions in these cases? In his later study Segal offered almost no explanation to reconcile the two findings beyond asserting that they were not contradictory 'because the units of analysis differ' (1989: 562). He is correct in the sense that the search and seizure study focused on court decisions as a whole while the attitude study focused on the votes of individual Justices. However, court decisions are a function of individual votes. Regrettably, not enough data has been provided to discern the correct explanation, which appears to be a function of the particular combination of strongly politicized and less politicized Justices. The crucial point is that given the right mix of circumstances, even in the politically charged atmosphere of the Supreme Court, legal factors can determine the outcome in cases, *consistent with* what the attitude studies show.

Finally, an intriguing recent study by Tracey George and Lee Epstein (1992) undertook directly to compare the legal and attitude models in Supreme Court death penalty cases from 1971 to 1988. The independent variables for the legal model were patterned after Segal's method of identifying criteria indicated in the case law, including the nature of the crime, whether the jury was death qualified, and the factors considered by the jury. The independent variables for the extralegal model include measuring the attitudes of the Justices, the level of expertise and nature of the counsel representing the defendant (organizations like the ALCU), and the political environment surrounding the decision (the political party of the President and controlling Congress). Their findings were quite similar to those of Segal's two separate studies: the legal model correctly classified 75 per cent of the cases and the extralegal model classified 81 per cent of the cases. *Both* models, legal and extralegal, were able to 'explain' the decisions.

Their conclusion was that these two models 'should be considered codependent explanations' (p. 332). The legal model is correct that the law has an influence on the outcome, within limits, and the extralegal model is correct that non-legal factors like the Justices' attitudes and surrounding political forces have an influence on the outcome, within limits. As between the two models, at least in the recent history of the US Supreme Court, it appears that when push comes to shove (as when Justice Roberts felt pushed and shoved by President Roosevelt's Court-picking plan), or when the law directly contradicts strongly-held political convictions of the Justices in a given case, politics wins out over law.

Unfortunately, social scientific studies of the Supreme Court have a long way to go to get to the root of the relationship between the dual influences of politics and law because only recently have they begun seriously to explore and test for the possibility that law matters.

B. *Studies of Appellate Court Decision-Making*

Understanding the nature of decision-making on the lower appellate level is crucial because only a miniscule proportion of cases make it to the US Supreme Court from the state courts and the federal appellate courts. 'In fact, fewer than one-half of 1 per cent of appeals courts decisions are reviewed now by the Supreme Court' (Songer and Haire 1992: 963). The Supreme Court gets all the attention, but it is just the glittering nail polish on the left hand of the arm of the law.

Social scientists have grouped the intermediate and highest state courts together with the federal appellate courts in the single category of appellate court decision-making. This grouping recognizes the unique position held by the US Supreme Court as *the* court of final resort—state high courts are final only on issues of purely state concern—as well as the unique history of the US Supreme Court and the political forces that buffet it. It also recognizes the fact that, though there are exceptions, the behaviour patterns of the highest state courts tend to be more akin to federal appellate courts than to the US Supreme Court. In contrast to convincing demonstrations of the influence of values in the latter, studies on the influence of personal values on appellate judges' decisions beneath the Supreme Court have been mixed, and 'the differences were far more modest than anticipated' (Brace and Hall 1995: 11). The only durable finding from these studies is that Democratic judges are more liberal than Republican judges, but even this is not a uniform pattern, and when it does show up the differences are often slight (see Songer and Davis 1990; Songer and Haire 1992; Goldman 1975).

Weighty threshold support for the conclusion that personal values have a limited impact on the judicial decisions of federal appellate courts and state supreme courts can be found in the plain fact that, unlike the recent history of the US Supreme Court in which about half of the decisions have not been unanimous, these lower appellate courts consistently produce a high proportion of unanimous decisions, generally upwards of 90 per cent (see Dubois 1988; Beiser 1974; Glick and Vines 1973), just as Judges Rubin and Edwards observed.

Increasing recognition that a mix of factors, legal as well as extra-legal, have an influence on judicial decisions has led to the development, in just the last five years, of the 'integrative approach' (see Brace and Hall 1995; Songer and Haire 1992). A study by Donald Songer and Susan Haire (1992) of obscenity cases in the federal courts compared five different models: attitude, impact of Supreme Court precedent, characteristics of the litigants ('repeat players' or 'underdogs'), fact patterns, and nature of legal arguments. They found that while each model 'explained' some of the variance in the decisions (the attitude model was the weakest), none of the correlations was strong. When combined in one integrated model, however, 79.2 per cent of the votes were predicted (p. 975).

Integrated approaches represent the first systematic attempt by social scientists to incorporate legal factors into their models. Because these kinds of studies have not been in existence for long, however, there is not much to report. Integrated approaches must still surmount several hurdles. They have yet to settle methodological questions such as how to quantify matters like legal precedent and the strength of legal arguments.

Most problematic, all of the integrated approaches constructed thus far contain a central defect, one shared by the mass of existing studies on judicial decision-making: less than a handful have actually ever tested for the influence of the judges' perceptions of their judicial role on their decision-making behaviour (see Songer and Haire 1992: 978). Role perception defines what judging is and means for the people doing it, yet there is rarely any mention of it in the legal model versus extra-legal model studies.

One reason for this gaping omission is that judges have traditionally been inaccessible, so social scientists have had difficulty investigating the role orientations of specific judges (Songer and Haire 1992: 978), and thus cannot test the influence of these orientations against their decisions. But there is an even more telling reason. The majority of studies conducted on the US Supreme Court as well as on the lower appellate courts have *focused exclusively on cases giving rise to judgments which are not unanimous*. Social scientists who limit their research in this fashion quietly assume that all the unanimous cases—about 50 per cent for the US Supreme Court and 85 per cent to 95 per cent for the various state supreme courts and federal appellate courts—are determined by *legal* factors. These scholars have ignored role orientation because to focus on that would lend support to the primacy of the legal model, and they set out to demonstrate the superiority of the extralegal model. 'For the attitudinalist then, role is a given, differences in role perceptions are not explored, and the explanation of judicial behavior is in terms of judicial attitudes and values' (Goldman and Sarat 1978: 468).

For reasons of strategy as well as convenience, the studies have been slanted. Social scientists have limited their studies mostly to situations of disagreement where the factors they wish to highlight operate, creating a disproportionate emphasis on these factors.

Let us now examine the few studies that have focused on the role orientation of appellate court judges. In the mid-1960s Kenneth Vines (1969) interviewed the state supreme court judges of Louisiana, Pennsylvania, Massachusetts, and New Jersey, eliciting information about how the judges viewed the nature of their decision-making. He divided their responses into three categories: the law-interpreter, the law-maker and the pragmatist. Over half of the judges viewed their role in law-interpreter terms, with the other half divided between law-makers and pragmatists (the distribution was not even among states).

According to Vines, the law-interpreter orientation received strong support from many of the judges. The judges articulated this position in relation to their institutional position. Here is one response by a judge:

We interpret the law. That's our function. We're not authorized to write the law. We can only act in one way. That is to be solely interpreters of the law. The moment he steps out of the role of interpreter, he violates the constitution which separates the legislature and the executive from the judiciary (p. 474).

The law-makers assumed two different but related stances. Some believed that law-making was an inevitable aspect of interpreting the law, while others felt that law-making involved filling in the gaps in the law. Here is a representative description by a judge which blends the two:

Inevitably a judge makes law as does a legislative body. No matter how you decide a case, you're making law . . . That whole idea about whether a judge makes law or whether he found what the law always was by looking somewhere up in the blue is not true. Judges always made law and always will . . . In interpretation you're trying to give answers to problems that were not considered by the legislature, and you try to guess what the legislature would have thought had they thought about this problem (p. 475).

Finally, the pragmatists felt that there were elements of both interpretation and law-making in judicial decisions. They tended to focus on outcome and described their role as achieving a balance between applying the law and 'achieving a just result. You can call it law making or law interpreting. It's a combination of all these things' (p. 476).

Vines tested whether these role orientations were related to the liberal-conservative axis. His findings were contrary to the popular view that law-makers tend to be liberals. A greater percentage of Democrats than Republicans assumed the law interpreter position, even when the conservative southern Democrats on the Lousiana court were excluded. He then tested role orientation against actual decisions in divided cases. Vines found that there was no significant relation between role orientation and liberal or conservative decisions. 'There are virtually no differences [along this axis] among law interpreters and law makers, and while pragmatists have a somewhat more liberal position, the difference is not great' (p. 481). Vines concluded that political attitudes are not directly linked to role orientation.

Vines did not, unfortunately, systematically test for whether judges acted in ways consistent with their claimed role orientation, although he did conclude, based upon impressionistic evidence, 'that role perceptions were consistent with role behavior and represented behavior observable in state judicial institutions' (p. 485).

A study by John Wold (1974) confirmed Vine's basic categories of judicial attitudes (law-interpreters, law-makers, and somewhere in the middle), and that half of the judges saw themselves as law-interpreters. Wold (p. 240) found that two distinct conceptions of role were in competition: 'a deferential, precedent-oriented view and an innovative, policy-oriented view.' Significantly, however, he (p. 23–4) emphasized that:

The dissimilarities between the two views of course should not be exaggerated. Regardless of his feelings about judicial creativity, no jurist advocated an unrestrained policy-making role for his court. Even the lawmakers believed that sponsorship of change in public policy was chiefly the perogative of the legislature, and only secondarily that of the judge . . . and even some interpreters admitted the necessity of legislating in the 'interstices' of the law.

Basically, all of the judges felt they should follow the law, but the law-makers felt more freedom to intervene when 'the legislature has abdicated its responsibilities' and to abandon precedent 'when convinced that the situation warranted it' (p. 240). Like Vine, Wold did not systematically test for the influence of role orientation on decision behaviour.

Finally, in the mid-1970s, J. Woodford Howard (1977) conducted a study of the role perceptions of the judges on three federal appellate courts, the Second, Fifth, and District of Columbia Circuits. Howard found that these judges 'shared a strong consensus' and that 'little disagreement . . . existed about their duty to enforce the laws of Congress, Supreme Court, and their Circuits' (p. 918). According to Howard, virtually all of the judges agreed that bold policy ventures should be left to the Supreme Court or Congress, although they also agreed that stare decisis is not an unbreakable rule. At most, differences in role orientation were one of degree. There was tension among these judges only with regard to 'the proper scope of judicial lawmaking in an estimated tenth of their cases having innovative potential' (p. 918).

Using the same three categories, there were nine interpreters, five law-makers (Howard labelled them 'Innovators'), and twenty judges in the middle ('Realists'). Howard then tested the influence of role orientation of judicial decisions. He grouped the judges by attitude into three categories, liberals, moderates, and conservatives, and he examined their voting behaviour to see if their role orientation had any intervening influence on decisions. His results were inconclusive: 'neither political nor professional orientations, alone or in concert with the other, were totally consistent with voting behaviour' (p. 939). Howard speculated that the reason for this might be that the judges didn't actually differ that much in role orientations or value orientations and that the large bulk of cases are routine with fairly settled rules. He confirmed the view expressed by many appellate judges that *stare decisis* 'is largely responsible for encouraging decisional consensus on the appellate courts' (Goldman 1973: 105).

In summary, studies of the role orientations of appellate courts have demonstrated that judges vary along a continuum from those who believe they are limited to interpreting the law to those who affirmatively see their role as involving policy-infused law-making. This range of views should not obscure the fact that even the law-makers believed they should apply the law when there is clear precedent on the subject, and the law interpreters generally recognized that gaps existed which had to be filled in. Perhaps the core of the difference lies in the sense of the realist/pragmatists and the law-makers that even settled law must sometimes give way if justice requires it. As one judge described the struggle to straddle this perennial dilemma,

> The primary role of the judge is to do justice. There are principles that must be adhered to. But the result must be a just and equitable one. Settled principles of law are used to guide a court to a just result. When it is clear that these principles or precedents will produce an injustice, then you must strain the principles to get a just result (Goldman 1973: 106).

Law-interpreters who feel compelled by justice will strain the rules but pull back before extending too far; realists/pragmatists will strain them to the limit; law-makers will strain them to the limit (and maybe beyond), but sooner and with less agonizing than the realists/pragmatists.

C. Studies of District Court Decision-Making

Studies of federal district court or state trial court decision-making have largely been limited to a narrow band of subjects. About two-thirds of these studies have focused on criminal sentencing with the primary objective to test whether judges show any racial bias. I will take up these studies first, then address several other studies of note, including a couple that examine the role orientation of the judge and their adherence to precedent.

Research on the influence of judicial attitudes and the race of offenders in criminal sentencing behaviour went through two distinct phases. Most, though not all, early studies tended to show that blacks received harsher treatment than whites. However, a flaw shared by these early studies is that they failed to control for differences in the severity of crime or the past record of the defendant, two aspects which are among the primary considerations for a judge in the formulation of a sentence. Later studies which controlled for these differences have—contrary to the expectations of most researchers in the field—almost uniformly shown that black offenders are not sentenced more severely than whites (see Kleck 1981; Hagan 1974). Surprisingly, several studies have found that blacks actually tend to receive shorter terms of imprisonment than whites (Peterson and Hagan 1984; Myers 1988); two such studies have found that blacks receive lighter sentences but are more likely to be imprisoned (Spohn, Gruhl, and Welch 1981–2). A major exception to this pattern is death penalty cases.

After several decades of work and many studies, the general consensus in the field is that 'assumptions of racial and social class sentencing have been exaggerated . . . There is no general policy of discrimination. In fact, we could conclude that there is a *general policy of even-handedness* in most sentencing' (Glick 1983: 279, emphasis in original). '[J]udicial background has little *direct* bearing on sentencing outcomes' (Myers 1988: 668), nor have uniform or consistent differences in treatment been demonstrated in relation to types of offenders. 'Social background factors generally explain little of the variance in sentencing behaviour. Similarities outweigh differences, or expected differences never materialize in the first place' (p. 651). And isolated studies have found that the sentencing behaviour of female judges is similar to that of male judges (although one study showed that female judges do not base their decisions on the offender's sex, whereas male judges tend to treat female offenders more leniently than male offenders) (see Gruhl, Spohn and Welch 1981; Myers 1981; Kritzer and Uhlman 1977), and that black judges sentence similar to white judges (Uhlman 1978).[6] These conclusions are especially powerful because the researchers *expected* to find that judges' backgrounds do influence their sentencing behaviour and that blacks are treated more harshly.[7]

The conclusion that blacks are not generally discriminated against should not obscure strong evidence that blacks disproportionately receive the death penalty, although the extent of this disproportion drops when taking into account the fact that blacks are charged with committing a disproportionately high number of murders. A review of the death penalty studies by Gary Kleck (1981) concluded that this pattern of discrimination is real but limited to Southern states. Outside the South blacks actually had a lower chance of receiving the death penalty for murder than whites, though this may also be evidence of discrimination because most murders are intra-racial and thus leniency may reflect a devaluation of black victims of murder.

Although studies have not, with the exception of death penalty cases in the South, found any general pattern of discrimination based upon the characteristics of offenders, judges clearly differ between one another in their sentencing patterns, even on the very same case (see

---

[6] Uhlman's study was flawed because he failed to control for prior record, but this does not affect the validity of his comparative analysis between the sentencing behaviour of black and white judges.

[7] There are indications that the situation is more complicated than these conclusions indicate. Gibson (1978a) did a study of eleven judges in a Georgia court which showed that there was pro-black and anti-black sentencing, which tended to offset one another. Thus the overall picture would show no discrimination, while in fact there was some discrimination.

Cook 1973). Criminal sentencing is the one area in which the law explicitly confers a great deal of discretion on the judge. 'It is something of an embarrassment to observe the great range of sentences that different judges assign to apparently indistinguishable crimes' (Saks and Hastie 1986: 271). Though most judges appear to fall within a middle range, there are indeed 'hanging' judges and 'bleeding heart' judges (as any prosecutor or public defender can attest to), and the fate of a defendant can vary greatly depending on the luck of the draw. In addition, there are regional differences, such that judges in certain districts sentence more severely than judges in others districts (Levin 1974; Glick 1983: 288–90). One study of sentencing patterns for people who violated the selected service law (requiring draft-aged people to register) during the Vietnam War demonstrated that sentencing is also sometimes influenced by public opinion; judges become more lenient as public support for this war dropped (Cook 1977).

Social scientists have also begun to look at the influence of other participants in the sentencing process. For example, consistent with my own prior experience as a public defender, studies have demonstrated that judges tend to sentence in close accord with the recommendation of probation officers. As one researcher concluded, the 'single most important predictor of sentencing severity in these data was probation officer recommendations' (Frazier and Bock 1982: 269). Recognition that judges rely upon and are heavily influenced by other participants like probation officers and prosecutors (though not defence attorneys, in my experience)[8] provides a more accurate, collaborative view of the situation and suggests another explanation for why judges' backgrounds may not show a direct relation to their sentencing behaviour. Instead of viewing judges in isolation, increasingly they are being viewed as participants in an interactive process within an organizational context (see Jacob 1991).

Beyond the field of criminal sentencing but still on the subject of race, a couple of studies have been conducted on the federal district courts' enforcement of the desegregation mandate of *Brown* v. *Board of Education*. Kenneth Vines (1978) examined Southern District Court decisions in these cases from 1954 to 1962. He found a wide disparity in decision patterns for and against black desegregation claimants. Vines divided the judges into three broad groups based upon their

---

[8] Saks and Hastie (1986: 263) report a study which showed that the prosecutor's recommendation had a great influence on the judge's setting of bail, whereas the 'defense attorney's recommendation had no influence on the judge'.

decision pattern: 'Segregationists' decided for blacks in less than one-third of the cases before them; 'Moderates' held for blacks in 34 to 67 per cent of the cases; 'Integrationists' rule in favour of blacks in more than 67 per cent of cases. He then tried to discover whether any background factors correlated with these different groups. On the whole, however, the judges had quite similar backgrounds—they were from the South, attended school in the South, and practiced law in the South. The main differences fell into just two categories: only one-third of the Integrationists were Protestants, in contrast to two-thirds of the Segregationists and Moderates; and 9 per cent of the Integrationists had held state office, compared to 57 per cent of the Segregationists and 41 per cent of the Moderates. Based upon this data, Vines speculated that Segregationists were more closely tied to Southern culture: '[t]he evidence points to the conclusion that Southern federal judges in district courts are influenced by their social and political environment' (p. 385). A problem with Vines' study, however, is that he made no attempt to examine the cases for differences in legal merit or the factual situation of the school districts involved.

A more careful follow-up study was conducted ten years later by Michael Giles and Thomas Walker (1975). They identified four groups of independent variables: social background, environment (percentage of blacks and percentage of the vote for George Wallace's presidential candidacy), community linkage (membership in clubs and location of the court), and the nature of the school district (percentage of black enrolment and size of school district). And rather than consider just the percentage of decisions for or against blacks, for the dependent variable they examined the degree of segregation the judges allowed to exist in the school systems. By 1970 every school system had some level of desegregation, in contrast to the early stage examined by Vines. Giles and Walker found that in general there was little or no relationship between the degree of segregation allowed by the judge and the judges' background characteristics, their links to the community or the surrounding environment.

The final two studies I will relate have specifically tested for the influence of the judge's role orientation and for whether judges adhere to precedent. In a study published in 1978 James Gibson attempted to test the relative influence of attitudes and role orientation in judges' sentencing behaviour in the Iowa district court system from 1972 through 1974, covering 2,715 cases and 26 judges. Gibson interviewed the judges and scaled their attitudes (liberal-conservative) as well as their role orientations, then he compared these measures against the severity of their sentences. He (1978: 915) found that 'Liberals are not in any meaningful sense less severe in sentencing than conservatives.' Gibson also conducted a more refined analysis which identified those judges who believed that social and environmental forces caused crime, or that rehabilitation should be the goal of the criminal justice system, along with several other attitudes. Although he hypothesized that judges favouring anti-defendant positions would be more severe, again he found that there was a 'lack of relationship between attitudes and behavior' (p. 916).

Gibson distinguished two basic types of role orientation. A 'narrow' orientation applied to those judges who believed that their decisions must be based upon strictly legal grounds (precedent, statutes); judges with a 'broad' orientation felt it was more permissible to allow their own values and sense of justice to influence their decisions. If role orientations do have an influence, Gibson surmised, it would follow that, regardless of whether the judge is a conservative or liberal, '[a]ttitudes are good predictors of behavior only for judges with "broad" role orientations' (p. 919). And that is precisely what he found. For the significant minority of judges who believed that it was permissible to consider attitudes, 'attitudes are a key determinant of behavior' (p. 922).

Gibson then compared and combined the two models. Attitudes alone accounted for 14 per cent in the variance of sentencing behaviour, role orientations alone accounted for 8 per cent, but the interaction of attitudes and role orientations accounted for 64 per cent. 'Thus, some judges believe that it is not proper for them, as judges, to allow their own values to influence their decisions. The data demonstrated that the role orientations of judges do indeed block the relationship between attitudes and behavior, a finding also consistent with the experimental literature' (p. 922).

Similar to the scant research on the subject of role orientations, few studies have been conducted on the issue of whether judges follow precendent. The basic problem is that it is difficult to conceptualize how this can be tested in a quantitative fashion, which is also why so many studies have been done on sentencing behaviour, where the dependent variable (severity of sentence) can be easily observed and scaled. Charles Johnson (1987) conducted a study in which he tested the lower federal courts' reactions to fourteen randomly selected decisions announced by the US Supreme Court from 1950 through 1975. Along with a panel of four law students, he then examined 311 court of appeals and district court decisions in which one of the fourteen decisions was cited. They found that, '[i]n very few instances did the lower courts clearly fail to follow one of the fourteen decisions when it was a determinative precedent' (p. 327). 'The fact is that lower courts in this study followed the Supreme Court's holding or reasoning in a substantial number of cases . . . The point is that judges must make choices but within limited options. This research demonstrates that their options are sometimes sufficiently limited so that legal considerations heavily influence outcomes' (p. 339).

Generalizations from Studies of Judicial Decision-Making

Several caveats are necessary before any generalizations can be drawn from the preceding studies. Each study was constructed through a series of abstractions involving a multitude of questionable decisions, resulting in a simplified, inevitably distorted, narrow slice of what was actually occurring. Furthermore, the reliability of each study depends upon the capacity, integrity, and rigorousness of the scholars involved, including Journal Referees, especially since the full data is never published with the study itself and a number of studies rely upon complicated mathematical formulas which only specialists can understand and check. Finally, it is all too easy for researchers to construct a study to prove what they already believe, and once the study has been completed, after much time and expense, the researchers have a strong interest in characterizing its findings as significant.

In view of these limitations, these studies are most reliable for negative purposes, to tell us what is *not* the case rather than what is. And even this negative application is safe only in two circumstances: 1) when a number of researchers with varying points of view have duplicated the same basic finding using several different techniques or approaches; and 2) when the expectations of the researchers are resisted by their own study, when what they expected to and wanted to prove was not in fact supported by what they found.

Having said that, it is fascinating to note that the history of social scientific studies—especially behaviouristic studies—of judicial decision-making is replete with confoundings of the expectations of researchers. At the outset the dominant view in the field was that extralegal factors were a more powerful influence on legal decision-making than legal factors, that judges were politicians in black robes. While this predisposition is still strong, increasing acknowledgement that background/

attitude models are weak beyond the Supreme Court is slowly but surely leading to a view closer to the legal model, as reflected in the recent trend towards the integrated approach.

I will now offer general observations drawn from these studies. From a descriptive standpoint, the above studies insist upon the necessity for a distinctly two-part view of judicial decision-making. The US Supreme Court is in a category by itself, whereas, in broad terms, the federal appellate courts, lower state appellate courts, federal district courts and state trial courts can be grouped together. State high courts have on the whole appeared more similar to lower courts than to the US Supreme Court, but that is a contingent matter which depends upon the time period and the particular state involved. I will therefore exclude the highest state courts from the following generalizations.

With regard to the US Supreme Court, at least in the last few generations, attitudes have had a dominant influence in determining the decision-making of many of the individual Justices, and by implication determining the outcome for the Court as a whole in many cases, though whether this holds true for any given case depends upon the issues involved and the particular configuration of Justices. This observation is a positive assertion, but the persistence and strength of the data is too compelling to dismiss, especially with regard to the consistently outcome-correlated voting behaviour (in certain subjects) of Justices like Brennan, Marshall, and Rehnquist. That is not to deny that law also has an influence, but the extent of this influence and its interaction with attitudes is entirely unclear, especially since no systematic study has been conducted on the role orientations of the Justices.

In contrast to the Supreme Court, 'ideological values play a less prominent role in the lower federal courts' (Songer and Haire 1992: 964). More strongly put, in most cases the background and attitudes of judges do not have a determinative influence on the decision-making of lower court judges, especially when judges believe it is inappropriate to consider personal values. Evidence in support of this negative conclusion is as strong as that behind the positive conclusion that attitudes do have a significant influence on the Supreme Court. There are of course rogue judges for whom attitudes do have a determining influence, and judges themselves openly acknowledge that cases regularly arise in which value judgements are called for; the assertion here is the more measured one that for a substantial majority of judges in a large proportion of their cases personal values do not determine their decisions.

On the appellate level the strongest support for this assertion comes from the high proportion of unanimous decisions, despite the different attitudes and backgrounds of judges. Even in the D.C. Circuit, the appellate court that is widely reported to be the most politicized and divided in the country, over 94 per cent of the decisions are unanimous, and the dissent rate of 'mixed' panels (those with liberal and conservative judges) is not higher than the general dissent rate (Edwards 1991: 856). In addition, studies on role orientation, though limited in number, generally indicate that appellate judges see their primary role as following the law, though they will depart from this presumptive orientation if a compelling sense of justice requires it, and some judges will depart more readily than others. On the trial court level the evidence comes from the many studies which show that differences in background and attitudes of judges (Republican, Democratic, liberal, conservative, white, black, male, female) are not substantially or consistently reflected in or correlated to their sentencing behaviour, especially when the particular judges' role orientation precludes such effect. Finally, the strongest overall support is comparative: the kinds of studies which have proven the undeniable influence of values at the Supreme Court level have been unable to show the same below, despite concentrated efforts to do so.

Because this generalization is a negative one—attitudes do not determine decisions—it does not directly tell us what does determine decisions. The few studies that have tested for the influence of legal factors have been affirmative. There have not, however, been many of these studies, though the development of the integrative approach promises to rectify this lack of information. Nevertheless, it seems fair to conclude, by default, that legal factors are the strongest candidate as the source of these decisions because there are no other viable possibilities—there is nothing else all these judges share which could explain the consistency in their decision behaviour.

The popular response that the similar backgrounds of judges (elite, white, middle-aged males) is what produces uniform decisions has initial plausibility and some merit, but the strong form of the thesis collapses upon closer inspection. First, without denying that shared attitudes make some contribution, it is absurd to suggest that this minimalist sense in which they have similar backgrounds would result in attitudes sufficiently identical to generate unanimity in 85 to 95 per cent of the cases. After all, the leaders of CLS are mostly elite, white, middle-aged males. Secondly, it cannot explain why there is so much disagreement on the Supreme Court, whose members tend to be selected from a much narrower band of the white male elite than appellate court judges (see Schmidhauser 1979). Thirdly, as I indicated, studies have shown that women judges do not significantly differ from men, and black judges from white (though critical scholars may assert that this is because they have bought into the dominant white male values).

The only unifying background characteristics all these judges share are that they were indoctrinated into the same intersubjective legal community, they operate within the same institutional settings, and they participate in the practice of judging within the same legal tradition. This shared indoctrination and institutional context, combined with shared attitudes and ways of doing that characterize the practice of judging in this tradition, especially the role orientation of following the law, enables them to see legal rules in much the same way, suppressing disagreement or alternative interpretations except for those cases where the law is genuinely open, incomplete, or contradictory, or when the end is so unacceptable to a given judge that the rules must be departed from, in which instance the judge purposefully exploits the latent indeterminacy in the legal rules. In the easy cases particularly, many of the legal rules are seen and followed in routine or habitual ways, requiring a conscious effort even to be seen otherwise.

To borrow Mead's phrase, these judges share the mind and ways of doing that make up the community of judges and the practice of judging, as conventionalist legal theorists have argued. Interpretivism suggests that this intersubjective view is what shapes their perspective. The insistence that it's all a matter of the judges' political views is reductionist in precisely the same way that the strong programmers were reductionist in asserting that scientific beliefs are all the product of external social interests. Critical scholars who hold to this skeptical position must account for the fact that judges widely *believe* that they are bound by the law and that the law largely, albeit not entirely, determines their decisions. As Judge Edwards (1983–4: 396) remarked, '[t]hat conviction could, of course, be the product of self-deception, but it seems unlikely that so many judges could have been so deluded for so long.' The insistence that this is false consciousness, without supporting evidence of some kind, is dogma.

A skeptic may nevertheless insist that the studies which show that judges vary widely in their sentencing behaviour is proof that personal attitudes determine decisions. Yes but no. Sentencing is one major area in which the law explicitly commits the decision to the discretion of the judge, but law still guides the exercise of this discretion by broadly specifying what factors should be taken into account (past record, prospects for rehabilitation, consistency in treatment, etc.) and by prohibiting the consideration of certain factors deemed improper or irrelevant (race, personal dislike).

Attitudes undoubtedly do have an influence on how judges interpret and apply the law, and many judges openly admit as much. The question is, how much? And the answer suggested by these studies is, in most cases, not extraordinarily much. One way to understand this relation is to say that conservative judges see the law through green-tinted legal glasses, while liberal judges see it through red-tinted legal glasses (there are other coloured legal glasses as well). Despite the tints, which do make a difference under certain circumstances, in a substantial majority of cases—below the Supreme Court—judges look through these lens to more or less interpret the law the same way because the tints colour what are still 'legal' glasses.

It must be emphasized that the conclusion that the attitudes of lower court judges do not systematically determine their legal decisions does not itself refute claims that, for example, the law exhibits a tilt in favour of the rich over the poor or that the 'haves' come out ahead. It says only that the source of this bias, if in fact present, is not located in the decision-making of judges, but must be found elsewhere, either among the other institutional players (like prosecutors who do not vigorously pursue white collar crimes, or elite lawyers who only serve clients who can afford exorbitant lawyer's fees), or embodied within the substantive content of the laws. Faithful judicial adherence to a tilted body of law leads to tilted outcomes.

A stark example of this can be found in the effect of the federal sentencing guidelines which limited judicial sentencing discretion by setting mandatory minimums and detailed guidelines for certain crimes. A recent study by the US Justice Department reveals that, prior to the implementation of the guidelines, blacks, whites, and hispanics received similar sentences; after the implementation of the guidelines blacks received substantially longer sentences than whites and hispanics (Carlson and McDonald 1993). The difference is explained by the fact that the guidelines required a substantially longer sentence for crack cocaine convictions, which involves mostly blacks. The sentencing guidelines have a built-in racial bias. Judges who had formerly been treating all defendants with an even hand were forced by law to do otherwise.

A Social View of Judging

In this final Section I will round off the picture of the social nature of judging revealed by these studies. Emerging from the studies is a differentiation between two units of investigation: the individual judge and the context within which the judge works. The *locus* of judging, the context within which judging takes place, is a crucial variable because the same individual judge operating within a different locus might well behave differently. Studies of judicial decision-making have established that there are two qualitatively distinct kinds of environments—social and institutional—surrounding each locus, each of which has an influence on judging.

The social environment consists of two populations or communities—the general social community, and the community of lawyers, legal scholars, and fellow judges. The immediate audience for judges consists of the latter. The legal community constantly monitors and writes about the Supreme Court, but pays less attention to federal appellate and district courts, with a similar pattern applying to the various levels of state courts. Scrutiny of judges by the social community as a general matter is low and limited to cases of particular concern, and even then attention is paid only to outcomes. At the Supreme Court level only highly politicized subjects (abortion, death penalty, gay rights, affirmative action) garner attention. Appellate courts toil in blissful anonymity. Trial courts get attention, but usually only in sensational cases dealing with celebrities or heinous crimes. The actual influence exerted by both communities varies greatly depending on the court as well as the case, in interaction with the receptivity of the individual judge (which is a function of the judge's role perception).

The institutional environment also has two distinct components, which I will distinguish as immediate and vertical. The immediate institutional environment are the surrounding circumstances within which judging takes place. For the Supreme Court that consists, on the one hand, of each Justice with their cadre of law clerks, and on the other hand, of their interaction in the 'small group' dymanics that envelop the nine Justices in their back-and-forth deliberation on cases, including negotiations, pressure from others, and sometimes vote trading. Appellate court judges have the same two basic aspects, though the 'small group' dynamics are more attenuated because the judges rotate and there are fewer on each panel. Trial court judges are also served by law clerks, but their immediate environment differs markedly from that of higher judges. Instead of dealing with other judges, the cast of players of which a trial judge is a part consists of a changing set of litigants and lawyers on the civil side, and a lot of familiar, repeat players (prosecutors, defenders, probation officers, and sometimes defendants) on the criminal side.

The vertical institutional environment refers to the position of the court within the entire complex of courts seen as a whole. Trial courts are the gatekeepers to whom social events are brought, already preselected and narrowed, transformed into legal terms by the lawyers involved. They are live participants in the collaborative construction of the legal framing of events, though most of their work involves a routine drudgery of taking pleas and processing cases, and ruling on evidence motions, much of which is handled through the application of practice-based heuristics and habits of thought rather than conscious deliberation (see Segal 1986; Schneider 1992: 80–1; Manning and Hawkins 1990). Their law application activities (like deciding evidence motions) are often peripheral to the substance of the case, though the resolution of these issues may have a determinative influence on outcomes. In this locus, trial judges operate in a variety of modes, as facilitors, negotiators, administrators, umpires, researchers and writers of legal opinions, and so forth (see Wice 1991: Chapter 8).

A large proportion of cases for intermediate appellate courts also involve routine processing (also dealt with through habits and heuristics), though a substantial remainder require close attention and difficult decisions. Behind the brief and often inconsequentional oral hearings, the bulk of their work, relying heavily upon law clerks, takes place in quiet offices and libraries and involves poring through thick piles of paper—briefs, transcripts and exhibits, and law reports. In contrast to the trial courts, law dominates more so than the facts and the scope of decision-making is more circumscribed, narrowed by the lawyers' framing of the appeal and by the actions of the trial court below.

Finally there is the Supreme Court. Many petitions to hear cases are routine, but cases accepted for consideration are not. They are the hard cases, winnowed and selected from the subsection of hard cases below, where the law does not clearly speak or issues of justice are of pressing concern. Other than this, their situation is similar to the appellate courts in the paper-based, already framed nature of the case, the narrowed scope of the review, and the focus on law over facts. The crucial difference is that the Supreme Court has the last word.

One pervasive factor that all three courts face within this vertical institutional environment is an overwhelming burden of cases which need to be managed and moved along. 'Trial judges spend nearly as much time on administrative tasks as on their adjudicative responsibilities . . . [M]anagerial functions even account for a large portion of the appellate judge's time, especially on the Supreme Court . . .' (Wice 1991: 253). The court system is a massive bureaucracy (see Edwards 1983), with judges perched at the top, and this has as a major influence on the shape that law takes.

The preceding description captures, I believe, all of the major influences social science researchers have identified with regard to judicial decision-making. It portrays the practice of judging within its social context. The most noteworthy aspect of this social science informed description is that it is so ordinary and unremarkable—it closely matches the already taken for granted views of most judges, legal academics, and lawyers.

8 Legal Theory and the Practice of Judging

The Realistic View of Judging

Critical scholars and social scientists are fond of asserting that judges are deluded about the nature of their own activities. Scientists have this attitude generally about their subjects of study, and the critical view is part of a tradition of the radical left of claiming that people who don't see things their way are deluded. Ever since the Realists, legal theorists have also too readily asserted that judges are either disingenuous or mistaken when they describe what judicial decision-making entails. Richard Posner (1990a: 189) presented a typical expression of this view:

> I am denying that judicial introspection, and *a fortiori* judges' avowals concerning the nature of judicial decision making, are good explanations for judicial action. It is a mistake to take at face value descriptions of judges as engaged always in a search for 'the' correct answer, rather than as exercising discretion under the influence of personal values and preferences determined by temperament and selective life experiences rather than by a considered, somehow self-chosen judicial philosophy. A teenager may honestly feel that he is deliberating over a choice of colleges that his parents know is foreordained by factors of which the teenager himself is unaware.

Never mind that *Judge* Posner has neatly (albeit inadvertently) situated himself within a 'self-deluded' variant of the 'liar's paradox', since he made the above comments in the course of describing his own view of how judge's really do decide cases.

Given the alleged pervasiveness of judicial self-delusion, the question is: by what precise means do we find out how judges decide cases? Posner (p. 186–96) asserted that he knew—presumably in his legal theorist capacity—and that the source and confirmation of this insight was to be found in behaviourist studies of judicial decision-making. Social scientists, in Posner's above analogy, were the knowing parents to the unaware judges. But the extensive discussion of behaviourist-dominated studies in the preceding Chapter suggests that social scientists are actually moving toward the judicial view of affairs.

Moreover, the description Posner sets out in his text is no different in substance from the views expressed by many of the judges quoted earlier, none of whom said anything about *the* correct answer in the course of describing how they decide cases. Talk about *the* correct answer derives from dated formalist declarations and, lately, from legal theorist Ronald Dworkin, who *claimed* to be representing the internal view of judges for the boost of legitimacy it provided to his account. Judges may properly insist that their decision is determined by the law and that it is the correct answer, without making the additional, metaphysical assertion that it is *the* one and only answer law provides. Legal theorists wallow in luxurious contemplation with their attention focused on the normative task of legitimating or delegitimating the law (depending upon their political ilk), which leads to extreme assertions like the 'one right answer' thesis, or the 'law is efficiency' thesis, or the 'law is politics' thesis. Judges, meanwhile, are doing the best they can to live up to their role obligations while wading through a daily grind of cases, a task which neither calls for, nor allows much time for, attention to the distant beckoning of concerns about system-wide legitimation.

As social science researchers in this area overcome their initial biases, the earlier quoted descriptions given by judges—many of which were made twenty or thirty years ago—are beginning to sound quite accurate. Social scientists, as well as critical scholars and a few legal theorists, have been beating up on a long defunct caricature of what judges believe, though judges bear partial responsibility because they still write decisions in the formalist style. Like scientists, judges also separate discovery from justification. Few social scientific articles list all the doubts and potential flaws that were overcome in reaching the final conclusions—so, too, with legal opinions. To find out how judges believe they make decisions they must be asked that specific question and given the opportunity to provide a reflective answer. Under these circumstances, judges tend to give quite realistic accounts. They admit that they make law, and that their values have an influence, and that there are gaps in the law, and that choices must be made; but they also insist that the law is often clear, and that in a large proportion of cases their decisions are determined by the law.

For many critical theorists and legal theorists, however, the very idea that judges could be bound by rules is a fraud. Quoting and paraphrasing Robert Cover, a legal theorist widely respected by the mainstream (Tushnet 1991: 1540 n.96), Margaret Jane Radin (1989: 813) expressed this view:

When judges slip into the old rhetoric and claim to act not as people but as functionaries whose hands are tied, they 'substitut[e] the hermeneutic of jurisdiction for the hermeneutic of the text.' In other words, they refuse to take responsibility for their actions by taking refuge in their role as rule-followers. 'Judges are people of violence': one way of being violent is to disavow responsibility for the consequences of their functionary behavior.

Strong words, these are, which aim to wrest a confession from judges that their talk of being ruled by rules is a bad faith subterfuge.

Probably no amount of scientific studies will shake this belief. Perhaps, however, the considered words of an authority will prompt them to reconsider. Justice Cardozo, as I mentioned in the Chapter on pragmatism, has recently been canonized, the recipient of virtually unanimous acclaim from the left, centre, and right, from critical scholars to Richard Posner. This reference to Justice Cardozo is not just a shameless resort to authority; the views expressed by the judges quoted earlier are consistent with, and were no doubt in part a product of, the views of Justice Cardozo.

Cardozo began his classic, *The Nature of the Judicial Process* (1921), by declaring that judge-made law is 'one of the existing realities of life', and that 'choice' is integral to the process (pp. 10–11). Citing William James' *Pragmatism*, Cardozo (pp. 12–13) also recognized that:

There is in each of us a stream of tendency, whether you choose to call it philosophy or not, which gives coherence and direction to thought and action. Judges cannot escape that current any more than other mortals. All their lives, forces which they do not recognize and cannot name, have been tugging at them—inherited instincts, traditional beliefs, acquired convictions; and the resultant is an outlook on life . . . which, when reasons are nicely balanced, must determine where choice shall fall. In this mental background every problem finds its setting. We may try to see things as objectively as we please. None the less, we can never see them with any eyes except our own.

Cardozo has unflinchingly acknowledged the ineradicable presence of what I described earlier as the 'ground', the enabling yet limiting conditions of our existence as thinking, interpreting beings, the 'prejudices' Gadamer identified as necessary aspects of the very ability to interpret. All judges and all judging are subject to these conditions.

Then Cardozo turns to describe the law, the ingredient with which and upon which judges exercise their judgment. Again he (p. 14) forthrightly declares: '[t]here are gaps to be filled. There are doubts and ambiguities to be cleared. There are hardships and wrongs to be mitigated if not avoided.' Cardozo (p. 14) also adds, however, that '[t]here are times when the source is obvious. The rule that fits the case may be supplied by the constitution or by statute. If that is so, the judge looks no farther. The correspondence ascertained, his duty is to obey.' Cardozo (pp. 20–3; see also Dewey 1931: 130–1) describes adherence to *stare decisis* as a complex process of searching, comparing, shaping, and following, undergirded on a psychological level by habits of mind. And he (p. 26) observed that through this process judges change the law, such that, '[h]ardly a rule of today but may be matched by its opposite of yesterday'; though he (p. 48) also recognized that over time, from a tentative and groping beginning, after repeated application, lines of precedent obtain 'a new permanence and certainty'.

Cardozo sets out most of the above in the first thirty pages of his text, and it comports well with the views of most legal theorists, critical scholars, and social scientists generally, but this was only the *beginning* of his analysis. Cardozo (p. 33) immediately thereafter made a crucial point about the attitude judges should bring to this malleable mass of law:

I am not to mar the symmetry of the legal structure by the introduction of inconsistencies and irrelevancies and artificial exceptions unless for some sufficient reason, which will commonly be some consideration of history or custom or policy or justice. Lacking such a reason, I must be logical, just as I must be impartial, and upon like grounds.

All lawyers know the difference between going with the flow presented by the law, versus exploiting the patent or latent indeterminacy of the law, and judges should not embark upon the latter path except for a 'sufficient' reason.

To guide the determination of this reason, Cardozo (p. 66—7) opined:

I do not mean, of course, that judges are commissioned to set aside existing rules at pleasure in favor of any other set of rules which they may hold to be expedient or wise. I mean that when they are called upon to say how far existing rules are to be extended or restricted, they must let the welfare of society fix the path, its direction and distance.

Many legal theorists will agree, though a few might diverge when Cardozo (pp. 88–91) insists that the standard to be applied to determine what is in the interest of social welfare is not the judge's 'own ideas of reason and justice', but rather an 'objective' (p. 108) one derived from the standards of the community. Whether in the course of interpreting the law or filling in gaps, Cardozo (ibid.) believed that a judge 'would err if he were to impose upon the community as a rule of life his own idiosyncracies of conduct or belief'. Again, however, he

(p. 110) displayed his philosophical sophistication by quickly adding that the difference between objective and subjective 'is shadowy and evanescent'; since, as he (p. 111) states in terms closely reminiscent of Mead, '[t]he personal and the general mind and will are inseparably united.'

With regard to the issue of the relative extent to which judges are rule-bound, Cardozo (p. 129) asserted:

> In countless litigations, the law is so clear that judges have no discretion. They have the right to legislate within gaps, but often there are no gaps. We shall have a false view of the landscape if we look at the waste spaces only, and refuse to see the acres already sown and fruitful. I think the difficulty has its origin in the failure to distinguish between right and power, between the command embodied in a judgment and the jural principle to which the obedience of the judge is due. Judges have, of course, the power, though not the right, to ignore the mandate of a statute and render judgment in spite of it. They have the power, though not the right, to travel beyond the walls of the interstices, the bounds set to judicial innovation by precedent and custom. None the less, by that abuse of power they violate the law . . .

Legal theorists who charge judges with bad faith when they claim to be rule-bound fail to recognize the crucial distinction drawn by Justice Cardozo. Judges are in fact rule-bound when they accept and undertake that obligation as a defining aspect of the nature of their activity. Judges know they have the de facto power to depart from the rules at any time, or to manipulate the rules with dexterous ease, but they *accept the responsibility* of having made the decision to forego the exercise of this power (but for exceptional circumstances); whereas Cover and Radin, in the earlier quotation, construe this decision as an abdication of responsibility. For the judge who accepts the duties of the position, Cardozo (p. 137) asserts, '[i]nsignificant is the power of innovation of any judge, when compared with the bulk and pressure of the rules that hedge him in on every side.'

According to Cardozo (p. 114), even when working within the gaps and intersticies of the law the judge is not given completely free reign:

> Even within the gaps, restrictions not easy to define, but felt, however impalpable they may be, by every judge and lawyer, hedge and circumscribe his action. They are established by the traditions of the centuries, by the example of other judges, his predecessors and colleagues, by the collective judgment of the profession, and by the duty of adherence to the pervading spirit of the law.

Cardozo thus identified surrounding social forces as providing the sources of restraint.

And to those who assert that judges invariably select an outcome, then reason backwards, manipulating the rules to achieve that outcome, Cardozo (p. 170) responds, without denying that a projection of ends is involved: 'I would not put the case thus broadly. So sweeping a statement exaggerates the element of free volition. It ignores the factors of determinism which cabine and confine within narrow bounds the range of unfettered choice.' Cardozo straddled a middle position. 'The judge, even when he is free, is still not wholly free' (p. 141).

Most judges serving today, and for the past thirty years at least, were taught by law professors influenced by Holmes, Cardozo, Pound, and the Realists. Their accounts of what judicial decision-making involves, scattered about in this and the preceding Chapter, differ little from Cardozo's. And, I have argued, social scientists are beginning to concur, or at least are being forced in that direction by the persistent weight of their recalcitrant findings. When all the rhetoric is cut through, it seems fair to say that most everyone in the US legal tradition—lawyers, law professors, social scientists, judges—more or less see matters the same realistic way, with the notable exception of critical scholars.

Socially Grounded Determinacy of Law—an Achievement of Behaviour

Many critical scholars will probably be unmoved by the above presentation, along with more than a few mainstream legal theorists and socio-legal scholars. It is easy to discount the views of participants—including someone of Cardozo's stature—as mere rationalization, and to reject out of hand positivist social scientific studies. Regardless of what anyone says, they know that law is substantially indeterminate and they know that judges make choices in the course of interpreting and applying the law. Cardozo's insistence that law still largely controls when choice exists is not convincing because to admit indeterminacy and choice means, *ipso facto*, law *cannot* control. Reaching into philosophy for support, I will now show how the presence of indeterminacy and choice is consistent with the conclusion that law still determines decisions.

The indeterminacy identified by critical scholars refers to the body of legal rules read in the abstract, or to the conflicting principles underlying the rules, or to the indeterminacy inherent within rules as such or language as such (see Solum 1987). It is correct that on this level legal rules are, or can be made to be, indeterminate. As Gadamer (1991: 307–9) argued, however, application is an integral aspect of interpretation. The context of actual legal interpretation and judicial rule application is where the sources of determinacy lie, stabilizing what appears indeterminate when the rules are viewed in the abstract. To assert that law 'determines' despite the indeterminacy of rules means that factors apart of the law—including habits and traditions, shared meaning, institutional structures (including review by higher courts), peer pressure, the nature of the practice of judging, etc., everything that goes into the social theory of judging I have been constructing, have an influence on the final decision. If, by necessity owing to an ambiguity or gap in the law, a choice must be made within this context, then it is still a choice controlled by the law (so conceived), even if the ultimate sources for the choice are personal values (what other source could there be?). Only when law and judging are viewed in these broader terms, as a social activity comprising of situated complexes of meaning and actions, can the source of the determinacy in law be located. Legal determinacy is the product of all of these influences in combination.

Perhaps counter-intuitively, the true strength of the behaviouristic social scientific studies elaborated earlier is that they do not actually pretend to tell us how judicial decisions are made. The decision-making process is concealed from purview within bracketed grey matter, sandwiched between independent variables and dependent variables. Anything can be going on inside that grey matter—we just don't know; even cognitive science doesn't know. All of our talk about thought and decision-making, from psychology to artificial intelligence, from schemata to interpretive schemes, consists of groping attempts at capturing unknown phenomena through approximate verbal formulations.[1] In a very real sense every attempt to gain access to the mind is behaviouristic because the only evidence we have to go on is behaviour—actions, what we do—and other behaviour—speech, what we say. Gilbert Ryle (1949) argued, and a number of prominent philosophers agree, that the mind doesn't even exist, that the mind is a fiction we postulate to account for functional brain states. Whether or not we agree with Ryle—my sense of realism says he is mistaken[2]—the point

---

[1] For an outstanding overview of this field, see Flanagan (1991).

[2] A powerful response to Ryle and his supporters is John Searle's, *The Rediscovery of the Mind* (1992). The response I would give adopts the position articulated by William James. He conceived of the mind as a natural phenomenon which evolved out of the need to make plans in order to survive.

is that arguments over indeterminacy are unlikely to ever be resolved through a deeper inquiry into the decision-making process.

That leaves only two other sources: an examination of patterns of behaviour, and recourse to phenomenological or hermeneutic accounts; that is, watch what people do, compare that with what they think they are doing, then try to understand the connections (or lack thereof) between the two.

We know with certainty that law is determinate in one important sense: the very fact of the high proportion of unanimous decisions in appellate cases is a behaviour pattern which reflects widespread agreement about the law. Judges behave in this context as if the law is determinate. Whether from a Realist view of law (law is what law does), a conventionalist view of rules (rules mean what the social group perceives them to mean), or a Wittgensteinian view of rules (rules exist through rule-following behaviour, through acting in conformity), the conclusion is the same: the fact that the judges behave in this way means the law *is* determinate. That still leaves the question of what, specifically, makes law determinate; but, as I argued earlier, by demonstrating that backgrounds and attitudes *are not* systematically correlated to decision behaviour, behaviourist studies have eliminated the only possible candidate other than the law. Thus the law—seen in toto, beyond just legal rules—and more specifically *the situated practice of judging*, renders law determinate. This conclusion holds regardless of the presence of an indeterminate body of rules, the existence of choice, and the fact that judges might regularly work backwards from ends and manipulate the rules in the course of justifying their decisions.

Put another way, if judges act (behave) as if the law is determinate (a large proportion of the time), then it is determinate; if judges assert and believe that legal rules determine their decisions (for the most part), that adds one more dimension; the combined weight of these two observations is that law *is* determinate. Judges have in effect created—have achieved as an accomplishment—law-based determinacy in their actions despite the indeterminacy of legal rules. Pragmatism says that is what matters.

The broader significance of this conclusion is that determinacy is always a contingent matter. As with all ongoing activities, practices change. If agreement in judicial behaviour diminishes beyond some critical point, or if the determinative influences shift from legal factors to non-legal, the law will no longer determine judicial decisions, as appears to be the case currently on the Supreme Court in a significant proportion of cases. A number of factors may prompt such changes, but the most immediate one would be if judges began to believe that they did not have an obligation to follow the law.

Legal Theory and the Changing Nature of Judicial Decision-Making

From the foregoing amalgamation of behaviourist, interpretive, and participant reports can be extracted the core elements of the structure (metaphorically speaking) of judicial decision-making. Judges within the US legal tradition think within this structure when making legal decisions. It is their framework of thought. It is the aspect which judges engaged in the practice of judging in the US legal tradition share regardless of their particular locus, though the relative distribution of the elements of this structure differs among individual judges and differs in relation to different judicial loci and different cases. This articulation will involve a speculative leap into the grey matter, though an informed leap grounded in consideration of the available sources of information.

A. The Shift from Rule Application to Instrumental Rationality

To understand the origin of and relation between the elements of the structure of judicial decision-making we must briefly resort to legal theory. In Chapter Six I asserted that the practice of judging in the United States has changed over time from the grand style, to the formalist style, to the current blend of law and policy. This change, specifically the shift from the formalist to the current period, has direct implications for the nature of judicial decision-making.

Aspects of this change were already evident to Cardozo in 1921. Under the formalist view, law, especially common law, had its own self-contained existence and integrity, derived from timeless principles connected to the natural order or from custom immemorial encapsulated by courts (see Atiyah and Summers 1987: 250). This view tended to shield law from criticism, specifically the criticism that law was out of step with social interests. Law went its sober, conservative way encrusted in formalisms and rigid, archaic pleading requirements, oblivious to the changing needs of society. That was the essential Holmes/Cardozo/Pound/Realist complaint. Citing Pound, Cardozo (1921: 73) observed that 'today in every department of the law . . . the social value of a rule has become a test of growing power and influence.' He (p. 160) saw evidence of 'a spirit and a tendency to subordinate precedent to justice'. This development has been labelled the 'instrumental' or 'purposive' view of law—that law is and should be an instrument to serve our social purposes. Cardozo endorsed this change, and *The Nature of the Judicial Process* was a substantial contribution to it.

At this point it will clarify matters to recognize two distinct, but closely related and sometimes confused senses of the shift toward justice, both of which have been called substantive justice. The shift Cardozo identified has to do with *social* justice in the sense that legal rules should serve social interests. But a second shift has also occurred, a shift towards a greater desire to do justice in the *individual* case (also referred to as equity). The two differ because a rule which furthers the general welfare (social justice) may still give rise to an injustice in the individual case (individual justice); though they converge in instances where the rule does not conform to social justice and the sense of injustice in the individual case is derived from the sense of what social justice requires. Although Cardozo supported the former shift, he (p. 136) was far less sanguine about the 'destruction of all rules and the substitution in every instance of the individual sense of justice . . .' 'That might result in benevolent despotism if the judges were benevolent men. It would put an end to the reign of law' (ibid.).

Approaching from different directions and political persuasions, in the mid-1970s several prominent legal theorists brought renewed attention to this change in the orientation of law. The clearest articulation was set out by Roberto Unger. Borrowing from Weber, Unger (1975: 89) distinguished legal justice and substantive justice as alternative ways of ordering human relations:

One way is to establish rules to govern general categories of acts and persons, and then to decide particular disputes among persons on the basis of the established rules. This is legal justice. The other way is to determine goals and then, quite independently of rules, to decide particular cases by a judgment of what decision is most likely to contribute to the predetermined goals, a judgment of instrumental rationality. This is substantive justice.

The core difference is that legal justice focuses on *rule application*, whereas substantive justice applies *instrumental rationality* to achieve designated social purposes or ends. The former system requires a sharp distinction between rule-making and rule-application, whereas the latter is not rule-based. According to Unger (p. 91), each system is internally unstable, and the two systems 'cannot be reconciled' with one another.

He argued that a system of rules cannot dispense with consideration of values, but is inconsistent with such consideration; and that judgments to further the general interest cannot be made without rules, but is not compatible with them. 'This is the antinomy of rules and values' (p. 91).

Unger then moved from this analytical discussion to observe that the law in Western welfare societies are marked by a rise of purposive reasoning (p. 99; see also Unger 1976: 192–200). Signs of this development can be found in the shift away from formalistic analysis, an increase in the use of open-ended standards in the law (like 'reasonableness' and 'unconscionability'), and more frequent discussions of policy. These developments, according to Unger, represent the disintegration of the rule of law. The generality of law is destroyed by the necessity for *ad hoc* determinations required in purposive instrumental reasoning, and the autonomy of law is lost as 'the style of legal discourse approaches that of commonplace political or economic argument' (1976: 199).

In these situations, the courts and agencies are caught between two roles with conflicting demands: the role of the traditional formalist judge, who asks what the correct interpretation of rules of law is, and the role of the calculator of efficiencies, who seeks to determine what course of action will most effectively serve a given goal, such as the maintenance of a competitive market (1975: 99).

The result of this change is that the entire legal system contains 'an unstable oscillation between generalizing rules and *ad hoc* decisions' (p. 99).

A couple of years later, legal sociologists Philippe Nonet and Philip Selznick (1978) propounded the same thesis though with a different outlook. Nonet and Selznick characterized the increased use of purposive, policy reasoning as progress toward a higher evolutionary stage of law, towards a more 'responsive' law which better serves social needs. Similar to Unger, they recognized that this development represented the 'death of law' as a distinct activity (pp. 115–18), though they did not shy away from this consequence.[3] They believed that this development was the 'true program of sociological and realist jurisprudence' (p. 115).

Finally, at the same time, writing from England, Patrick Atiyah (1978) pointed to the same factors and observed the same basic trend

---

[3] Although their text suggests the 'death' of law, my reaction is the opposite. In their prescription law is democratized, but conversely everything else in government is legalized, to the point that we have 'law-government' (p. 110). Their utopian-leaning text conveys an extraordinary faith in law which, from my standpoint, leads to a frightening vision of what law and government should be, even though I agree with the political position they assert.

in law, which he labelled the shift 'from principles to pragmatism'. There is, however, one major analytical difference with Atiyah's version, a difference which matches the distinction I set out between two conceptions of substantive justice. Unger, Nonet, and Selznick characterized purposive reasoning in terms of the achievement of social goals or ends. Atiyah (p. 5) characterized the change as one from a system of legal rules (he called 'principles') which is forward looking, to a pragmatic system in which a decision is 'designed to achieve justice in the particular circumstances of the case, irrespective of the possible impact of the decision in the future.'

Atiyah argued that the shift he identified was attributable to a variety of factors, prominent among which was a general decline in faith about principles and taking the 'longer view' of affairs which prevailed among intellectuals from the mid-18th to 19th centuries. Another contributing factor, which Atiyah implies but does not articulate, would seem to be the general rise in the sanctity accorded to each individual. The old justification that general rules are good and necessary even if in the occasional case an injustice is done no longer sounds persuasive when individuals come to be seen as bearing rights and entitled to justice.

Like Unger, Nonet, and Selznick, Atiyah believed that the change he observed is a structural change which threatens the very idea of a system of law. Although he speculated that some kind of accommodation might be worked out in practice, he (pp. 31–2) also projected the possibility of dire consequences: 'as discretion succeeds principle, the individual may have escaped one yoke only to bow before a heavier one. For one consequence of the growth of discretion has been a vast decrease in the individual's freedom to plan and order his own life and a corresponding growth in the power and paternalism of the state.'

Thus, similar to Cardozo's observations over fifty years earlier, all four legal theorists noted the same basic decline in the strict adherence to rules, replaced by a greater degree of instrumental reasoning for the purpose of furthering social interests or doing justice in the individual case. These observations indicate that the legal system (as least in Anglo-America)[4] has achieved a kind of hybrid state. Although the conceptualist/essentialist formalism of the Classical period expired long ago, under pressure from the Realists as well as from social and

[4] Atiyah and Summers (1987) argue that the English system is formalistic and the American system substantive. They also recognize (p. 32), however, that both systems contain a mixture.

political factors, and from a change in our cultural beliefs, the formalistic orientation to rule application has basically survived; but in the process space has been made for the operation of instrumental reasoning that is usually associated with substantive justice (in one or the other variant). Judicial decision-making today, as the result of a long term trend, partakes of both rule orientation and instrumental rationality.

B. *The Internal Judicial Attitude*

It is now possible to articulate the structure of judicial decision-making. To provide a concrete focus, I will use what I earlier called the *internal judicial attitude* to refer to judges engaged in the process of decision-making. It is the cognitive style or framework of thought applied in the course of this activity (see Tamanaha 1993a: 117–24). In the US legal tradition there are four elements to the internal judicial attitude: an overarching orientation, an overarching end, a technique, and a disposition. Decision-making as a generic process—like deciding where to go on vacation or deciding whether to go to a theater or rent a video—provides the context within which these elements operate. This generic decision-making context involves a complex dialectical interaction between the projection of ends and the evaluation of means, between objectives and reasons, preferences and possibilities (see Fuller 1966: 1626–7).

The *overarching orientation* of judges in the internal judicial attitude, at least for those judges who accept the responsibility of their role, is well known. It consists of an orientation of impartiality or even-handedness or fairness, a sense that neither party should be favoured over the other except for valid reasons of legal substance. Many judges cite this as *the* characteristic element of judging (a characteristic, it should be noted, which many scientists, and the pragmatists, cite as essential to the practice of science). Essential as this orientation is, it does not get us very far in the decision-making process because it is mostly a negative restraint.

The *overarching end* of judges is, in plain language, to do the right thing.[5] In itself this overarching end is empty of content. For some judges the right thing is to follow the law no matter what the outcome,[6]

---

[5] One former politician turned state judge put it in these words: '. . . when you go on the bench a chemical reaction takes place. [A judge] only wants to do the right thing within his limitations' (Glick 1983: 226).

[6] Atiyah (1978: 23) notes that under the view of Mill and others of his time, 'adherence to principle was justice.'

for others it is to do what is in the social welfare, for others it is to do justice in the individual case, or some other possibility or combination thereof. A judge may uniformly adopt one notion or may shift in response to different cases. Regardless, all judges are trying to do what is right.

The *technique* is central to the internal judicial attitude, and directly reflects the change in the law identified by Unger and the others. The technique is characterized, in a phrase, by *rule-oriented instrumental rationality*. Judges follow and apply rules—hence rule-oriented—yet they do this in an instrumental fashion to achieve outcomes—hence instrumental rationality. The outcomes they aim toward are determined by the specific end they identify. The relative proportion of rule orientation to instrumental rationality depends upon the judge, the case, and the difficulty of achieving the end aimed toward.

In contrast to Unger, who analysed rule orientation and instrumental rationality in analytical terms as irreconcilable elements of competing systems, I describe them here as co-existing aspects of a mental technique, with the judge moving back and forth between the two usually without noticing the shift. Although Unger claimed that the injection of purposive reasoning alongside rule application created an unstable oscillation, when viewed in terms of a total mental arsenal these apparently conflicting impulses in fact generate flexibility. Instead of opposed, they serve as complementary alternatives (subconsciously) called upon as necessary to advance toward the specified end (to do what is right). Rule orientation and instrumental rationality also interact to modify the projected end where one or the other (the rule or the attempt to reason from it) stiffly resists or does not work out.

Actually, the presence of instrumental rationality along side rule orientation did not originate in the collapse of formalism. To the extent that well intentioned judges have always felt compelled by the overarching end to do what is right, even in highly formalistic systems instrumental reasoning is at play. The proliferation of legal fictions, which are designed to avoid unacceptable outcomes forced by the rules, is evidence of that fact. The difference today, reflecting the changes identified by Unger and Atiyah in particular, is that—concurrent with the discrediting of and diminished use of legal fictions, and the demise of equity as separate from law—instrumental reasoning is more openly accepted. From the formalist period to the present, the relative proportion of rule orientation has lessened in comparison to the play of instrumental reasoning, though it is still more dominant as between the two.[7] One point implied by this change is that formalism was not just a rhetorical facade, as legal theorists sometimes indicate; it reflected a real way of judicial decision-making in which the judges were in fact more rule bound (though never totally), just as English judges today tend to be more rule bound than American judges (Atiyah and Summers 1987).

The *disposition* can best be characterized as a sense of being *bound yet not bound*. It is the dispositional (attitudinal) concomitant the technique. To the extent that judges are rule-oriented they are bound, but to the extent that they apply instrumental reasoning they are not bound. Cardozo (1921: 141) wrote that even when the judge is free, he is 'still not wholly free'. CLS doyen Duncan Kennedy (1986: 522), in his phenomenological account of judging, observed that the 'judge is neither free nor bound . . . Or you could say the judge is both free and bound.' Judges are bound yet not bound. No contradiction is entailed by this assertion because it does not refer to a logical relation but to a felt disposition.

C. *The Internal Judicial Attitude and Legal Theory*

To fill out the notion of the internal judicial attitude I will briefly show how it relates to the findings of social scientific studies of judicial decision-making. Necessarily, I will be speaking in terms of generalizations. The first two elements of the internal judicial attitude—the overarching orientation and the overarching end—are constant regardless of locus, judge, and case. By this I mean that all good faith judges strive to be impartial and even-handed, and strive to do the right thing, whenever engaging in judicial decision-making. The crucial variations, then, relate to the technique and the disposition.

The starting points are individual judges and their specific role orientations. The judges who undertake as their primary role orientation the faithful interpretation and application of the law—a large majority of judges, according to role studies to date—will have a high degree of rule orientation relative to instrumental rationality. They will be much more bound than not bound. They will not purposely exploit the inconsistencies and indeterminacies within the legal rules but will make a sin-

---

[7] In this respect I differ from Atiyah's and Summer's (1987) thesis that American law is substantive more so than formal. While they are correct in their comparative thesis that American law is more substantive than English law, the social scientific studies recited indicate that in both behaviour and attitude American judges continue to be more formal than substantive.

cere effort to find out what the law is (in the conventionalist sense), setting aside their personal attitudes when the law requires it.

But cases arise which alter this general relative proportion. These are the exceptional cases which stand out from the daily, weekly, monthly stream. They are not so much the hard cases in the sense of incompleteness or ambiguous legal terms. Most judges today recognize that in certain cases the law runs out or is ambiguous and the judge will have to make law and make choices—no serious role conflict arises. The hard cases I am referring to are the ones in which there is law, clear law, but it runs contrary to the judge's most deeply held personal values and attitudes; these are the cases which put pressure on and test the judge's role orientation, so much so that the judge may even be compelled to articulate explicitly and evaluate his or her role orientation, which is normally taken for granted and seldom a matter of conscious contemplation. The two basic situations in which this conflict arises are when the judge is strongly disposed against the social policy contained within the applicable body of legal rules, or against the particular outcome the legal rules direct in the case at hand.

In such cases (and leading up to it by degrees), the judges are less rule-oriented than usual and reason more instrumentally than usual. Judges will purposely exploit the inconsistencies and indetermincies in the legal rules to avoid the outcome dictated by the rules and arrive at the preferred one; they will explicitly thematize the legal rules and manipulate them with all of their considerable skill. The difference among individual judges (to borrow the labels applied by social scientists) is that the law interpreter-oriented judge will do this less quickly and to a lesser extent; the law-maker will do this more readily and to a more significant degree; and the realist/pragmatist (which probably describes most judges today) is more restrained than the law-maker but less so than the law-interpreter. All judges in this situation are less bound by the rules but not to the point that they are totally not bound. For, if in the final analysis the rules cannot be instrumentally shaped as the judge desires, the good faith judge will rule as the law requires, withdraw from the case, or resign. Ultimately, judges are bound by their sense of responsibility to their office.

The final variation has to do with locus. As a general matter, the strong correlation of attitudes with Supreme Court decision-making demonstrated by social science research, along with statements by the Justices, indicates that Supreme Court Justices for most of this century have had a lesser proportion of rule orientation and a greater proportion of instrumental reasoning when compared to lower court judges. This depends upon the individual Justice and the individual case (i.e. Brennan, Marshall, and Rehnquist in civil liberties cases) and on the time periods involved (just after Roosevelt's court-packing plan and during the heady reformist days of the Warren Court). It may be due to different role orientations adopted by the Justices or as a consequence of the kind of cases they confront—if there are a preponderance of sharply contradictory rules or no clearly applicable rules, one cannot be completely rule-oriented for then no decision could be made. Whatever the reasons, Justices on the Supreme Court are proportionally less bound by the law than lower court judges.

These generalizations—which can be tested by social scientists, although such research will require a much more sophisticated inquiry into role orientations and the influence of legal factors than these studies have achieved up to the present—have direct implications for current discussions in legal theory. In Chapter Two, I argued that the recent espousal of pragmatism among critical theorists is an attempt to open up judicial decision-making to a greater consideration of substantive justice (in both the social and individual sense). Assuming I am correct, this proposed development has in fact already occurred, and for some time now. The continued call for this development partially reflects the fact that these critical theorists—still boxing with formalist phantoms—have failed to recognize the reality of the situation. But it also reflects the fact that they are not satisfied with the outcome wrought by this change—with how things actually work out when judges bring in greater consideration of ends. If this conclusion is correct, there is no reason to believe that more of the same development will satisfy them. The solution they press may not solve the ails they seek to rectify.

For legal theory more broadly, these generalizations provide an answer, albeit a loose one, for the issues raised by Unger, Atiyah, Nonet, and Selznick. The increase in purposive, instrumental reasoning in a rule-oriented system does not spell the end of law, nor does it increase instability. Judges are human actors dealing with human situations, and have demonstrated the capacity to resolve the tension between the two. What maintains this resolution is the attitude that rules will be faithfully applied unless, in the exceptional case, a compelling reason mandates departure. As long as most of the judges most of the time are more rule-bound than not, as is the case in the United States today, a rule of law system will exist.

Three Last Words

Before summarizing what this work has established with regard to the three objectives specified at the outset, I will briefly point out the strengths and limitations revealed in this sustained application of pragmatism. All of the strengths derive from the seminal insight of pragmatism that the key to truth, knowledge, meaning, understanding, and science lies in our acting in the world. Each of these are the products of our actions in the pursuit of our projects, a process which is constructive and creative, yet always influenced by the traditions, habits, and ways of thinking which constitute our social inheritances. Out of this single insight I have derived the social theory of law, the fact-value distinction, the view of institutions as co-ordinated complexes of action, the description of the nature of social practices, the argument that determinacy in law is an achievement, and more. Consistently looking at law and socio-legal studies through the lens of pragmatism leads to a thoroughly social, non-essentialist, behaviour-based view of law. And that, I believe, is the most accurate, descriptive perspective available on law.

The limitation of pragmatism is its substantive emptiness, mentioned in Chapter Two, which plays out in two different ways in this context. In social science terms it is empty in that it makes no claims about the nature of law or social life other than the minimalist descriptive ones set out above. Beyond that, an answer to a particular question about law can be provided only after the study of a given context. In contrast, structuralism, functionalism, autopoiesis, scientific socialism, Black's behaviourism etc., are substantively rich theories—they all assert that law and social life consist of the elements and relations touted by their respective theory. These substantively rich theories provide prescriptively detailed research agendas aimed at verifying the content of their theories; whereas my only basic suggestions are to urge close observation and keep and open mind. The pragmatic approach I present may thus appear uninspired by comparison, although the advantage it offers is that it can accommodate the insights generated by each of the other approaches (assuming they are reflected in observable behaviour), while maintaining a sceptical distance from each, and it does not suffer from the narrow framework each provides.

The second respect in which it is empty is in terms of values. Although I have said a lot about many aspects of law, thus far I have not made assertions about whether it is good or bad, fair or unfair. Pragmatism provides no basis for making such claims. It is about how to acquire reliable knowledge. Pragmatism has nothing affirmative to offer precisely at the point at which the hard questions begin, when we are called upon to make and justify judgements about good and bad, right and wrong. However, pragmatism does continue to serve as a negative check on normative arguments in three ways. First, it insists that any normative arguments based upon an alleged special insight into the Absolute are based upon a false claim; secondly, it suggests that what counts when determining which normative assertions we should accept is whether, when acted upon, the assertions result in consequences we find desirable; thirdly, it reminds us that the best way to determine whether the consequences are desirable is to play close attention to the facts of the matter.

These limitations are the flip side of the strengths of pragmatism, as I indicated earlier, because a theory about the nature of, and acquisition of, knowledge presents no substantive knowledge claims. Although these limitations of pragmatism are not insignificant, in the context of realistic socio-legal studies they are outweighed by its strengths. Legal theory is surfeit with normative claims about law, and socio-legal studies is dominated by substantively rich theories and politically committed theories. The role for realistic socio-legal studies, I have argued, is to be a non-normative testing grounds for these theories. I will now end by returning to the three objectives set out in the Foreward to elaborate several of the insights gained from the realistic approach applied in this book.

Socio-legal Studies

The first last word involves drawing out the tripartite social science related interaction woven through the course of this work. This involved exploring the complementary aspects of participant reports, behaviourism and interpretivism. In everyday terms, these coincide with listening to what people say, carefully observing what they do, considering others' interpretations of what is going on, and trying to figure out how it all comes together. These are the elements of ordinary social interaction. The development of socio-legal studies has been stunted by its disregard for the participant view, its initial positivism-induced obsessive focus on behaviour to the exclusion of meaning, and more recently by the opposite error of rejecting positivism for interpretivism.

Although each of the three makes an integral contribution to the understanding of social life, and I have tried to treat them in a balanced fashion, at the same time I have given a particular prominence to the participant view. My first reason for doing this is to offset a strong tendency among critical scholars and social scientists, positivists as well as interpretivists, to reject participant accounts as biased or deluded. This tendency, I believe, says more about the occupational insecurity of social scientists and academics than it does about the reliability of participant accounts—'[c]oncern with the right to speak with authority is an artifact of academic life' (Bauman 1989: 53).

My second reason is the substantive one that interpretivism (and the Charity Principle) requires that a presumption of credibility be extended to participants. A core tenet of interpretivism is that meaningful actions and beliefs substantially constitute social life. This presupposes that people generally know what they are doing, and that the results of intentional actions are generally as people intend. There are two major exceptions: the unintended consequences of action, and mistake. These can result from a lack of attention or information, or from inadequate reasoning, but neither entails false consciousness or systematic and widespread self-delusion. False consciousness is a real phenomenon, but one that arises under extreme circumstances like brainwashing of prisoners, indoctrination into cults, or cradle to grave control of socialization and access to information as has occurred, for example, in North Korea. In each of these instances there is a concerted, intentional, and overwhelming effort by certain actors to inculcate a particular set of attitudes and beliefs in a target group. Seldom do these circumstances hold in the arena covered by Anglo-American socio-legal studies. Socio-legal discussions of false consciousness presuppose a social teleology—Marx's class dynamics—which operates in a law-like fashion behind the backs of everyone, oppressors and oppressed alike. These ideas are simply incompatible with interpretivism. Nothing prohibits socio-legal scholars from arguing that participants/subjects are unaware of the negative implications of their ideas and beliefs, or that these beliefs operate against their interests. This approach fills the explanatory role now filled by ideology, it points to phenomena which are amenable to observation and verification, and it accords a greater measure of moral respect for participants/subjects.

While an understanding of social life requires input from all three sources, they are not on an entirely equal footing. Behaviourism has a slight priority, for the sound reason captured by the adage that actions speak louder than words. Behaviourism goes only so far, however, because behaviour is underdeterminative with regard to meaning. Participant reports come close to behaviourism, because it always helps to know what people think they are doing. Knowing this, and knowing whether they are actually doing what they say or think they are doing, is essential to an understanding of any situation. Interpretivism, when it consists of the observations of outsiders, simultaneously promises to offer the most insight—by informing participants of a perspective on their own activities they might otherwise be oblivious to—or the least insight, when it reveals what is obvious or already known. And it entails the greatest risk of error, because outsider observers often have their own agenda which they project onto their subjects in the course of interpretation, and they lack the understanding of an activity which can only come from experience. That is not to demean interpretism—many of my own observations in this work are interpretivist—but to remind us that engaging in interpretism involves participating in ordinary social discourse, a fact which tends to be obscured by the heavy overlay of theory talk and citation to authorities.

On the level of application, I have tried to demonstrate that these three perspectives can be fruitfully combined by working on what I have called the behaviour/talk (including meaning) axis. This methodological orientation has dominated throughout, leading to repeated comparisons and contrasts between: what people do and what they say, the rules legal actors enforce and the rules in the law books, the behaviour of people in the community and the rules in the law books, what judges do and what they think they are doing, what judges do and what observers say they are doing, what legal theorists do and what they claim they are doing. That is the focus I have singlemindedly pursued. The behaviour/talk axis roughly matches the positivism-interpretivism distinction, and thus joining the latter two naturally leads to a focus on the former two.

Overall, my discussion of social science was designed to serve the objective of establishing a realistic approach to socio-legal studies. This included laying a pragmatic philosophical foundation regarding the nature of social science and how it must understand the fact-value distinction, and laying a methodological foundation built upon careful and impartial observation, close description, and an openness to testing. And it involved presenting the social theory of law. The social theory of law, I must emphasize, is merely one way of looking at law, a way grounded in interpretive analysis which focuses on how law is constructed as a social presence through shared meaning and participation in practices and co-ordinated complexes of action, through social interaction. But it is not the only way of looking at law. The realistic approach suggests that we should try to understand law from every angle possible, as long as we remember not to mistake the analytical constructs applied (functions, autopoiesis, etc.) for being reality.

In addition to establishing comprehensively the theoretical base, I have tried to demonstrate the power of the realistic approach by applying it to explore issues of relevance to legal theory, including the concept of law, law's role in maintaining social order, legal positivism's claim to being grounded in social behaviour, the problem of indeterminacy, and the nature of the practice of judging. The cost of this focus is that I said very little about many other aspects of the social presence of law; I have not extensively reviewed empirical studies of law other than those dealing with judging; and I have especially neglected how non-legal actors use and view the law. There is much more to learn about law that the realistic approach, and the social theory of law articulated herein, is well suited to uncover.

Finally, I should admit that the approach I have set out is so mundane that to give it a name—'realistic approach'—is pretentious. My description of this 'approach'—keep an eye on what people are doing and listen to what they are saying, strive to be impartial and observe closely, test when possible, be open to information from all sources—consists of common sense rules of thumb we should follow whenever we embark upon an attempt to understand any aspect of social life. Were it not for the overheated atmosphere (with contributors from all sides), much of what I say would be truistic. Rather than claim to have set out an approach, perhaps I should say that this book has been a sustained argument for doing socio-legal studies more realistically.

Legal Theory

The second last word is on the misplaced focus of legal theory. In the course of taking up some of the more prominent issues in legal theory, I have attempted to shift the way in which these issues are approached in the direction of a social theory of law. My conviction is that legal theorists are talking in old ways when the world of law has changed, and that much of what is said is irrelevant to the everyday reality of law (cf. Edwards 1992).

The assumption that law represents consensual social order (that it reflects prevailing social norms), and the assumption that legitimation matters (which underwrites the practice of legal theory), have long been taken for granted by legal theory. These two assumptions are connected: a legitimate law is one that represents a consensual social order. From a descriptive standpoint, however, both assumptions are suspect. In Chapter Four on the concept of law and Chapter Five on legal positivism and the social theory of law, I pressed the points that, descriptively speaking, legal institutions are apparatuses of the state, complexes of co-ordinated actions which are coercive resources of power that do all kinds of things with norms, and are used for all kinds of purposes and have all kinds of functions. Consent and social order are connected to social patterns of behaviour, more so than legal, and legal norms are only contingently (if at all) connected to social norms.

Although what I describe applies in various ways and degrees to law everywhere, it is most evident in situations of recently transplanted law, especially in developing countries, where the laws are not the consensual norms of society and the law often does not substantially contribute to the maintenance of social order (though it is still a significant presence in society). In many countries the law operates to: keep rulers in power and dissenters quiet; serve as a source of income for legal actors; facilitate commercial transactions; give appearance of modernity (despite lying unused), etc. Furthermore, the infrastructure of commercial legal rules that are contained within many legal systems and are steadily spreading around the world have their own impetus and momentum, and generate their own needs and requirements. Consent, at least general social consent, seems to have little to do with the actual formulation or application of a great deal of the law, and social order is substantially generated by social phenomena other than law, yet they remain enthroned within the legal theory view of law.

The necessity, role and influence of legitimation are also, from a descriptive standpoint, highly questionable. A good deal of legal theory assumes that legitimation—or delegitimation—is of central importance. Descriptively speaking, however, at least in Western countries, law just is. Law is a social presence with a concrete and rather stable form that is here to stay as long as society does not collapse. It's existence is strongly rooted in its own institutional and meaning-based permanence and it has increasingly been insinuated as an aspect of social transactions. Many people do law or have something to do with law; it is grounded in legal and academic institutions; it undergirds economic and political institutions; it is carried generation after generation as a tradition, collection of habits and practices, and body of meaning. Law has a social existence entirely apart from legal rules, and this existence is the basis upon which it is perpetuated.

Legal theory generated legitimation—'law provides one right answer'—or delegitimation—'law is politics'—alike seem largely beside the point to the massive intertial presence of law in the United States, and perhaps elsewhere in the West. The source of whatever legitimation or delegitimation that does occur, at least in relation to members of society, comes from the mass media: news reports, dramatic series, sensational cases. As for judges and lawyers, their views of law largely come from the practices they engage in every day, practices which theories about legitimation almost completely ignore, regardless of claims about the internal view. Much of the work in legal theory today has little apparent connection to the actual practice of law.

Legal theory must be prompted to bring the conversation closer to reality. If the reality is that, at least in the West, legal systems have acquired a social permanence, a fixed and largely unmoveable form that can only be patched and trimmed here and there, weighed down by the legal tradition that is passed on to each new generation, what does that mean? Is law one of those social realities that has achieved objectification (like the morning rush hour), not just as a matter of reification but as a matter of sedimented social fact? We don't know because these are not the questions being asked by legal theorists. Descriptions which shake existing assumptions will be an effective means of prompting legal theorists to move in this direction. This is where realistic socio-legal studies have something to offer.

To say that legal theory has little influence in relation to the views of members of the community at large, and few connections to the realities of judging and the practice of law today, does not mean it will not have an influence on the shape that law takes in the future. The Legal Realists had a monumental impact in prompting the instrumental turn in law. The various critical schools of legal theory that dominate the discussion today also have the potential for leading to a change in the longer term.

These critical schools, however, are in a different position from the Realists. First, because the Realists already prompted the overdue paradigm shift in US law away from mechanistic analysis and conceptual formalism, toward more open consideration of social purposes and justice in the individual case, no further major change is possible unless we give up rules altogether for a completely substantive justice regime, which would be deeply problematic given the pluralistic circumstances of modern society. Secondly, much of the critical theory of the past ten years is too theoretical to make a difference. Hermeneutics, Wittgenstein's language analysis, anti-foundational philosophy, and postmodernism, I have argued, either address the conditions of our existence, which cannot be changed and therefore discussing them changes nothing, or address issues within philosophical debates (like the nature of truth) which have absolutely no impact on everyday activities. Ironically, the point of all of these theories is that what counts are ongoing social practices, and that to make a difference one must give up the view that theory can govern from above and engage in the practices on their own terms (Fish 1989), leading to change from within. For all the espousal of pragmatism, the recent flight to theory is precisely what the pragmatists argued against.

Nonetheless, it is presently impossible to assess the full impact of CLS and its critical compatriots and progeny, including critically oriented socio-legal studies. In the short term it appears impotent in relation to the practice of law. What we don't know yet is the long term impact on generations of law students influenced by this literature (assuming it is read). The resilience of practice, grounded in ongoing activities and needs, suggests that it will have little effect. But the more subtle influence will operate in the realm of attitudes. If the next generation of judges are raised on the belief that law is a fraud, and whoever becomes a judge aggressively and without restraint manipulates the law in every case to achieve the outcome they desire, law will be a fraud.

Concern about this possible outcome is what led me to respond to the indeterminacy thesis. Law can certainly be made indeterminate, if judges so desire. But their actions show that by and large they do not act in this way, thereby rendering law determinate. My application of social science to refute the indeterminacy argument is not a repudiation of the critical position. Rather, it indicates that blame was being laid by critical scholars in the wrong place. The problem is not with the judges or with the liberal system of rule application (which has opened up to considerations of substantive justice); the problem is, first, with the substantive content of legal rules and, secondly, with the inequitable structures and distributions of wealth and opportunity in society. These are political, economic, and social problems. To be sure, the liberal rule of law system enforces and perpetuates these inequities, but so would any legal system except one run by benevolent dictators.

Law is law, not politics. State law is a collection of institutions attached to the state, having to do with the subject of law, involving the community of those trained in law. Law is a resource which can be used or called upon to advance political purposes. CLS got the idea wrong. Instead of 'law is politics', the rallying cry should have been 'law for politics'. To draw upon law for politics is to take action in the world, utilizing what law has to offer, as every dedicated legal aid attorney or public interest lawyer does, often at significant personal sacrifice.

Politics

The final last word is about politics, and about why I have aggressively promoted a descriptive, non-normative approach. It is a reaction against what I believe to be a profoundly mistaken attitude and approach that exists today in socio-legal studies. My conviction is that critical scholars have harmed their cause far more so than advanced it. Critical scholars made the mistake of attacking everything about law from every conceivable angle. This wholesale and unrestrained resort to criticism and scepticism carried two consequences that have haunted them ever since. The first consequence is that the failure to be judicious in the critique led to a failure to recognize that law does much good for many people. Critical scholars were defenceless when it was argued in response that rights talk has been a powerful tool in the advancement of the treatment of minorities. In their well nigh total denouncement of the rule of law and of rights, they were living in the elites-only world of theory, out of touch with the reality below (cf. Delgado 1987). People teaching at law schools might not need law (though they are not reluctant to use it when the need arises), but the people they were trying to help sometimes do because they have nowhere else to resort to in times of trouble. Destroying law does not further any political interest other than that of those in society so powerful, so able to call upon resources, that they have the capacity to thrive regardless of law. Contrary to the intentions of critical scholars, the politically inspired systemic assault on law—the attack on the rule of law and legal liberalism in the absence of any viable alternatives—advances only the interests of the elite.

The second consequence is that after the orgy of criticism, there was no basis upon which to build. It is easy to show that there are serious problems with law. The hard part is suggesting what to do about it. Their almost total silence on this, with the exception of Roberto

Unger's utopian proposals, has led more than anything else to the demise of the movement. Critique without construction is indulgence in negativism. Suggestions by critical scholars that more conversation is needed, or more theory, or attention to context, would be laughable were they not so disappointing.

Ironically, matters have come full circle. In recent exchanges, the leftist self-declared 'postmodernists' who were spawned by CLS, at least indirectly by taking CLS views to their logical extension, are now being criticized by CLSers as lacking in any positive normative vision (Tushnet 1992). Mark Tushnet, who in his CLS salad days declared (1988: 317–18) that, '[c]ritique is all there is,' now complains that postmodernists have taken the critique so far that the very possibility of normative argument has been destroyed. A related development can be found in other schools with connections to CLS, including certain versions of critical feminism and critical race theory. Drawing upon the theory as well as the tactics of CLS, group-based advocates are setting themselves up with a kind of epistemological privilege, claiming to represent a particular point of view which must be judged by its own internal standards (which, according to some theorists, are superior to the middle-aged white male standards). Although we have learned a great deal from these schools of thought about the silent biases contained within law, the long term destructive potential entailed by such exclusive and excluding group-bound-standards is reason for concern. What used to be plain old disagreement is now construed as incommensurable discourse and a battle against hegemonic ideology. Promoting a cause of social justice shared by many of the mainstream, left-leaning academics in law faculties, CLS took its trashing of law to such an extreme that it left nowhere to go except ever narrower spin-offs.

Socio-legal studies have also been harmed by these developments. The close association of socio-legal scholars with CLS, either as participants or cheering on the sidelines, has had a negative influence on the field. A good deal of socio-legal work is avowedly critical, with no constructive suggestions. Much of it transparently perpetuates the leftist view of the world and thus is easily dismissed as pure politics. Like much CLS work, these critical socio-legal studies are read mostly by people who already agree (the rest of the group), and largely ignored by everyone else. As a form of transformative politics, it is an abject failure.

It is time to switch tactics. It is time for socio-legal studies to get back to its scientific basics, to get back to impartial and disinterested investigation, to give up the impotent politics and the debunking anti-law attitude. The accumulation of knowledge is a valuable project that stands on its own merit. Socio-legal scholars can no more completely efface their biases than can judges, of course, but they can at least strive to meet the level of success attained by many judges, as indicated by social scientific studies of judicial decision-making. Only in this way can we uncover what specifically is wrong with law and how it can be made better.

To critics who assert that I have revived the fact/value distinction buried by postmodernism, my response is that I have built a non-foundational version of this distinction out of philosophical pragmatism (which presaged postmodernism). I would not assert, as Llewelyn did, that the 'ought' should be put on hold while figuring out the 'is'. Rather, I am proposing a division of labour: legal theory continues with the ought, as it has always done; realistic socio-legal studies takes care of the is. For those who claim this is an abdication of moral responsibility, I respond, with Dewey, that science has an inherently critical capacity in relation to values because it provides the check and testing ground for ideas and beliefs. In this work I have applied science to test the beliefs of legal and socio-legal theorists across the political spectrum.

A commitment to engage in non-political social scientific inquiry is, I believe, a political commitment, made in the faith that increased understanding of the truth—the facts of the matter about law—is a necessary prerequisite to positive change.

Bibliography

Abel, R. L. (1973), 'A Comparative Theory of Dispute Institution in Society', *Law and Society Review* 8: 217–347.
—— (1976), 'Law Books and Books About Law', *Stanford Law Review* 26: 175–228.
—— (1980), 'Law & Anthropology', *American Journal of Comparative Law* 28: 128–42.
—— and P. S. C. Lewis (1989) (eds.), *Lawyers and Society, Vol. 3: Comparative Theories* (Berkeley, Calif.: University of California Press).
Aldisert, R. J. (1985), 'The Role of Courts in Contemporary Society', in M. W. Cannon and D. M. O'Brien (eds.), *Views From the Bench* (Chatham, NJ: Chatham House Publishers), 257–65.
Alexander, J. C., et al, (1987) (eds.), *The Micro-Macro Link* (Berkeley, Calif.: University of California Press).
Atiyah, P. S. (1978), *From Principles to Pragmatism: Changes in the Function of the Judicial Process and the Law* (Oxford: Clarendon Press).
—— and Summers, R. S. (1987), *Form and Substance in Anglo-American Law* (Oxford: Clarendon Press).
Auerbach, C. A. (1966), 'Legal Tasks for the Sociologists', *Law and Society Review* 1: 91–104.
Baker, L. (1992), ' "Just Do It": Pragmatism and Progressive Social Change', *Virginia Law Review* 78: 697–718.
Barnes, B. (1974), *Scientific Knowledge and Sociological Theory* (Boston: Routledge and Kegan Paul).
—— (1977), *Interests and the Growth of Knowledge* (Boston: Routledge and Kegan Paul).
Bauman, Z. (1989), 'Hermeneutics and Modern Social Theory', in D. Held and J. B. Thompson (eds.), *Social Theory of Modern Societies* (New York: Cambridge University Press), 34–55.
—— (1992), *Intimations of Postmodernity* (New York: Routledge and Kegan Paul).
Baumgartner, M. P. (1992), 'The Myth of Discretion', in K. Hawkins (ed.), *The Uses of Discretion* (New York: Oxford University Press), 129–62.
Baynes, K., Bohman, J., and McCarthy, T. (1987) (eds.), *After Philosophy: End or Transformation?* (Cambridge, Mass.: MIT Press).
Beiser, E. N. (1974), 'The Rhode Island Supreme Court: A Well-Integrated Political System', *Law and Society Review* 8: 167–86.
Berends, M. (1992), 'Review Essay: An Elusive Profession? Lawyers in Society', *Law and Society Review* 26: 161–88.
Berger, P., and Luckmann, T. (1966), *The Social Construction of Reality* (Garden City, NY: Doubleday).

Black, D. J. (1972), 'The Boundaries of Legal Sociology', *Yale Law Journal* 81: 1086–1100.
—— (1976), *The Behavior of Law* (New Haven, Conn.: Yale University Press).
—— (1984), 'Social Control as a Dependent Variable', in D. J. Black (ed.), *Toward a General Theory of Social Control-Volume I* (New York: Academic Press), 1–36.
—— (1989), *Sociological Justice* (New York: Oxford University Press).
—— (1995), 'The Epistemology of Pure Sociology', *Law and Social Inquiry* 20: 829–70.
Bleicher, J. (1980), *Contemporary Hermeneutics: Hermeneutics as Method, Philosophy and Critique* (Boston: Routledge and Kegan Paul).
Bloor, D. (1976), *Knowledge and Social Imagery* (Boston: Routledge and Kegan Paul).
—— (1984), 'The Sociology of Reasons: Or Why "Epistemic Factors" Are Really "Social Factors" ', in J. Brown (ed.), *Scientific Rationality: The Sociological Turn* (Boston: D. Reidel Publishing Co.), 295–324.
Blumer, H. (1969), *Symbolic Interactionism* (Englewood Cliffs, NJ: Prentice-Hall).
Bohannan, P. (1967), 'The Differing Realms of the Law', in P. Bohannan (ed.), *Law and Warfare* (Garden City, NY: Natural History Press), 43–56.
Bohman, J. (1991), *New Philosophy of Social Science: Problems of Indeterminacy* (Cambridge, Mass.: MIT Press).
Brace, P., and Hall M. G. (1993), 'Integrated Models of Judicial Dissent', *Journal of Politics* 55: 914–35.
—— (1995), 'Studying Courts Comparatively: The View From the American States', *Political Research Quarterly* 48: 5–29.
Brenner, S. and Dorff, R. H. (1992), 'The Attitudinal Model and Fluidity Voting on the United States Supreme Court: A Theoretical Perspective', *Journal of Theoretical Politics* 4: 195–205.
Bronner, S. E. (1994), *Of Critical Theory and Its Theorists* (Cambridge, Mass.: Blackwell).
Brown, J. (1984) (ed.), *Scientific Rationality: The Sociological Turn* (Boston: D. Reidel Publishing Co.).
Burton, S. J. (1985), *An Introduction to Law and Legal Reasoning* (Boston: Little, Brown and Co.).
Calavita, K., and Seron, C. (1992), 'Postmodernism and Protest: Recovering the Sociological Imagination', *Law and Society Review* 26: 765–71.
Cardozo, B. N. (1921), *The Nature of the Judicial Process* (New Haven, Conn.: Yale University Press).
—— (1924), *The Growth of Law* (New Haven, Conn.: Yale University Press).
Carlson, K. E. and McDonald, D. C. (1993), *Sentencing in the Federal Courts: Does Race Matter?* (Washington, D.C.: U.S. Department of Justice).
Carson, D. (1988), 'Psychologists Should be Wary of Involvement With Lawyers', in P. J. van Koppen, D. J. Hessing, and G. van Den Heuvel (eds.),

Lawyers on Psychology and Psychologists on Law (Amsterdam: Swets & Zeitlinger), 28–34.

Chow, D. C. K. (1992), 'A Pragmatic Model of Law', *Washington Law Review* 76: 755–825.

Cohen, F. S. (1935), 'Transcendental Nonsense and the Functional Approach', *Columbia Law Review* 35: 809–49.

—— (1960), *The Legal Conscience* (New Haven, Conn.: Yale University Press).

Cohen, I. J. (1987), 'Structuration Theory and Social Praxis', in *Social Theory Today* (Stanford, Calif.: Stanford University Press), 273–308.

Comaroff, J. L., and Roberts, S. (1981), *Rules and Processes: The Cultural Logic of Dispute in an African Context* (Chicago: University of Chicago Press).

Conant, J. (1990), 'Introduction', in H. Putnam (ed.), *Realism With a Human Face* (Cambridge, Mass.: Harvard University Press), xv–lxxiv.

Conley, J. M., and O'Barr, W. (1993), 'Legal Anthropology Comes Home: A Brief History of the Ethnographic Study of Law', *Loyola University of Los Angeles Law Review* 27: 41–64.

Cook, B. B. (1973), 'Sentencing Behavior of Federal Judges: Draft Cases—1972', *University of Cincinnati Law Review* 42: 597–633.

—— (1977), 'Public Opinion and Federal Judicial Policy', *American Journal of Political Science* 21: 567–600.

Coombe, R. J. (1995), 'Finding and Losing One's Self in the Topoi: Placing and Displacing the Postmodern Subject in Law', *Law and Society Review* 29: 600–09.

Cooney, M. (1986), 'Review Article: Behavioral Sociology of Law: A Reference', *Modern Law Review* 49: 262–71.

Coser, L. (1982), 'The Notion of Control in Sociological Theory', in J. Gibbs (ed.), *Social Control: Views from the Social Sciences* (Beverly Hills, Calif.: Sage Publications), 13–22.

Cotterrell, R. (1983), 'The Sociological Concept of Law', *Journal of Law and Society* 10: 241–55.

—— (1984), *The Sociology of Law* (London: Butterworths).

—— (1989), *The Politics of Jurisprudence* (Austin, Tex.: Butterworths).

—— (1995), *Law's Community: Legal Theory in Sociological Perspective* (Oxford: Clarendon Press).

Davidson, D. (1984), *Inquiries Into Truth and Interpretation* (New York: Oxford University Press).

Delgado, R. (1987), 'The Ethereal Scholar: Does Critical Legal Studies Have What Minorities Want?', *Harvard Civil Rights Civil Liberties Law Review* 22: 301–22.

Dewey, J. (1925), *Experience and Nature* (New York: Norton).

—— (1931), 'Logical Method and Law', in *Philosophy and Civilization* (New York: Minton, Balch & Company), 126–40.

—— (1948), *Reconstruction in Philosophy* (enlarged edn.) (Boston: Beacon Press).

Dreyfus, H. (1986), 'Why Studies of Human Capacities Modeled on Ideal Natural Science Can Never Achieve Their Goal', in J. Margolis, M. Krausz, and R. M. Burian (eds.), *Rationality, Relativism, and the Human Sciences* (Boston: M. Nijhoff).

DuBois, P. L. (1988), 'The Illusion of Judicial Consensus Revisited: Partisan Conflict on an Intermediate State Court of Appeals', *American Journal of Political Science* 32: 946–67.

Duxbury, N. (1995), *Patterns of American Jurisprudence* (Oxford: Clarendon Press).

Dworkin, R. M. (1986), *Law's Empire* (Cambridge, Mass.: Belknap Press).

—— (1987), 'Legal Theory and the Problem of Sense', in R. Gavison (ed.), *Issues in Contemporary Legal Philosophy* (Oxford: Clarendon Press), 9–20.

Edgerton, R. (1985), *Rules, Exceptions, and the Social Order* (Berkeley, Calif.: University of California Press).

Edgeworth, B. (1986), 'Legal Positivism and the Philosophy of Language: A Critique of H. L. A. Hart's "Descriptive Sociology" ', *Legal Studies* 6: 115–39.

Edwards, H. T. (1983), 'The Rising Work Load and Perceived "Bureaucracy" of the Federal Court: A Causation-Based Approach to the Search for Appropriate Remedies', *Iowa Law Review* 68: 871–936.

—— (1983–4), 'The Role of a Judge in Modern Society: Some Reflections on Current Practice in Federal Appellate Adjudication', *Cleveland State Law Review* 32: 385–430.

—— (1985), 'Public Misconceptions Concerning the 'Politics' of Judging: Dispelling Some Myths About the D.C. Circuit', *University of Colorado Law Review* 56: 619–46.

—— (1991), 'The Judicial Function and the Elusive Goal of Principled Decisionmaking', *Wisconsin Law Review* 1991: 837–65.

—— (1992), 'The Growing Disjunction Between Legal Education and the Legal Profession', *Michigan Law Review* 91: 34–78.

—— (1993), 'The Growing Disjunction Between Legal Education and the Legal Profession: A Postscript', *Michigan Law Review* 91: 2191–219.

Ehrlich, E. (1922), 'The Sociology of Law', *Harvard Law Review* 36: 130–45.

—— (1975), *The Fundamental Principles of the Sociology of Law* (New York: Russell & Russell).

Emerson, R. M., and Paley, B. (1992), 'Organizational Horizons and Complaint-Filing', in *The Uses of Discretion* (Oxford: Clarendon Press), 231–47.

Ewick, P., and Silbey, S. (1995), 'Subversive Stories and Hergemonic Tales: Toward a Sociology of Narrative', *Law and Society Review* 29: 197–226.

Farber, D. A. (1988), 'Legal Pragmatism and the Constitution', *Minnesota Law Review* 72: 1331–78.

—— and Sherry, S. (1993), 'Telling Stories Out of School: An Essay on Legal Narratives', *Stanford Law Review* 45: 807–55.

Feeley, M. M. (1976), 'The Concept of Laws in Social Science: A Critique and Expanded View', *Law and Society Review* 10: 497–523.

Fish, S. E. (1980), *Is There a Text in This Class?* (Cambridge, Mass.: Harvard University Press).
—— (1989), *Doing What Comes Naturally* (Durham, NC: Duke University Press).
—— (1990), 'Almost Pragmatism: Richard Posner's Jurisprudence', *University of Chicago Law Review* 57: 1447–75.
Fiss, O. M. (1985), 'Conventionalism', *Southern California Law Review* 58: 177–97.
—— (1982), 'Objectivity and Interpretation', *Stanford Law Review* 34: 739–63.
Flanagan, O. (1991), *The Science of the Mind* (2nd edn.) (Cambridge, Mass.: MIT Press).
Frankford, D. M. (1995), 'Social Structure of Right and Wrong: Normativity Without Agents', *Law and Social Inquiry* 20: 787–803.
Frankfurter, F. (1916), 'The Constitutional Opinions of Justice Holmes', *Harvard Law Review* 29: 683–99.
Frazier, C. E., and Bock, E. W. (1982), 'Effects of Court Officials on Sentence Severity', *Criminology* 20: 257–72.
Friedman, L. M. (1969), 'Legal Culture and Social Development', *Law and Society Review* 4: 29–44.
—— (1975), *The Legal System: A Social Science Perspective* (New York: Russell Sage Foundation).
—— (1986), 'The Law and Society Movement', *Stanford Law Review* 38: 763–80.
Fuller, L. L. (1964), *The Morality of Law* (New Haven, Conn.: Yale University Press).
—— (1966), 'An Afterword: Science and the Judicial Process', *Harvard Law Review* 79: 1604–28.
Gadamer, H. G. (1979), 'The Problem of Historical Consciousness', in P. Rabinow and W. Sullivan (eds.), *Interpretive Social Science* (Berkeley, Calif.: University of California Press), 103–60.
—— (1991), *Truth and Method* (2nd ed.), trans. J. Weinsheimer and D. G. Marshall (New York: Crossroad).
Galanter, M. (1981), 'Justice in Many Rooms: Courts, Private Ordering, and Indigenous Law', *Journal of Legal Pluralism* 19: 1–47.
Garfinkel, H. (1967), *Studies in Ethnomethodology* (Englewood Cliffs, NJ: Prentice-Hall).
Geertz, C. (1973), *The Interpretation of Cultures* (New York: Basic Books).
—— (1983), *Local Knowledge: Further Essays in Interpretive Anthropology* (New York: Basic Books).
George, T. E., and Epstein, L. (1992), 'On the Nature of Supreme Court Decision Making', *American Political Science Review* 86: 323–37.
Gibbs, J. P. (1982), 'Law as a Means of Social Control', in J. P. Gibbs (ed.), *Social Control: Views from the Social Sciences* (Beverly Hills, Calif.: Sage Publications), 83–113.
Gibson, J. L. (1978a), 'Race as a Determinant of Criminal Sentences: A

Methodological Critique and a Case Study', *Law and Society Review* 12: 455–78.

—— (1978b), 'Judges' Role Orientations, Attitudes, and Decisions: An Interactive Model', *American Political Science Review* 72: 911–24.

Giddens, A., and Turner, J. (1987) (eds.), *Social Theory Today* (Stanford, Calif.: Stanford University Press).

Giles, M. W., and Walker, T. G. (1975), 'Judicial Policy-Making and Southern School Segregation', *Journal of Politics* 37: 917–36.

Glick, H. R., and K. N. Vines (1973), *State Court Systems* (Englewood Cliffs, NJ: Prentice-Hall).

—— (1983), *Court, Politics, and Justice* (New York: McGraw Hill).

Goldman, S. (1968), 'Conflict and Consensus in the United States Courts of Appeals', *Wisconsin Law Review* 1968: 461–82, reprinted in S. Brenner (1973) (ed.), *American Judicial Behavior* (New York: MSS Information Corp.), 102–8.

—— (1975), 'Voting Behavior on the United States Courts of Appeals Revisited', *American Political Science Review* 69: 491–506.

—— (1978), 'Judicial Appointments to the United States Courts of Appeals', in S. Goldman, and A. Sarat (eds.), *American Court Systems: Reading in Judicial Process and Behavior* (San Francisco, Calif.: W. H. Freeman and Co.), 270–9.

—— and Sarat, A. (1978) (eds.), *American Court Systems: Reading in Judicial Process and Behavior* (San Francisco, Calif.: W. H. Freeman and Co.).

Gordon, R. (1990), 'New Developments in Legal Theory', in D. Kairys (2nd ed.), *The Politics of Law: A Progressive Critique* (New York: Pantheon Books), 413–25.

Grey, T. (1989), 'Holmes and Legal Pragmatism', *Stanford Law Review* 41: 787–863.

Griffiths, J. (1986), 'What is Legal Pluralism?', *Journal of Legal Pluralism* 24: 1–55.

Grossman, J. B. (1966), 'Social Backgrounds and Judicial Decision-Making', *Harvard Law Review* 79: 1551–64.

Gulliver, P. H. (1973), 'Negotiations as a Mode of Dispute Settlement: Towards a General Model', *Law and Society Review* 7: 667–91.

Habermas, J. (1988), *On the Logic of the Social Sciences* (Cambridge, Mass.: MIT Press).

Hagan, J. (1974), 'Extra-Legal Attributes and Criminal Sentencing: An Assessment of a Sociological Viewpoint', *Law and Society Review* 8: 357–83.

Hall, D. (1994), *Richard Rorty: Prophet and Poet of the New Pragmatism* (Albany: State University of New York Press).

Hamnett, I. (1975), *Chieftainship and Legitimacy* (Boston: Routledge and Kegan Paul).

—— (1977), 'Introduction', in I. Hamnett (ed.), *Social Anthropology and Law* (New York: Academic Press), 1–13.

Handler, J. (1992), 'Postmodernism, Protest, and the New Social Movements: The Presidential Address, 1992', *Law and Society Review* 26: 697–731.

—— (1992), 'Discretion: Power, Quiescence, and Trust', in K. Hawkins (ed.), *The Uses of Discretion* (New York: Oxford University Press), 331–60.
Harrington, C. B., and Yngvesson, B. (1990), 'Interpretive Sociolegal Research', *Law and Social Inquiry* 15: 135–48.
Hart, H. L. A. (1957–8), 'Positivism and the Separation of Law and Morals', *Harvard Law Review* 71: 593–629.
—— (1961), *The Concept of Law* (Oxford: Clarendon Press).
—— (1983), *Essays in Jurisprudence and Philosophy* (New York: Oxford University Press).
—— (1994), *The Concept of Law* (2nd ed.) (Oxford: Clarendon Press).
Hawkins, K. (1992), 'The Use of Legal Discretion: Perspectives from Law and Social Science', in K. Hawkins (ed.), *The Uses of Discretion* (New York: Oxford University Press), 11–46.
Hempel, C. (1965), *Aspects of Scientific Explanation* (New York: Free Press).
Hesse, M. (1980), *Revolutions and Reconstructions in the Philosophy of Science* (Bloomington, Ind.: Indiana University Press).
Hiley, D., Bohman, J., and Shusterman, R. (1991) (eds.), *The Interpretive Turn: Philosophy, Science, Culture* (Ithaca, NY: Cornell University Press).
Hoebel, A. (1954), *The Law of Primitive Man* (Cambridge, Mass.: Harvard University Press).
Hollis, M., and Lukes, S. (1982) (eds.), *Rationality and Relativism* (Cambridge, Mass.: MIT Press).
Holmes, O. W. (1897), 'The Path of the Law', *Harvard Law Review* 10: 457–78.
—— (1955), 'Law in Science and Science in Law', in J. J. Marke (ed.), *The Holmes Reader: The Life, Writings, Speeches, Constitutional Decisions, etc., of the Late Oliver Wendell Holmes* (New York: Oceana Publications), 124–47.
Homans, G. (1987), 'Behaviorism and After', in A. Giddens and J. Turner (eds.), *Social Theory Today* (Stanford, Calif.: Stanford University Press), 58–81.
Horwitz, A. V. (1990), *The Logic of Social Control* (New York: Plenum Press).
Horwitz, M. J. (1977a), 'The Rule of Law: An Unqualified Human Good?', *Yale Law Journal* 86: 561–6.
—— (1977b), *The Transformation of American Law 1780–1860* (Cambridge, Mass.: Harvard University Press).
—— (1988),'Rights', *Harvard Civil Rights Civil Liberties Law Review* 23: 393–406.
—— (1992), *The Transformation of American Law 1870–1960* (New York: Oxford University Press).
Howard, Jr., J. W. (1968), 'On the Fluidity of Judicial Choice', *American Political Science Review* 62: 43–56.
—— (1977), 'Role Perceptions and Behavior in Three U.S. Courts of Appeals', *Journal of Politics* 39: 916–38.
Hunt, A. (1983), 'Behavioral Sociology of Law: A Critique of Donald Black', *Journal of Law and Society* 10: 19–46.
—— (1985), 'The Ideology of Law: Advances and Problems in Recent

Application of the Concept of Ideology to the Analysis of Law', *Law and Society Review* 19: 11–37.
—— (1987), 'The Critique of Law: What is "Critical" About Critical Legal Theory?', in P. Fitzpatrick and A. Hunt (eds.), *Critical Legal Studies* (New York: Basil Blackwell), 5–19.
—— (1990), 'The Big Fear: Law Confronts Postmodernism', *McGill Law Journal* 35: 507–40.
—— (1993), *Explorations in Law and Society* (New York: Routledge and Kegan Paul).
Jacob, H. (1991), 'Decision Making in Trial Courts', in J. B. Gates and C. A. Johnson (eds.), *The American Courts: A Critical Assessment* (Washington, DC: CQ Press), 213–33.
James, W. (1890), *The Principles of Psychology, Vol. I* (New York: Dover Publications).
—— (1975), *Pragmatism and the Meaning of Truth* (Cambridge, Mass.: Harvard University Press).
Janowitz, M. (1978), 'The Intellectual History of "Social Control"', in J. S. Rouek (ed.), *Social Control for the 1980's* (Westport, Conn.: Greenwood Press), 20–45.
Jarvie, I. (1984), 'A Plague on Both Your Houses', in J. Brown (ed.), *Scientific Rationality: The Sociological Turn* (Boston: D. Reidel Publishing Co.), 165–82.
Joas, H. (1993), *Pragmatism and Social Theory* (Chicago: University of Chicago Press).
Johnson, A. M. (1991), 'Think Like a Lawyer, Work Like a Machine: The Dissonance Between Law School and Law Practice', *Southern California Law Review* 64: 1231–60.
Johnson, C. A. (1987), 'Law, Politics, and Judicial Decision Making: Lower Federal Court Uses of Supreme Court Decisions', *Law and Society Review* 21: 325–40.
Just, P. (1992), 'History, Power, Ideology, and Culture: Current Directions in the Anthropology of Law', *Law and Society Review* 26: 373–411.
Kennedy, D. (1979), 'The Structure of Blackstone's Commentaries', *Buffalo Law Review* 28: 205–382.
—— (1986), 'Freedom and Constraint in Adjudication: A Critical Phenomenology', *Journal of Legal Education* 36: 518–62.
King, M. (1993), 'The Truth About Autopoiesis', *Journal of Law and Society* 20: 218–36.
Klare, K. (1978), 'Judicial Deradicalization of the Wagner Act and the Origin of Modern Legal Consciousness, 1937–41', *Minnesota Law Review* 62: 265–339.
Kleck, G. (1981), 'Racial Discrimination in Criminal Sentencing: A Critical Evaluation of the Evidence With Additional Evidence on the Death Penalty', *American Sociological Review* 46: 783–805.

Kress, K. (1989), 'Legal Indeterminacy', *California Law Review* 77: 283–337.
Kritzer, H. M., and Uhlman, T. M. (1977), 'Sisterhood in the Courtroom: Sex of Judge and Defendant in Criminal Cases Disposition', *Social Science Journal* 14: 77–88.
Kronman, A. T. (1983), *Max Weber* (Stanford: Stanford University Press).
—— (1990), 'Precedent and Tradition', *Yale Law Journal* 99: 1029–68.
Krygier, M. (1980),'Anthropological Approaches', in E. Kamenka and A. Erh-Soon-Tay (eds.), *Law and Social Control* (New York: St. Martin's Press), 27–59.
Kuhn, T. S. (1977), *The Essential Tension* (Chicago: University of Chicago Press).
Laudan, L. (1984), 'The Pseudo-Science of Science', in J. Brown (ed.), *Scientific Rationality: The Sociological Turn* (Boston: D. Reidel Publishing Co.), 41–73.
Leiter, B. (1992), 'Intellectual Voyeurism in Legal Scholarship', *Yale Journal of Law and the Humanities* 4: 79–104.
Levin, M. A. (1974), 'Urban Politics and Judicial Behavior', *Journal of Legal Studies* 3: 339–75.
Levinson, S. (1991), 'Book Review: Strolling Down the Path of the Law (And Toward Critical Legal Studies?): The Jurisprudence of Richard Posner', *Columbia Law Review* 91: 1221–52.
Llewellyn, K. (1930), *The Bramble Bush: Some Lectures on Law and Its Study* (New York: Columbia University School of Law).
—— (1962), *Jurisprudence: Realism in Theory and Practice* (Chicago: University of Chicago Press).
Lloyd-Bostock, S. M. (1981), 'Psychology and the Law: A Critical Review of Research and Practice', *Journal of Law and Society* 8: 1–28.
—— (1988), 'Psychology and Law: From Understanding to Influencing Law in Practice', in P. J. van Koppen, D. J. Hessing, and G. van Den Heuvel (eds.), *Lawyers on Psychology and Psychologists on Law* (Amsterdam: Swets & Zeitlinger), 9–23.
Luhmann, N. (1982), *The Differentiation of Society* (New York: Columbia University Press).
—— (1985), *A Sociological Theory of Law* (Boston: Routledge and Kegan Paul).
Macaulay, S. (1963), 'Non-Contractual Relations in Business: A Preliminary Study', *American Sociological Review* 28: 55–67.
—— (1992), 'On Rattling Cages: Joel Handler Goes to Philadelphia and Gives a Presidential Address', *Law and Society Review* 26: 825–30.
MacCormick, N. (1981), *H. L. A. Hart* (Stanford, Calif.: Stanford University Press).
MacIntyre, A. (1984), *After Virtue: A Study in Moral Theory* (Notre Dame, Ind.: University of Notre Dame Press).
Mair, L. P. (1962), *Primitive Government* (Baltimore, Md.: Penguin Books).
Malinowski, B. (1926), *Crime and Custom in Savage Society* (New York: Harcourt, Brace and Company).
—— (1934), 'Introduction', in H. I. Hogbin, *Law and Order in Polynesia* (New York: Harcourt, Brace and Company).

Malinowski, B. (1942), 'A New Instrument for the Interpretation of Law—Especially Primitive', *Yale Law Journal* 51: 1237–54.
—— (1944), *A Scientific Theory of Culture* (Chapel Hill, NC: The University of North Carolina Press).
Manning, P. K., and Hawkins, K. (1990), 'Legal Decisions: A Frame Analytic Perspective', in S. Riggens (ed.), *Beyond Goffman* (Berlin: Aldine De Gruyter), 203–33.
Marcus, G. E., and Fischer, M. M. J. (1986), *Anthropology as Cultural Critique: An Experimental Moment in the Human Sciences* (Chicago: University of Chicago Press).
Margolis, J. (1986), 'Rationality and Realism', in J. Margolis, M. Krausz, and R. M. Burian (eds.), *Rationality, Relativism, and the Human Sciences* (Boston: M. Nijhoff), 223–40.
Marke, J. J. (1955) (ed.), *The Holmes Reader* (New York: Oceana Publications).
Marshall, T. (14 Mar. 1977) remarks, in W. F. Murphy and C. H. Pritchett (4th ed. 1986), *Courts, Judges and Politics* (New York: Random House), 176–80.
Matsuda, M. (1990), 'Pragmatism Modified and the False Consciousness Problem', *Southern California Law Review* 63: 1763–82.
Mead, G. H. (1934), *Mind, Self, and Society* (Chicago: University of Chicago Press).
Mensch, E. (1990), 'The History of Mainstream Legal Thought', in D. Kairys (2nd ed.), *The Politics of Law: A Progressive Critique* (New York: Pantheon Books), 13–37.
Merriam-Webster (1981), *Webster's Third New International Dictionary of the English Language, Unabridged* (Springfield, Mass.: G. & C. Merriam Company).
Merry, S. E. (1988),'Legal Pluralism', *Law and Society Review* 22: 869–96.
—— (1992), 'Anthropology, Law and Transnational Processes', *American Review of Anthropology* 21: 357–79.
—— (1994), 'Courts as Performances: Domestic Violence Hearings in a Hawai'i Family Court', in M. Lazarus-Black and S. F. Hirsch (eds.), *Contested States: Law, Hegemony, and Resistance* (New York: Routledge and Kegan Paul), 35–58.
—— (1995), 'Resistance and the Cultural Power of Law: 1994 Presidential Address', *Law and Society Review* 29: 11–12.
Merton, R. K. (1968), *Social Theory and Social Structure* (New York: Free Press).
Mertz, E., (1994), 'A New Social Constructionism for Sociolegal Studies', *Law and Society Review* 28: 1243–65.
Mitchell, W. J. T. (1990) (ed.), *Against Theory: Literal Studies and the New Pragmatism* (Chicago: University of Chicago Press).
Minda, G. (1989), 'The Jurisprudential Movements of the 1980's', *Ohio State University Law Journal* 50: 599–662.
—— (1993), 'Jurisprudence at Century's End', *Journal of Legal Education* 43: 27–59.

—— (1995), *Postmodern Legal Movements: Law and Jurisprudence at Century's End* (New York: New York University Press).
Minow, M., and Spelman, E. (1990), 'In Context', *Southern California Law Review* 63: 1597–1652.
Moore, M. S. (1985), 'A Natural Law Theory of Interpretation', *Southern California Law Review* 58: 277–398.
—— (1989), 'The Interpretive Turn in Modern Theory: A Turn for the Worse?', *Stanford Law Review* 41: 871–957.
Moore, S. F. (1978), *Law as Process: An Anthropological Approach* (Boston: Routledge and Kegan Paul).
—— (1986), 'Legal Systems of the World', in L. Lipson and S. Wheeler (eds.), *Law and the Social Sciences* (New York: Russell Sage Foundation), 11–62.
Mulkay, M. J. (1979), *Science and the Sociology of Knowledge* (Boston: G. Allen & Unwin).
Munger, F. (1993), 'Sociology of Law for a Postliberal Society', *Loyola University of Los Angeles Law Review* 27: 89–125.
Murphy, J. P. (1990), *Pragmatism: From Peirce to Davidson* (Boulder: Westview Press).
Myers, M. A. (1988), 'Social Background and the Sentencing Behavior of Judges', *Criminology* 26: 649–75.
Nader, L. (1965), 'The Anthropological Study of Law', *American Anthropologist* 67: 3–32.
—— and Yngvesson, B. (1973), 'On Studying the Ethnography of Law and Its Consequences, in J. Honigmann (ed.), *Handbook on Social and Cultural Anthropology* (Chicago: Rand McNally Company), 883–921.
Nagel, S. S. (1969), *The Legal Process from a Behavioral Perspective* (Homewood, Ill.: Dorsey Press).
Nelson, R. L. (1988), 'Ideology, Scholarship, and Sociolegal Change: Lessons from Galanter and the "Litigation Crisis" ', *Law and Society Review* 21: 677–93.
Nonet, P. (1976), 'For Jurisprudential Sociology', *Law and Society Review* 10: 525–45.
—— and Selznik, P. (1978), *Law and Society in Transition: Toward Responsive Law* (New York: Octagon Books).
Oaks, D. H. (1985), 'When Judges Legislate', in M. W. Cannon and D. M. O'Brien (eds.), *Views From the Bench* (Chatham, N.J.: Chatham House Publishers), 147–54.
Parsons, T. (1980), 'The Law and Social Control', in W. Evan (ed.), *The Sociology of Law* (New York: Free Press), 60–8.
Patterson, D. M. (1990a), 'Law's Pragmatism: Law as a Practice and Narrative', *Virginia Law Review* 76: 937–96.
—— (1990b), 'Book Review, Law's Practice', *Columbia Law Review* 90: 575–600.
—— (1992), 'Postmodernism/Feminism/Law', *Cornell Law Review* 77: 254–317.
—— (1994) (ed.), *Postmodernism and Law* (New York: New York University Press).

Payne, M. A. (1982), 'Law Based on Accepted Authority', *William & Mary Law Review* 23: 501–28.
Peterson, R. D., and Hagan, J. (1984), 'Changing Conceptions of Race: Towards an Account of Anomalous Findings of Sentencing Research', *American Sociological Review* 49: 56–70.
Posner, R. (1990a), *The Problems of Jurisprudence* (Cambridge, Mass.: Harvard University Press).
—— (1990b), 'What Has Pragmatism to Offer Law?', *Southern California Law Review* 63: 1653–70.
Pospisil, L. (1971), *Anthropology of Law: A Comparative Theory* (New York: Harper & Row).
Pound, R. (1942), *Social Control Through Law* (New Haven, Conn.: Yale University Press).
—— (1959a), *Jurisprudence, Vol. I* (St. Paul: West Publishing Company).
—— (1959b), *Jurisprudence, Vol. II* (St. Paul: West Publishing Company).
Pritchett, C. H. (1969), 'The Development of Judicial Research', in J. B. Grossman and J. Tanenhaus (eds.), *Frontiers of Judicial Research* (New York: J. Wiley), 27–42.
Putnam, H. (1990), *Realism with a Human Face* (Cambridge, Mass.: Harvard University Press).
—— (1995), *Pragmatism: An Open Question* (Cambridge, Mass.: Blackwell).
Quine, W. V. O. (1953), *From a Logical Point of View* (Cambridge, Mass.: Harvard University Press).
—— (1975), 'On Empirically Equivalent Systems of the World', *Erkenntnis* 9: 316.
Rabinow, P., and Sullivan, W. M. (1979) (eds.), *Interpretive Social Science* (Berkeley, Calif.: University of California Press).
Radin, M. J. (1989), 'Reconsidering the Rule of Law', *Boston University Law Review* 69: 781–819.
—— (1990), 'The Pragmatist and the Feminist', *Southern California Law Review* 63: 1699–1726.
Raz, J. (1979), *The Authority of Law: Essays on Law and Morality* (New York: Oxford University Press).
Review Symposium (1989), 'Critical Empiricism and Sociolegal Studies', *Law and Social Inquiry* 14: No. 1.
Rheinstein, M. (1954), *Max Weber on Law in Economy and Society* (New York: Simon and Schuster).
Ricouer, R. (1979), 'The Model of a Text: Meaningful Action Considered as a Text', in P. Rabinow and W. Sullivan (eds.), *Interpretive Social Science* (Berkeley, Calif.: University of California Press), 73–101.
Roberts, S. (1979), *Order and Dispute: An Introduction to Legal Anthropology* (New York: St. Martin's Press).
Root, M. (1993), *Philosophy of Social Science: The Methods, Ideals, and Politics of Social Inquiry* (Cambridge, Mass.: Blackwell).

Rorty, R. (1979), *Philosophy and the Mirror of Nature* (Princeton, NJ: Princeton University Press).
—— (1983), 'Method and Morality', in N. Hann (ed.), *Social Science as a Moral Inquiry* (New York: Columbia University Press).
—— (1989), *Contingency, Irony, and Solidarity* (New York: Cambridge University Press).
—— (1990), 'The Banality of Pragmatism', *Southern California Law Review* 63: 1811–19.
—— (1991), 'Feminism and Pragmatism', *Michigan Quarterly Review* 30: 231–58.
—— (1992a), 'What Can You Expect from Anti-Foundationalist Philosophers?: A Reply to Lynn Baker', *Virginia Law Review* 78: 719–27.
—— (1992b), 'The Professor and the Prophet', *Transition* 52: 70.
Rosenberg, A. (1988), *Philosophy of Social Science* (Boulder: Westview Press).
Roth, P. (1987), *Meaning and Method in the Social Sciences: A Case for Methodological Pluralism* (Ithaca, NY: Cornell University Press).
Roucek, J. (1978), 'The Concept of Social Control in American Sociology', in J. Roucek (ed.), *Social Control for the 1980's* (Westport, Conn.: Greenwood Press), 3–19.
Rubin, A. B. (1987), 'Does Law Matter? A Judge's Response to the Critical Legal Studies Movement', *Journal of Legal Education* 37: 310–14.
Ryle, G. (1949), *The Concept of Mind* (London: Penguin Books).
Saks, M. J., and Hastie, R. (1986), 'Social Psychology in Court: The Judge', in H. R. Arkes and K. R. Hammond (eds.), *Judgment and Decision Making* (New York: Cambridge University Press), 255–74.
Sarat, A. (1990), 'Off to Meet the Wizard: Beyond Validity and Reliability in the Search for a Post-Empiricist Sociology of Law', *Law and Social Inquiry* 15: 155–70.
—— (1994), 'A Prophesy of Possibility: Metaphorical Explorations of Postmodern Legal Subjectivity', *Law and Society Review* 29: 615–30.
Schanck, P. (1992), 'Understanding Postmodern Thought and Its Implications for Statutory Interpretation', *Southern California Law Review* 65: 2505–97.
Schapera, I. (1957), 'Malinowski's Theories of Law', in R. Firth (ed.), *Man and Culture: An Evaluation of the Work of Malinowski* (London: Routledge and Kegan Paul), 139–55.
Schauer, F. (1988), 'Formalism', *Yale Law Journal* 97: 509–48.
—— (1991), *Playing By the Rules: A Philosophical Examination of Rule-Based Decision-Making in Law and Life* (Oxford: Clarendon Press).
Schlegel, J. H. (1984), 'Notes Toward an Intimate, Opinionated, and Affectionate History of the Conference on Critical Legal Studies', *Stanford Law Review* 36: 391–411.
Schmidhauser, J. R. (1978), 'The Social and Political Backgrounds of the Justices of the Supreme Court: 1789–1959', in S. Goldman and A. Sarat

(eds.), *American Court Systems: Reading in Judicial Process and Behavior* (San Francisco, Calif.: W. H. Freeman and Co.), 280–9.

—— (1979), *Judges and Justices: The Federal Appellate Judiciary* (Boston, Mass.: Little, Brown and Co.).

Schneider, C. E. (1992), 'Discretion and Rules: A Lawyer's View', in K. Hawkins (ed.), *The Uses of Discretion* (New York: Oxford University Press), 47–88.

Schur, E. M. (1968), *Law and Society: A Sociological View* (New York: Random House).

Schutz, A. (1962), *The Problem of Social Reality* (The Hague: M. Nijhoff).

—— (1967), *The Phenomenology of the Social World* (Evanston, Ill.: Northwestern University Press).

Sciulli, D. (1995), 'Donald Black's Positivism in Law and Social Control', *Law and Social Inquiry* 20: 805–28.

Searle, J. R. (1992), *The Rediscovery of the Mind* (Cambridge, Mass.: MIT Press).

Segal, J. A. (1984), 'Predicting Supreme Court Cases Probabilistically: The Search and Seizure Cases, 1962–1981', *American Political Science Review* 78: 891–900.

—— (1986), 'Supreme Court Justices as Human Decision Makers: An Individual-Level Analysis of the Search and Seizure Cases', *Journal of Politics* 48: 938–55.

—— and Cover, A. D. (1989), 'Ideological Values and the Votes of U.S. Supreme Court Justices', *American Political Science Review* 83: 557–64.

Seidman, R. B. (1972), 'The Communication of Law and the Process of Development', *Wisconsin Law Review* 1972: 686–719.

Selznick, P. (1968), 'The Sociology of Law', *International Encyclopedia of the Social Sciences* (New York: MacMillan), 9: 50–9.

—— (1969), *Law, Society and Industrial Justice* (New York: Russell Sage Foundation).

Shiner, R. A. (1992), 'The Acceptance of a Legal System', in D. M. Patterson (ed.), *Wittgenstein and Legal Theory* (Boulder: Westview Press), 59–84.

Silbey, S., and Sarat, A. (1987), 'Critical Traditions in Law and Society Research', *Law and Society Review* 21: 165–74.

—— (1991), 'Loyalty and Betrayal: Cotterrell's Discovery and Reproduction of Legal Ideology', *Law and Social Inquiry* 16: 809–33.

Simon, R. J., and Lynch, J. P. (1989), 'The Sociology of Law: Where We Have Been Going and Where We Might Be Going', *Law and Society Review* 23: 825–47.

Singer, J. W. (1984), 'The Player and the Cards: Nihilism and Legal Theory', *Yale Law Journal* 94: 1–70.

—— (1988), 'Legal Realism Now', *California Law Review* 76: 465–544.

—— (1989), 'Book Review: Should Lawyers Care About Philosophy?', *Duke Law Journal* 1989: 1752–83.

Skolnick, J. H. (1966), 'Social Research on Legality: A Reply to Auerbach', *Law and Society Review* 1: 105–10.
Smelser, N. (1992), 'Culture: Coherent or Incoherent?', in R. Munch and N. Smelser (eds.), *Theory of Culture* (Berkeley, Calif.: University of California Press), 3–28.
Smith, G. A. (1992), 'Wittgenstein and the Sceptical Fallacy', in D. M. Patterson (ed.), *Wittgenstein and Legal Theory* (Boulder: Westview Press), 157–88.
Smith, S. D. (1990), 'The Pursuit of Pragmatism', *Yale Law Journal* 100: 409–49.
Snyder, F. (1981), 'Anthropology, Dispute Processes and Law: A Critical Introduction', *British Journal of Law and Society* 8: 141–80.
Solum, L. B. (1987), 'On the Indeterminacy Crisis: Critiquing Critical Dogma', *University of Chicago Law Review* 54: 462–503.
Songer, D. R., and Davis, S. (1990), 'The Impact of Party and Region on Voting Decisions in the United States Courts of Appeals, 1955–1986', *Western Political Quarterly* 43: 317–33.
—— and Haire, S. (1992), 'Integrating Alternative Approaches to the Study of Judicial Voting: Obscenity Cases in the U.S. Courts of Appeals', *American Journal of Political Science* 36: 963–82 .
Special Issue (1988), 'Law and Ideology', *Law and Society Review* 22: No. 4.
Special Issue (1995), 'Socio-Legal Studies in Context: The Oxford Centre Past and Present', *Journal of Law and Society* 22: No. 1.
Spohn, C. (1981), 'Women as Policymakers: The Case of Trial Judges', *American Journal of Political Science* 25: 308–22.
——, Gruhl, J., and Welch, S. (1981–2), 'The Effect of Race on Sentencing: A Re-Examination of an Unsettled Question', *Law and Society Review* 16: 71–88.
Starr, J., and Collier, J. F. (1989), 'Introduction: Dialogues in Legal Anthropology', in J. Starr and J. F. Collier (eds.), *History and Power in the Study of the Law: New Directions in Legal Anthropology* (Ithaca, NY: Cornell University Press), 1–28.
Suedfelf, P., and Tetlock, P. E. (1991), 'Psychologists as Policy Advocates: The Roots of Controversy', in P. Suedfelf and P. E. Tetlock (eds.), *Psychology and Social Advocacy* (Washington, D.C.: Hemisphere Press).
Summers, R. S. (1982), *Instrumentalism and American Legal Theory* (Ithaca: Cornell University Press).
Symposium (1990), 'The Renaissance of Pragmatism in American Legal Thought', *Southern California Law Review* 63: No. 6.
Symposium (1995), 'Charting a Course for Sociolegal Scholarship', *Law and Society Review* 29: No. 4.
Tamanaha, B. Z. (1992), 'The Issue of Politics and the Judge in the United States', *Ars Aequi* 41: 733–42.
—— (1993a), *Understanding Law in Micronesia: An Interpretive Approach to Transplanted Law* (Leiden: Brill Publishers).

Tamanaha, B. Z. (1993b), 'The Folly of the "Social Scientific" Concept of Legal Pluralism', *Journal of Law and Society* 20: 192–217.

Tanenhaus, J. (1966), 'The Cumulative Scaling of Judicial Decisions', *Harvard Law Review* 79: 1583–94.

Tarnas, R. (1991), *The Passion of the Western Mind: Understanding the Ideas That Have Shaped Our World View* (New York: Harmony Books).

Tate, C. N. (1981), 'Personal Attribute Models of Voting Behavior of United States Supreme Court Justices: Liberalism in Civil Liberties and Economics Decisions, 1946–1978', *American Political Science Review* 75: 355–60.

—— and Handberg, R. (1991), 'Time Binding and Theory Building in Personal Attribute Models of Supreme Court Voting Behavior, 1916–88', *American Journal of Political Science* 35: 460–80.

Taylor, C. (1979), 'Interpretation and the Sciences of Man', in P. Rabinow and W. Sullivan (eds.), *Interpretive Social Science* (Berkeley, Calif.: University of California Press), 25–71.

Tetlock, P. E., Bernzweig, J. and Gallant, J. L. (1985), 'Supreme Court Decision Making: Cognitive Style as a Predictor of Ideological Consistency of Voting', *Journal of Personality and Social Psychology* 48: 1227–39.

—— and Mitchell, G. (1993), 'Liberal and Conservative Approaches to Justice: Conflicting Psychological Portraits', in B. A. Mellers and J. Baron (eds.), *Psychological Perspectives on Justice: Theory and Applications* (New York: Cambridge University Press), 234–55.

Teubner, G. (1988) (ed.), *Autopoietic Law: A New Approach to Law and Society* (New York: W. de Gruyter).

Thompson, J. D. (1990), *Ideology and Modern Culture* (Stanford: Stanford University Press).

Travers, M. (1993), 'Putting Sociology Back Into the Sociology of Law', *Journal of Law and Society* 20: 438–51.

Trubek, D. M., and Galanter, M. (1974), 'Scholars in Self-Estrangement: Some Reflections on the Crisis in Law and Development Studies in the United States', *Wisconsin Law Review* 1974: 1062–1102.

—— (1984), 'Where the Action Is: Critical Legal Studies and Empiricism', *Stanford Law Review* 36: 575–622.

—— and Esser, J. P. (1989), '"Critical Empiricism" in American Legal Studies: Paradox, Program, or Pandora's Box?', *Law and Social Inquiry* 14: 3–52.

—— and Esser, J. P. (1990), 'From "Scientism Without Determinism" to "Interpretation Without Politics": A Reply to Sarat, Harrington and Yngvesson', *Law and Social Inquiry* 15: 171–80.

Turner, S. P. (1981), 'Interpretive Charity, Durkheim, and the "Strong Programme" in the Sociology of Science', *Philosophy of the Social Sciences* 11: 231–43.

Tushnet, M. V. (1988), *Red, White, and Blue: A Critical Analysis of Constitutional Law* (Cambridge, Mass.: Harvard University Press).

—— (1991), 'Critical Legal Studies: A Political History', *Yale Law Journal* 100: 1515–44.

—— (1992), 'The Left Critique of Normativity: A Comment', *Michigan Law Review* 90: 2325–47.

Uhlman, T. M. (1978), 'Black Elite Decision Making: The Case of Trial Judges', *American Journal of Political Science* 22: 884–95.

Ulmer, S. S. (1986), 'Are Social Background Models Time-Bound?', *American Political Science Review* 80: 957–67.

Unger, R. M. (1975), *Knowledge and Politics* (New York: Free Press).

—— (1976), *Law in Modern Society: Toward a Criticism of Social Theory* (New York: Free Press).

Vines, K. N. (1969), 'The Judicial Role in the American States', in J. B. Grossman and J. Tanenhaus (eds.), *Frontiers of Judicial Research* (New York: J. Wiley), 461–85.

—— (1978), 'Federal District Judges and Race Relation Cases in the South', in S. Goldman, and A. Sarat (eds.), *American Court Systems: Reading in Judicial Process and Behavior* (San Francisco, Calif.: W. H. Freeman and Co.), 376–85.

Watson, A. (1974), *Legal Transplants: An Approach to Comparative Law* (Charlottesville: University Press of Virginia).

Weaver, W. (1992), 'Richard Rorty and the Radical Left', *Virginia Law Review* 78: 729–57.

Weber, M. (1964), *The Theory of Social and Economic Organization* (New York: Free Press).

Wells, C. (1990), 'Situated Decisionmaking', *Southern California Law Review* 63: 1727–46.

West, R. (1985), 'Liberalism Rediscovered: A Pragmatic Definition of the Liberal Vision', *University of Pittsburgh Law Review* 46: 673–738.

Whitford, W. C. (1989), 'Critical Empiricism', *Law and Social Inquiry* 14: 61–7.

Wice, P. (1991), *Judges and Lawyers: The Human Side of Justice* (New York: Harper Collins Publishers).

Wilkinson, P. (1981), 'The Potential of Functionalism for the Sociological Analysis of Law', in A. Podgorecki and C. Whelan (eds.), *Sociological Approaches to Law* (New York: St. Martin's Press), 67–90.

Wilson, J. (1983), *Social Theory* (Englewood Cliffs, NJ: Prentice-Hall).

Winch, P. (1964), 'Understanding a Primitive Society', *American Philosophical Quarterly* 1: 307–24.

—— (1958), *The Idea of a Social Science and Its Relation to Philosophy* (Atlantic Highlands, NJ: Humanities Press).

Wittgenstein, L. (1958), *Philosophical Investigations* (3rd ed.) (New York: MacMillan).

Wold, J. T. (1974), 'Political Orientations, Social Backgrounds, and Role Perceptions of State Supreme Court Judges', *Western Political Quarterly* 27: 239–48.

Ziegert, K. A. (1979), 'The Sociology Behind Eugen Ehrlich's Sociology of Law', *International Journal of the Sociology of Law* 7: 225–73.
—— (1980), 'A Sociologist's View', in E. Kamenka and A. Erh-Soon Tay (eds.), *Law and Social Control* (New York: St. Martin's Press), 60–85.

Subject Index

Anti-foundationalism ix, 3–5, 43, 47, 54, 55, 161, 193, 252
Appellate court decision making 201–2, 205, 210–15, 221–2, 224–37, 235

Behaviourism ix, x, xi, 8, 19, 25, 46–7, 58–70, 101–3, 126–7, 187–95, 203–4, 220, 228, 234, 245, 246–9

Coercion 97, 110–14, 250
Conceptualism 35–6, 43, 239
Consensus 109, 110–14, 121, 130, 250
Context 29, 31, 39–42, 48–50, 57, 77–80, 81, 83, 240, 254
Conventionalism 151, 165, 200, 223
Critical empiricism 22, 25, 54–5
Critical legal studies x, 7, 21, 36–7, 43–7, 59–61, 71–3, 153–4, 184, 188–91, 192, 193, 199–200, 207, 222, 223, 228–30, 231, 233, 242, 244, 247, 251–4

Essentialism 6, 35–7, 43, 127–8, 239
External view 153, 154–6, 162, 163–7, 175–81, 192

Fact/value distinction x, 22, 24, 25, 32–4, 46–7, 50–5, 245, 248, 255
False consciousness 79–81, 84, 162–3, 190, 223, 247
Formalism 35–7, 86, 236, 238, 240, 241–2, 244
Functionalism 8, 25, 104–7, 112–13, 122, 127–8, 156, 245

Gap problem 38, 102, 117–18
Ground, as enabling and limiting conditions 48–51, 72–3, 230

Holism 30–3, 160–1, 164–7, 194

Ideology 16, 22, 71, 84–9, 189, 191n. 247, 254
Indeterminacy xi, 40, 144, 158, 164–6, 171, 173, 190, 196–203, 223, 231, 233–6, 252

Instrumental approach to law 6–7, 36, 44, 251, 236–7
Instrumental rationality 236–44
Internal judicial attitude 148–9, 240–4
Internal legal attitude 148–9
Internal view 153, 156–9, 162, 163–7, 175–83, 186–7, 188–91, 229
Interpretivism ix, x, xi, 3, 18, 24, 25, 48–9, 58, 61–70, 71–90, 92, 102–3, 127, 130, 142–51, 155–8, 175, 187, 189–90, 191–2, 193, 194, 223, 246–9
Intersubjective legal community 148–9, 175, 185, 223

Knowledge, instrumental view of 28–34, 54–5, 166, 245

Law and economics x, 7, 12, 36–7, 43–5, 174, 184
Legal meaing system 149, 171, 185
Legal positivism xi, 91, 98, 115–16, 126, 130–7, 152
Legal realism ix, 6, 7, 16, 25, 36, 44–7, 69, 102, 106, 117, 122, 173, 199, 204, 208, 228, 235, 236, 238, 239, 251
Legal tradition 149–50, 223, 251

Meaning for social actors 77–81
Meaning of social events or situations 81–4

Observed 175–81, 190, 191
Observer 175–81, 191, 192, 248

Politics of socio-legal scholars 20–5, 53–5, 75–6, 82–4, 248, 253–4
Positivism 3, 19, 22, 24, 25, 46–7, 58–70, 155–7, 162, 163–4, 175, 188, 189, 190, 191, 246–9
Postmodernism 4–10, 20, 22, 24, 25, 33, 52, 54, 57, 252, 254, 255
Practices xi, 147–9, 151, 167–75, 182–3, 184–5, 194, 202, 251–2

Subject Index

Realism, scientific 8, 32–3
Relativism 31–4
Role orientation 144, 148, 172, 211–215, 218–19, 222–3, 225, 229, 242–4
Rule orientation 140, 158, 230, 232, 236–44

Social construction of reality 4, 17, 71–3, 82, 84–5, 89, 188, 190, 247
Social control/social order 100, 104–7, 109–11, 114, 123, 124, 127–8, 129–30, 250
Social theory of law x, 130, 143–52, 225–7, 234, 248–9, 250–3
Social theory of science 55–6, 143

Strong programme of the sociology of science 162–7, 189, 190, 223
Substantive justice 41–2, 215, 237–40, 251–2
Supreme Court decision making 205–10, 211, 212, 221–2, 224–7, 235, 243–4
Symbolic interactionism x, 130, 143–152

Transplanted law 117, 133, 136–140, 250
Trial court decision making 215–20, 222, 224–7
Truth, instrumental view of 28–43, 53–4, 245

Author Index

Abel, R. L. 13, 91, 98, 102
Aldisert, R. J. 204
Alexander, J. C. 58 n.
Atiyah, P. S. 236, 238, 239 & n., 240 n., 241, 242 & n., 244
Auerbach, C.A. 20 n.

Baker, L. 43 n.
Barnes, B. 163 n., 165
Bauman, Z. 6, 10, 193, 247
Baumgartner, M.P. 61, 65, 66, 67
Baynes, K. 3 n., 5
Beiser, E. N. 211
Berends, M. 13
Berger, P. 85
Black, D. J. 1, 19, 60, 61, 62, 63, 64, 65 & n., 66, 67, 68, 69, 70, 100, 101, 110, 124 n., 127, 156, 156 n., 177, 245
Bleicher, J. 82
Bloor, D. 163 n., 164, 165
Blumer, H. 145
Bock, E. W. 217
Bohannan, P. 97, 98, 117, 121
Bohman, J. 3 nn., 5, 154 n., 155 n., 158 & n., 161 n., 162, 164, 165
Brace, P. 204, 205, 210, 211
Brenner, S. 206 n.
Bronner, S. E. 43 n.
Brown, J. 163 n.
Burton, S. J. 151

Calavita, K. 3
Cardozo, B. N. 44, 97, 172, 176, 177, 178, 181, 201, 202 n., 204, 230, 231, 232, 233, 236, 237, 239, 242
Carlson, K. E. 224
Carson, D. 2
Chow, D. C. K. 38 n., 42
Cohen, F. S. 35, 44, 46, 47, 53, 95, 106, 119
Cohen, I. J. 145
Collier, J. F. 1 n., 21
Comaroff, J. L. 91
Conant, J. 33 n.
Conley, J. M. 1 n., 129
Cook, B. B. 217

Coombe, R. J. 10
Cooney, M. 65 n.
Coser, L. 109 n., 110
Cotterrell, R. 3, 12 n., 18, 61 n., 84, 85, 86, 87, 101, 153, 191, 192, 193, 194 n.
Cover, A. 206, 229, 232

Davidson, D. 33 n., 159, 161, 166
Delgado, R. 88, 253
Dewey, J. 26, 27, 28, 29, 31 & n., 32, 37, 38 & n., 44, 46, 48, 49, 50, 51, 52, 55, 56, 60, 80, 82, 231, 255
Dorff, R. H. 206 n.
Dreyfus, H. 157 n.
DuBois, P. L. 211
Durkheim, E. 105, 155
Duxbury, N. 8, 20, 21, 61 n.
Dworkin, R. M. 7 n., 36, 153, 176, 177, 183, 184, 185, 186, 187 & nn., 193, 229

Edgerton, R. 158 & n.
Edgeworth, B. 135
Edwards, H. T. 1, 13, 187 n., 202 & n., 211, 222, 223, 227, 249
Ehrlich, E. 69, 93, 94, 95, 96 & n., 97, 98, 101, 102, 104, 107, 108, 111, 112, 117, 118, 119, 133, 136
Emerson, R. M. 146 n.
Epstein, L. 209
Esser, J. P. 2, 11, 17, 22, 54, 86
Evans-Pritchard, E. E. 159
Ewick, P. 18, 23, 24, 74, 75, 86, 87

Farber, D. A. 23 n., 37, 75
Feeley, M. M. 97, 109
Fischer, M. M. J. 20, 22, 23
Fish, S. E. 35, 48, 57, 73 n., 148, 149, 151, 167, 169, 170, 171, 200, 201, 252
Fiss, O. M. 151, 200, 201
Flanagan, O. 32, 48, 234 n.
Frankford, D. M. 64
Frankfurter, F. 207
Frazier, C. E. 217
Friedman, L. 1 n., 12, 85

Author Index

Fuller, L. L. 128 n., 240

Gadamer, H. G. 49 & n., 82, 230, 234
Galanter, M. 96, 108, 119 n.
Geertz, C. 72, 76, 78 & n., 147, 148, 158
George, T. E. 209
Gibbs, J. P. 98
Gibson, J. L. 216 n., 218, 219
Giddens, A. 58 n., 145, 154 n.
Giles, M. W. 218
Glick, H. R. 203, 211, 216, 217, 240 n.
Goldman, S. 206 n., 210, 212, 214, 215
Gordon, R. 188, 189
Gouldner, A. 61
Grey, T. 6, 7 n., 31 n., 39 & n., 126 n.
Griffiths, J. 96, nn.
Grossman, J. B. 205
Gruhl, J. 215, 216
Gulliver, P. H. 98

Habermas, J. 71, 124, 125
Hagan, J. 215
Haire, S. 210, 211, 221
Hall, M. G. 204, 205, 210, 211
Hamnett, I. 91, 93, 96
Handberg, R. 208 n.
Handler, J. 20, 79, 80
Harrington, C. B. 76
Hart, H. L. A. xi, 36, 91, 98, 115, 131, 132, 133, 134 & nn., 135, 136, 137, 141, 153, 157, 178, 179, 180, 181, 182, 183, 193, 200, 204
Hawkins, K. 23, 152, 226
Hempel, C. 105 n., 159
Hesse, M. 155, 160, 163, 166
Hiley, D. 3 n., 155 n.
Hoebel, A. 69, 91, 97, 101, 102, 106, 117, 121
Hollis, M. 159
Holmes, O. W. 6, 44, 46, 97, 102, 106, 126 n., 172, 204, 233, 236
Holstein, J. 74
Homans, G. 156
Horwitz, A. V. 109, 110
Horwitz, M. J. 7, 44, 45, 46, 47, 53, 88, 189 n.
Howard, Jr., J. W. 63 n., 206 n., 214
Hunt, A. 10, 17, 20, 65, 84, 86, 87, 111 & n., 124, 125, 191 n., 192

Jacob, H. 217

James, W. 9, 26, 27 & n., 28, 29 n., 30 & n., 31 & n., 32 & n., 34, 37, 38 & n., 46, 48, 52, 55, 56, 60, 230, 234 n.
Janowitz, M. 109, 110
Jarvie, I. 166, 167, 168
Joas, H. 28, 31 n., 52, 56, 61, 143
Johnson, A. M. 13
Johnson, C. A. 219
Just, P. 1 n., 21, 22, 53, 83

Kennedy, D. 89, 176, 242
King, M. 20, 21, 103
Klare, K. 88
Kleck, G. 215, 216
Kress, K. 200, 201
Kritzer, H. M. 216
Kronman, A. T. 7 n., 38 nn., 97, 157
Krygier, M. 100 n., 102, 109
Kuhn, T. S. 4, 55, 160, 164 & n.

Laudan, L. 165
Leiter, B. 3
Levin, M. A. 217
Levinson, S. 42 n.
Llewellyn, K. 44, 45, 97, 106 n., 117 n., 119 & n., 255
Lloyd-Bostock, S. M. 1 n., 14 & n., 15, 21
Luckmann, T. 85
Luhmann, N. 19, 103, 106, 111, 112, 113, 122, 124, 125
Lukes, S. 159
Lynch, J. 1, 13, 14 & n., 15, 17

Macaulay, S. 15, 21 n., 118
MacCormick, N. 131, 180, 181
MacIntyre, A. 159, 167, 168, 169, 170, 171
Mair, L. P. 91
Malinowski, B. 69, 93, 94, 95, 96, 97, 98, 101, 102, 104, 105 & n., 107, 108, 111, 112
Manheim, K. 163
Manning, P. K. 151, 226
Marcus, G. E. 20, 22, 23
Margolis, J. 159
Marshall, T. 207
Matsuda, M. 7
McCarthy, T. 3 n., 5
McDonald, D. C. 224
Mead, G. H. 52, 143, 144 & n., 145, 146, 148, 150, 223

Author Index

Mensch, E. 172 n.
Merriam-Webster 108
Merry, S. E. 1 & n., 20, 67, 96
Merton, R. K. 105 n., 107
Mertz, E. 17, 71
Mitchell, G. 23 & n.
Minda, G. 7, 36 n., 44
Minow, M. 7, 39 & n., 40, 41, 42
Moore, M. S. 7, 153, 185
Moore, S. F. 19 n., 91, 95, 96 & n., 119
Mulkay, M. J. 163
Munger, F. 1 n., 129
Murphy, J. P. 33 & n., 46
Myers, M. A. 215, 216

Nader, L. 22, 53, 83, 84, 91, 109
Nagel, S. S. 55, 69
Nelson, R. L. 20 n.
Nonet, P. 19, 20 n., 238, 239, 244

Oaks, D. H. 204
O'Barr, W. 1 n., 129

Paley, B. 146 n.
Parsons, T. 61, 106
Patterson, D. M. 9, 151 n.
Payne, M. A. 134 & n.
Peirce, C. S. 26, 29, 32
Peterson, R. D. 215
Posner, R. 7, 16, 36 & n., 42 & n., 44 & n., 178, 189, 228, 230
Pospisil, L. 93, 104
Pound, R. 96 n., 100, 102, 106, 233, 236
Pritchett, C. H. 204
Putnam, H. 29, 30 n., 31, 33 & n., 52

Quine, W. V. O. 30 & n., 46, 160 & n., 164 n.

Rabinow, P. 3 n., 156
Radin, M. J. 7, 38, 39, 229, 232
Raz, J. 122 n., 179, 180, 181
Rheinstein, M. 97
Ricouer, R. 81, 82
Roberts, S. 91, 99, 120
Root, M. 157, 161, 176
Rorty, R. 3 n., 32, 34, 35, 43 & n., 46, 47, 55, 72, 73, 162
Rosenberg, A. 154 n.
Roth, P. 160 & n., 161, 164, 166
Roucek, J. 110

Rubin, A. B. 201, 202 & n., 203, 204, 211
Ryle, G. 234 & n.

Saks, M. J. 217 & n.
Sarat, A. 10 n., 20 n., 21, 24, 54, 55, 206 n., 212
Schanck, P. 9
Schapera, I. 95, 111
Schauer, F. 35 n., 136, 198
Schlegel, J. H. 21, 60
Schmidhauser, J. R. 223
Schneider, C. E. 226
Schur, E. M. 93, 95, 97 n., 128
Schutz, A. 48, 53 & n., 77, 78 & n., 80, 143, 144 n., 148, 158
Sciulli, D. 19
Searle, J. R. 234 n.
Segal, J. A. 206, 208, 209, 226
Seidman, R. B. 119 n.
Selznick, P. 19, 101, 238, 239, 244
Seron, C. 3
Sherry, S. 23 n.
Shiner, R. A. 134 nn.
Shusterman, R. 3 n., 155 n.
Silbey, S. 18, 20 n., 21, 23, 24, 74, 75, 76, 86, 87
Simon, R. J. 1, 13, 14 & n., 15, 17
Singer, J. W. 7, 8, 21, 36, 37, 38, 43, 44, 173, 201 n.
Skinner, B. F. 60, 156 & n.
Skolnick, J. H. 20 n.
Smelser, N. 76, 86
Smith, G. A. 10 n.
Smith, S. D. 7 n., 36, 37
Snyder, F. 1 n., 18
Solum, L. B. 201 n., 233
Songer, D. R. 210, 211, 221
Spelman, E. 7, 39 & n., 40, 41
Spohn, C. 215, 216
Starr, J. 1 n., 21
Suedfelf, P. 24 n.
Sullivan, W. M. 3 n., 156
Summers, R. S. 6, 236, 239 n., 242 & n.

Tamanaha, B. Z. 36 n., 48 n., 53 n., 74, 78 n., 92, 96, 99, 136, 144 n., 240
Tanenhaus, J. 63 n.
Tarnas, R. 4
Tate, C. N. 205, 206, 207, 208 n.
Taylor, C. 66, 76, 157 n.

Author Index

Tetlock, P. E. 23 & n., 24 n.
Teubner, G. 19
Thompson, J. D. 78, 86
Thurow, L. C. 125
Travers, M. 1 nn., 13, 17, 18
Trubek, D. M. 2, 11, 17, 22, 54, 59, 60, 71, 72, 84, 86, 119 n., 153, 188, 189, 190
Turner, J. 58 n., 154 n.
Turner, S. P. 167
Tushnet, M. V. 21 n., 45 & n., 199, 200, 203, 229, 254

Uhlman, T. M. 216 & n.
Ulmer, S. S. 207, 208 & n.
Unger, R. M. 19, 42, 237, 238, 239, 241, 244, 254

Vines, K. N. 211, 212, 213, 214, 217, 218

Walker, T. G. 218

Watson, A. 117
Weaver, W. 43 n.
Weber, M. 22, 90, 97 & n., 124, 125, 126, 157, 237
Welch, S. 215, 216
Wells, C. 39 n., 41, 50
West, R. 7 n.
Whitford, W. C. 16
Wice, P. 226, 227
Wilkinson, P. 106
Wilson, J. 58 n., 90, 144
Winch, P. 156, 157, 158, 159, 160, 166, 167, 181, 182, 186
Wittgenstein, L. 4, 51, 54, 151 & n., 164, 165, 166, 196, 197, 198, 200, 203, 235, 252
Wold, J. T. 213, 214

Yngvesson, B. 76, 109

Ziegert, K. A. 18, 93